Front Office

Front Office

Procedures, social skills and management

Peter Abbott and Sue Lewry

Butterworth-Heinemann Ltd
Linacre House, Jordan Hill, Oxford OX2 8DP

A member of the Reed Elsevier group

OXFORD   LONDON   BOSTON
MUNICH   NEW DELHI   SINGAPORE   SYDNEY
TOKYO   TORONTO   WELLINGTON

First published 1991
Reprinted 1992, 1993 (twice)

British Library Cataloguing in Publication Data
Abbot, Peter
  Front office
  1. Hotels. Reception. Management
  I. Title   II. Lewry, Sue
  647.94068

ISBN 0 7506 0024 1

Typeset by Deltatype Ltd, Ellesmere Port, Cheshire
Printed in Great Britain by Martins the Printers Ltd., Berwick upon Tweed.

Contents

Introduction

This book is intended for students studying Front Office Operations at BTEC National Diploma, BTEC Higher Diploma, HCIMA Professional examination or degree and post-graduate level.

Although this is a wide range of qualifications, the operations themselves remain the same whatever the academic level of the recruit, and we do not subscribe to the view that undergraduate-level material necessarily has to be presented in long words.

One important difference between this book and the more traditional front office texts is that it tries to reflect the relative importance of different aspects of the receptionist's job. This can be divided into three elements:

1 Dealing efficiently with enquiries and reservations, room allocations, bills and checkouts. All these are *clerical* functions, calling for a methodical approach with a strong emphasis on accuracy and tidiness.
2 Dealing with people, either over the telephone or on a face-to-face basis. This calls for an entirely different set of abilities, notably tact, sympathy and the capacity to project *'hospitality'*.
3 Selling. Hotels are almost always profit-making concerns, and receptionists have certain obligations towards the owners who ultimately employ them. Selling is not necessarily the same as providing 'hospitality', although a satisfied guest is one of the best advertisements a hotel can have.

Clerical operations require a knowledge of procedures and this makes up a very large part of the traditional front office textbook. Procedures are important, but they are also usually straightforward. We have tried to cover them as simply and clearly as possible in Part One of this book in order to leave room for what we consider to be even more important aspects, namely the 'social skills'.

Hospitality and selling are both social skills. These are much more difficult to teach. It is all very well saying that receptionists ought to be 'neat', 'tidy', 'polite', 'helpful' and so on, but there is no evidence that this kind of exhortation has very much effect in practice. What is needed is an approach which will actually *change* the would-be receptionist's behaviour. This requires both a conceptual structure and some effective practice material. We have tried to provide both, in the first case drawing largely on Michael Argyle's 'behavioural' approach, and in the second by devising a set of role-playing problems which can be rehearsed (the choice of term is deliberate) over and over again until the students are reasonably proficient. The application of social skills to reception, selling and marketing forms the main theme in Part Two.

A second important difference between this book and traditional front office texts is that we have included a number of management aspects. This doesn't mean that every reader has to be an aspiring front office manager, though there is no reason why a bright and hard-working receptionist should not climb to the top of the ladder, as indeed many have done in the past. In our view a receptionist who does not understand what the front office department is trying to achieve in terms of profitability and overall guest satisfaction is unlikely to be very effective. The days of 'Think? You're not paid to think, you're paid to do as you're told!' are long over, and receptionists ought to know not only *what* they are doing, but *why*.

This explains why we have tried to incorporate a management dimension. It is important to be clear about what we mean by this. We are not trying to produce a book about management for front office managers, but rather to extend the scope of the traditional front office textbook to cover a number of topics which are usually excluded. For example, although marketing is a separate discipline in its own right and a separate department in most hotel companies, there are a number of topics (such as the activities of the Tourist Information Centres) which fall halfway between it and front office operations, and which increasingly affect the work of the latter. Our view is that receptionists ought to know something about these various intermediaries. In the same way, we think that receptionists ought to know something about how a hotel goes about setting a price for its accommodation, or establishing criteria for the purchase of new equipment, or a variety of other 'management' considerations. These make up Part Three.

We ought to say a word about our use of 'you', 'he' and 'she'. Usually, we have addressed our material to 'you', because this seems the simplest and most direct way of doing it. The 'you' we have in mind is a student who knows relatively little about front office operations at the outset, but who wants (or at least needs) to learn more.

However, there are occasions on which we have to quote examples, describing what a receptionist might say to a guest, for instance. Unfortunately, the English language has no neutral word which can replace 'he' or 'she' in the third person singular. We can write 'the guest' or 'the receptionist' to start with, but we cannot continue like this throughout the text without it becoming impossibly stilted. In short, we have to choose whether to make our characters male or female.

We have chosen to call the receptionist 'she' and the guest 'he'. This choice is a matter of expediency, based on the fact that we don't want to use the clumsy construction 'he or she' every time we describe what a receptionist does. It does *not* reflect any unconscious sexist bias on our part, and you should not allow it to affect your own perceptions either. It is true that in the past most receptionists have been female and the majority of guests male, but there is no reason at all why this should continue to be the case. We expect to see many more female front office managers in the future, and have tried to emphasize this by using 'she' for the manager as well. In the same way, we expect to see many more female 'FITs' (Frequent Independent Travellers) as guests in future. If on occasion we have mentioned the special problems of the single woman guest, this is simply because such problems do exist, and there is no point in ignoring them.

We should perhaps also apologize for mentioning one or two other unsavoury operational problems, such as theft and vice. This last topic is generally omitted from standard front office textbooks, but we think it needs to be covered. This does not reflect any preoccupation on our part with the twilight world of pimps and call girls, but rather a recognition that they also represent a problem which exists and which must not be ignored.

We do not want to suggest that hotels are unusually immoral, but it should be obvious that single travellers finding themselves at a loose end in the evening and at the same time free from all the constraints of their home environment will sometimes succumb to temptation. And where there is a demand, there will always be people prepared to cater for it. It is important to realize that a hotel runs very considerable risks if it caters for this particular kind of demand. Any would-be receptionist ought to know what the risks are and how to avoid them.

Another point we need to explain is our approach to computerization. Computerized reservation systems spread rapidly during the 1980s and something like two-thirds of British hotels now use them. This means, of course, that the remainder still use the older manual (i.e. paper-based) systems, though many of these will undoubtedly switch to computers as time goes by. We feel that it is still necessary for you to know something about the manual systems for the following reasons:

1 As we have indicated, many hotels still use them. In fact, there are sometimes good reasons for preferring a manual system, especially in smaller hotels.
2 Although manual systems can be simpler and faster in some respects, computers do offer great advantages. Understanding the limitations of the manual systems helps you to appreciate these advantages.
3 Manual systems form the basis of most of the computerized routines. It is easier to understand what a computer's screen is showing you if you have followed the same procedure through on paper first.
4 Computers are still liable to break or 'go down'. It makes sense to have a manual system ready to go as a back-up system. Front office staff need to know how to operate such a system. This means *you*.

For these reasons, we propose to cover the manual procedures before going on to consider their computer-based alternatives. We shall try to bring out the strengths and weaknesses of each, so that you can arrive at a balanced and informed judgement.

As far as the computer systems themselves are concerned, we have tried to provide an overview rather than describe any one system in particular. This is a rapidly evolving field, and both the hardware and the software currently available are constantly being improved and extended. Each major group has its own system, and it would be foolish to restrict ourselves to just one.

In fact, we have tried to avoid mentioning proprietary names throughout except where (as in the case of Whitney) they have become 'industry standard'. Our sample forms are generalized models rather than examples taken from specific hotels. Each hotel's system has its own peculiarities, and we have tried to concentrate on the common factors. You will find that one of the standard assignments at the end of many chapters invites you to collect a representative sample of such forms and to compare with the models shown in the text.

A final word of apology is due to those of you who don't like figures very much. Unfortunately, the nature of business means that numbers are its very life blood. Hotels exist by letting rooms, and occupancy percentages are one of their key measures of success. Rooms also have to be let at a profit, so revenue and cost figures constitute another key set of measures. In other words, you *have* to understand the basic figures.

Fortunately, most of these are reasonably straightforward, and we will not be asking you to follow anything very complicated. We may invite you to do the occasional addition, subtraction, multiplication or division, or to work out the occasional percentage, but there will be nothing that can't be dealt with by the ordinary hand calculator.

The one thing we would suggest above and beyond this is to familiarize yourself with the workings of computer spreadsheets. These can be very useful, especially in dealing with 'what if?' type problems like overbooking ('What if we did overbook and *everybody* came . . ?'). Many students are reluctant to create their own spreadsheets because they are afraid they won't be able to work out the formulae they have to put in. In fact the formulae are usually quite simple, and we have detailed them where we think that a problem will respond to a spreadsheet-based approach.

What is front office?

'Front office' is a term used in hotels to cover the various sections which deal with reservations, room allocation, reception, billing and payments.

The first contact most would-be guests have with a hotel is usually with its telephone switchboard. The telephonist puts the guest through to someone in the reservations department, who takes his booking and deals with any subsequent correspondence such as confirmations, amendments or cancellations.

When the guest arrives, he may be assisted by a uniformed porter, though this is by no means always the case nowadays. What *is* certain is that he will have to go to the reception desk to register and obtain his room key.

During his stay he may well have occasion to go back to reception several times, sometimes for information or to pick up messages, and sometimes for help with tickets or further travel. He will probably have to call there at the end of his stay in order to hand in his room key and deal with his bill.

This does not end his connection with the hotel. His registration form must be kept for a specified period, and the information it contains can be used for a variety of follow-up communications designed to get him to come back at some time.

All these vitally important contacts are the job of 'front office', an American term which is now commonly used in place of the older word 'reception'. Strictly speaking, it only covers those staff who come into direct, face-to-face contact with the guests, the other associated sections being known as 'back office'. However, the term 'front office' is now generally used to describe the whole range of 'front of house' sections, namely:

- Uniformed staff
- Switchboard
- Reservations
- Reception
- Enquiries

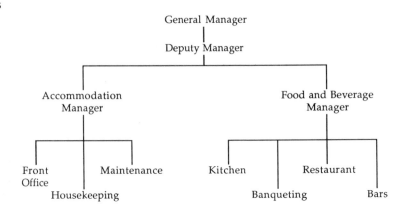

Figure 1   *Organization chart*

- Bill office
- Cashier
- Guest relations

We will use the term in this way, reserving 'reception' and 'receptionist' to describe the desk and the staff who work behind it.

Front office is only one of the hotel's departments. The hotel's actual organization structure will vary according to its size, grade, clientele and equipment, but the structure shown in Figure 1 may be taken to be representative of one of the larger establishments:

As Figure 1 shows, front office is part of the accommodation division. The Accommodation Manager is also responsible for housekeeping (the department which deals with the cleaning of the rooms) and maintenance (the department which looks after the premises, the fixtures and the fittings).

Traditionally, the uniformed staff (doormen, porters, liftmen, pages etc.) have formed a separate department in their own right, usually coming under the supervision of the Head Porter. These staff have tended to decrease in numbers in recent years because:

1 Airline weight restrictions have reduced the amount of luggage carried and thus the need for porters.
2 Modern clothing materials have reduced the need for valeting services.
3 Passenger-operated lifts have led to the disappearance of lift attendants.
4 Modern methods of communication have reduced the need for in-hotel messengers such as pages.

Uniformed staff still exist (doormen are still needed to summon taxis or park guests' cars for them), but they no longer form a separate department except in the largest luxury hotels. Even

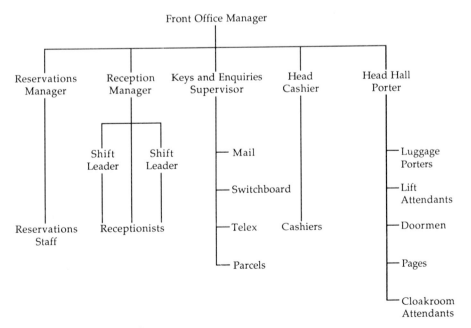

Figure 2   *Front office organization chart*

there, it is increasingly common to find them placed under the Front Office Manager, as the specimen organization chart for the Front Office Department of a 500 room luxury hotel shown in Figure 2 indicates.

Although we are mainly concerned with hotels, you should not forget that there are many other forms of accommodation letting, most of which face many of the same problems and require much the same kind of skills. Examples include:

1   *Ships*   Cruise liners are really 'floating resort hotels', with bars, restaurants, dance floors and other entertainments. Passengers have to be allocated cabins, and may send or receive messages to the outside world. There are often foreign exchange and immigration formalities to be handled. Passenger ferries have their guests on board for a shorter period, but they too must provide cabins, meals, drinks and a variety of services.

2   *Boats*   These can range from the chartered luxury yacht in the Mediterranean or Caribbean through to the canal-based narrow boat or Broads-based cabin cruiser. Here the accommodation is mobile and is often not under the immediate control of its owner, but the booking process still has to be completed, and the boats have to be cleaned and maintained between lets.

3   *Holiday camps*   This is another form of holiday letting. The traditional camp accommodated its customers in chalets and fed them in large restaurants. Nowadays many of the chalets are self-catering and some of the visitors (especially in the off-season) are conference delegates, but the basic operation remains much the same.

4   *Camp sites*   Although in this case the guests may provide their own accommodation (tents or caravans), there are still bookings to handle and various facilities and services to be provided and maintained (water, power, toilets and shops for example).

5   *Timeshare complexes*   In theory, the residents are also part-owners of the accommodation. Usually they buy the right to use a particular unit for one specific week or fortnight every year. In practice, many 'swop' units with owners from other countries, or let their relations or employees use them, or even rent them out themselves, so that many of the occupiers are not owners at all. The units are usually self-catering, but most timeshare complexes include resort hotel facilities such as restaurants and swimming pools. Their offices have to keep track of the various lettings, and oversee the cleaning of the apartments between guests.

6   *Student halls of residence*   In the past, these resembled residential hotels with a restricted type of clientele. Nowadays, more and more of them are used to accommodate short course or conference delegates during the academic holidays, and have moved correspondingly closer to the normal commercially-motivated hotel in that short-term lettings have to be arranged and bills made out and presented.

7   *Hospitals*   Once again, the tendency has been for hospitals and hotels to move closer towards each other. Not only have hospitals themselves become more relaxed in terms of open access (the rigid, rule-fixated ward sister is thankfully a thing of the past) but hotels are increasingly catering for their guests' concern with their own health. There have always been spa hotels and sanatoriums catering for guests who wanted to take 'the cure' in comfort, but swimming pools and health club facilities are extending the concept into everyday life. At the same time, more and more hospitals are beginning to think in terms of profitability (or at least effective cost control), or are setting up 'hotel services' departments for other reasons.

To sum up, any establishment providing food, drink and accommodation for a fluctuating group of residents is faced with similar problems to those of a hotel's front office. Their accommodation booking processes may differ in terms of organization and terminology, but their basic function remains the same, namely to make sure that every valid reservation is honoured, and nobody is unwittingly double booked.

There are other institutions which display certain similarities to hotels, such as residential homes. Their inmates are permanent residents, so it is not really appropriate to compare them with hotels. There is always some turnover amongst them, of course, but it is more like that found in a block of residential apartments, and is somewhat outside the scope of this book.

There is one last type of institution whose operations are very similar to those of a hotel, but whose atmosphere is so different that it also falls outside the scope of this work. We refer to prisons, detention centres and the like. Here there is a constantly-shifting population of 'guests' (inmates), some staying for extended periods (those serving long sentences), others a short while. They have to be allocated to rooms (cells) as well as being fed, exercised and given something to do during the day (consider the parallel with a holiday hotel). Their belongings have to be looked after during their stay (safe keeping for valuables), and they must be given certain (admittedly limited) opportunities to communicate with the outside world.

The parallels are obvious, yet nobody ever confuses the two kinds of experience. This brings us back to one of our main themes, namely that an essential ingredient of the hotel 'package' is *hospitality*. Staff at prisons, detention centres and the like are expected to treat their charges correctly and in accordance with the rules, but they are not usually expected to try to make them feel 'at home'. Hotels, cruise ships, timeshares, halls of residence and modern hospitals *do* try to make those who stay in them feel at home, and therein lies a fundamental difference.

There are many different kinds of hotels. They vary according to four main factors:

1 *Location*   This tends to determine the type of clientele. A hotel on a tiny tropical island with limited communication facilities may have plenty of holidaymakers, but it will attract relatively few business travellers. The main types of locations are as follows:

   - City centre
   - Suburban
   - Airport
   - Main road (motel)
   - Resort
   - Country

2 *Size*   This is related to the amount of business likely to be generated by the hotel's location, and the presence or absence of competition. Other things being equal, city centre establishments will be larger than country hotels because more people are likely to be drawn to the city. As far as Britain is concerned, the main categories are:

Less than 25 bedrooms:	Small
25–99 bedrooms:	Medium
More than 100 bedrooms:	Large
More than 300 bedrooms:	Major

The proportion of small to large hotels decreased during the 1970s and 1980s. This was partly because of the general decline of the traditional seaside resorts, which was due to the expansion of package tour holidays. However, there are still far more small hotels than large ones.

3   *Length of stay*   This is influenced by the hotel's location and type of clientele. Hotels catering for transient customers (motels and airport hotels) will seldom have average stays longer than one night, whereas the traditional resort hotel may attract holidaymakers who stay for a week or more. However, this latter type of business has declined with the increase in car ownership, since more and more people now prefer to spend their holidays touring, staying for shorter periods in any one location.

4   *Grade*   Hotels vary considerably in terms of price. It is possible to pay as little as £20 or as much as £200 per night in hotels which are only a mile or so apart. The differences are due to:

(a)   Location (desirable sites are very expensive to build on).
(b)   The extent and quality of the facilities.
(c)   Service standards. Here the ratio of staff to rooms is critical (luxury hotels can have up to three employees per room, sometimes even more).

There are a number of classification schemes in existence. The Automobile Association (AA) offers one well-known example. In this system hotels are graded in terms of an ascending number of stars on the basis of the facilities they offer, as follows:

*   Hotels and inns generally of small scale with good facilities and furnishings; adequate bath and lavatory arrangements. Meals are provided for residents, but their availability to non-residents may be limited.

**   Hotels offering a higher standard of accommodation; 20 per cent of bedrooms containing a private bathroom or shower with lavatory.

***   Well-appointed hotels with more spacious accommodation with two-thirds of the bedrooms containing a private bathroom/shower with lavatory. Fuller meal facilities are provided.

****   Exceptionally well-appointed hotels offering a high standard of comfort and service with all bedrooms providing a private bathroom/shower with lavatory.

*****   Luxury hotels offering the highest international standards.

A special 'Country House' symbol is used to indicate a secluded hotel with a relaxed and informal atmosphere, red stars are used to denote hotels of outstanding merit, and one to three rosettes are added if the food is specially recommended. Other merit indicators are a red 'H' (hospitality), a red 'B' (bedrooms) and a red 'P' (public areas). These show that these particular aspects are of a standard significantly higher than that implied by the star classification.

The tourist Boards use a parallel system. Basic bed and breakfast type accommodation is 'Listed' and other hotels are graded in terms of 'Crowns' as follows:

'Listed'   Accommodation is clean and comfortable, though the range of facilities and services may be limited.

👑   Accommodation with additional facilities, including wash basins in all bedrooms, a lounge area and the use of a telephone.

👑👑   Accommodation with a wider range of facilities and services including tea/coffee, calls, bed lights, colour TV in lounge or rooms, and assistance with luggage.

👑👑👑   Accommodation with at least one-third of the rooms with en suite WC and bath/shower plus easy chair and full length mirror, shoe cleaning facilities and hair dryers.

♛♛♛♛ Accommodation with at least three-quarters of the rooms with en suite WC and bath/shower, colour TV, radio and telephone in all rooms, twenty-four hour access and lounge service until midnight.

♛♛♛♛♛ All rooms with WC, bath and shower en suite, trouser press or valet services, and a wide range of services and facilities including room service, all night lounge service and laundry service.

Five *gold* crowns are used to indicate hotels which have reached exceptionally high standards in the provision of service and hospitality. The terms 'Approved', 'Commended' and 'Highly Commended' are being introduced as additional quality indicators at all levels.

Membership of these schemes is optional rather than obligatory, and Britain has not yet gone as far as many European countries, which have compulsory hotel grading and classification schemes. However, the AA and Tourist Board classification is carried out by impartial inspectors. Because the criteria differ slightly, AA and Tourist Board classifications may differ, though there is generally a large measure of agreement.

One of the most important things to remember about front office procedures is that no *one* system is ideal for all circumstances. As we have seen, hotels vary very much in size, grade and type of customer, and what suits one establishment may not suit another.

To make this point clearer, we invite you to look at two different kinds of hotel, which we think sum up the range of establishments you might find in operation. We shall be using these as the basis for various assignments. There are of course many other types of hotel, ranging from the seaside boarding house, through the small country pub and the private residential establishment, up to the exclusive five star establishments offering the highest possible standards of luxury and personal service. However, the two we have chosen allow us to look at the kind of systems you are most likely to meet.

One (the Tudor) is typical of a lot of medium-sized provincial hotels in that it dates from the heyday of the British seaside holiday and is consequently now rather elderly. It has been progressively refurbished, of course, but nothing can change the fact that its rooms still differ significantly in terms of their size and the facilities they offer. As we shall see, this affects the way that it runs its booking system. One very important aspect of this is that (as far as the 1980s were concerned, at least) it would not necessarily have benefited from the introduction of a computer, and since the management has been a little bit old-fashioned, it has not acquired one yet. This allows us to look at the kind of manual systems still in widespread (and perfectly satisfactory) use.

The other hotel (the Pancontinental) is a very different type of establishment. Since it is located close to an airport and a motorway intersection (both creations of the 1950s and 1960s), you would expect it to be much newer, and so it is. It has the standardized rooms typical of most post-war hotels, which allows it to operate a different kind of booking system. It is also larger and busier, with more facilities and a different kind of clientele. These factors mean that it benefits considerably from computerization, and (since the management has been anything *but* old-fashioned) it has had a computer since the early 1980s, and indeed has already upgraded its facilities twice.

We have described these two hotels as fully as possible because we want you to use them in subsequent assignments. Your standpoint should be that of the Head Receptionist or Front Office Manager, and your job will include staffing and running the front office, trying to maximize occupancy and room revenue, and making decisions about systems and equipment. Even if you can't expect to make the *final* decisions about some of these matters in real life, you will still be invited to submit recommendations, so you should have some ideas. You should also *know* your hotel thoroughly, which is why we have provided you with what may at first seem like some irrelevant information.

You may well find that you know a local hotel or hotels which share some of the characteristics of either the Tudor or the Pancontinental, in which case you are perfectly entitled to draw on these for additional detail. Of course, you shouldn't assume that one hotel's system will necessarily fit another's requirements in every particular. However, don't be afraid to borrow someone else's good ideas. If they work, it is the guest who benefits.

The Tudor Hotel

The Tudor Hotel is located in Abergelyn, a small town situated on the Welsh coast between Aberystwyth and Caernarvon. Abergelyn was a small fishing village at the start of the nineteenth century, but it possesses a reasonable beach and with improvements in communication it had developed into a minor tourist resort by the end of the century.

Abergelyn now has a population of 25,000. The fishing industry has virtually disappeared, but the town continues to act as a market centre for the farming population of the Gelyn valley, and there is also a small industrial park with three or four light manufacturing concerns attracted by the relatively low local rates and wages. Local unemployment currently stands at 8.3 per cent, and there is competition for part-time employment.

There is a plan to build a major new nuclear power station on the nearby Pen-set peninsula. This is being vociferously opposed by some local environmental interests, but there is an equally widespread view that it will bring increased prosperity to the area. The proposal has been the subject of a planning enquiry, but this is due to report in the near future and it is confidently expected that it will go ahead. The planned power station will be hidden from the town and it is claimed that it will not affect the tourist amenities.

Abergelyn has a sandy beach backed by a promenade. The small, picturesque port has become a thriving sailing centre. At the moment most of the boats are privately owned, but there is increasing interest in day hire and weekend or week-long sailing tuition. The town is also a base for walkers and mountain climbers, and there is a pony trekking centre a mile or two inland. In addition, there is a light railway up the Gelyn Valley to Lake Alwryt which was restored in 1965 and is now a considerable tourist attraction.

The main coast road and railway both pass through the town. The road originally ran along the promenade, but through traffic is now diverted around a new bridge and a ring road which circles the town further inland.

The Tudor Hotel is one of three hotels in the town. The others are The Grand, which is rather larger and more up-market, and The Station, which is smaller and cheaper. There are also a dozen or so guest houses offering bed and breakfast accommodation, mainly during the summer season, and large camp and caravan sites within a quarter of a mile of the town centre. The town has a Tourist Information Centre which operates a local booking service.

The Tudor Hotel is located about two-thirds of the way along the promenade on the town side and about 1 km from the main shopping centre. It is set back from the road itself by an area which was originally a garden but which was converted into a tarmac surfaced car park in 1964 and holds forty cars. There is plenty of twenty-four hour car parking along the promenade itself (though this tends to become full at peak holiday periods) and a large public car park within 0.5 km.

The hotel itself looks out onto the sea, and the view from the front bedrooms is excellent. It

Figure 3 *The Tudor Hotel (courtesy Val Slomka)*

was built in 1904 but has been considerably modified at various times since. Two lifts were installed in 1949 and the original mechanisms replaced in 1974. A coal-fired central heating system was installed in 1951 and converted to natural gas in 1977.

The public rooms consist of a bar, a restaurant (capable of seating eighty-eight covers) and a residents' lounge used for the service of morning coffee, afternoon teas and after dinner coffees. The hotel holds a restaurant and residential licence.

A side extension originally designed as a function room-cum-ballroom was modified during the mid 1970s so that it could also provide conference facilities: the main area can still seat sixty covers as a function room but is able to accommodate 100 delegates when used for conference purposes. It has adequate AV equipment (microphone, screen, video and slide projector etc.) and there are three smaller seminar rooms plus separate cloakroom facilities.

The general style of decoration has been chosen to retain the original atmosphere and appearance of the building, though with some modern concessions such as fitted carpets in the bedrooms, corridors and stairways. The furniture is traditional in style, and though it is mainly reproduction the dining room does contain a magnificent and genuine Welsh dresser and sideboard. The bedrooms are individually decorated in a variety of soft pastel shades, and the public areas contain a good deal of wood panelling and moulded plaster work. Considerable use has been made of old paintings and prints throughout.

All rooms are equipped with bedside lamps, colour television sets, telephones and tea and coffee makers. All now have a washbasin (with overhead strip light and electric razor socket) and shower cubicle as a minimum provision, and a considerable amount of work has been done to add en suite toilet facilities to as many rooms as possible, though this has not been possible in all cases. The current room situation is as follows:

- Ten singles with shower
- Ten singles with bath and toilet
- Ten doubles/twins with shower

- Fifteen doubles/twins with bath and toilet
- Five executive doubles/twins with bath, toilet and balcony

Ten of the doubles/twins interconnect with other doubles or with singles. The rooms within each category are comparable in terms of furnishings, but vary significantly in terms of views and proximity to the stairs and lifts. Some guests have complained about the first floor rooms immediately over the bar area on the grounds of noise.

The average monthly occupancies over the past year were as shown in Table 1. (Note that these are *room* occupancies, though we have added the number of sleepers underneath.)

Table 1   The Tudor – average monthly occupancies

	No.	Jan	Feb	Mar	Apr	May	Jun	Jul	Aug	Sep	Oct	Nov	Dec
Singles	10	5.8	5.9	6.1	6.2	6.3	6.9	7.2	7.7	7.6	6.6	5.9	6.2
Singles/bath	10	4.5	4.6	5.0	6.1	7.1	8.0	8.4	8.9	8.6	6.9	4.9	4.3
Twins	10	6.5	6.9	7.6	7.9	8.0	8.4	8.9	9.0	8.0	6.5	5.1	5.9
Twins/bath	15	3.9	4.3	4.8	6.4	7.7	8.4	11.1	12.7	13.3	8.0	4.2	5.8
Executive twins	5	0.9	1.3	1.6	2.1	2.4	2.2	3.3	4.2	4.0	2.2	1.3	2.0
Total rooms	50	21.6	23.0	25.1	28.7	31.6	33.9	39.0	42.5	41.5	30.2	21.5	24.2
Total beds	80	32.9	35.5	39.1	45.2	49.7	52.8	62.3	68.5	66.9	46.9	32.2	38.0

The hotel caters for a number of different types of business. These are:

1   Business traffic, mainly sales representatives and travelling professionals of various kinds. Such guests almost invariably occupy single rooms and stay for one or two nights, the actual average being about 1.5 nights.
2   Touring traffic. These are people who are travelling through the area for some reason (perhaps on the way to visit friends, or tourists during the summer) and who require overnight accommodation. They occupy both twins and singles, and their average length of stay is one night.
3   Resort business. These are people who come to the town to stay (perhaps using the hotel as a base for day trips of various sorts). This business is mainly seasonal, but there are always a certain number who come in the off-periods, and even one or two longer-term residents. Holidaymakers occupy mainly twins and usually stay for four to seven days, the actual average being 5.5 nights.
4   Groups. These are divided more or less equally between small conferences and the more traditional kind of coach tour. This business is highly seasonal, with a small surge at Christmas time. The conferences might book for two to three days, but the tours are almost always overnight stays, so that the average stay is 1.75 nights.

Over the past year, the average number of sleepers per night in each category has been as shown in Table 2.

Weekday (i.e. Monday to Thursday night) occupancies are significantly higher than the weekend (Friday to Sunday) ones. During the winter season (October to March) the proportions are 1:2, mainly because there are fewer business travellers. During the summer season (April to August) the proportion becomes 2:3, mainly because there are considerably more tourists.

Table 2   The Tudor – average numbers of sleepers per night

Category	Jan	Feb	Mar	Apr	May	Jun	Jul	Aug	Sep	Oct	Nov	Dec
Business	13.7	12.8	12.9	13.6	13.6	13.4	13.0	13.1	13.7	12.9	12.2	13.2
Touring	13.4	15.9	16.3	16.6	17.4	19.2	20.0	22.3	22.9	18.9	15.2	17.0
Resort	5.8	6.8	8.2	9.1	9.8	9.9	15.2	17.3	17.2	11.3	5.8	6.0
Group	–	–	1.7	5.9	8.9	10.3	14.1	15.8	13.1	3.8	–	1.8
Total	32.9	35.5	39.1	45.2	49.7	52.8	62.3	68.5	66.9	46.9	33.2	38.0

Tudor Hotel: Profit and loss account for year ended 31.12.9–

	Rooms	Food	Bar	Total
Sales	325,450	267,520	137,991	730,961
Payroll	58,581	109,683	48,297	216,561
Materials	24,409	104,333	55,196	183,938
Other expenses	4,768	12,528	5,781	23,077
Departmental income	237,692	494,064	28,717	307,385

Operating expenses		
Salaries	32,893	
Bad debts	1,096	
Fees and other expenses	3,655	
Advertising	16,081	
Entertainment etc.	4,386	
Energy costs	25,584	
Sundry expenses	5,482	89,177
Operating profit		218,208
Property expenses		
Depreciation	58,477	
Interest	4,175	
Property taxes etc.	19,005	
Repairs and maintenance	25,584	107,241
Net operating profit		110,967
Taxation		38,839
Profit and Loss b/fwd		20,529
Dividends		35,000
Profit and loss c/fwd		16,600
		110,967

Figure 4   *The Tudor – profit and loss account*

Tudor Hotel: Balance sheet as at 31.12.9–

	Cost	Depreciation	Net
Fixed assets:			
Land and buildings			1,000,000
Fixtures and fittings	525,000	288,750	236,250
Current assets:			
Stocks		15,350	
Debtors		5,848	
Cash in hand and at bank		8,041	
		29,238	
Current liabilities		13,888	15,350
Net assets:			1,251,600
Long-term liabilities			35,000
		Total	1,216,600
Represented by:			
Share capital (350,000 ordinary shares of £1 each)			350,000
Share premium A/c			25,000
Revaluation reserve			825,000
Profit and Loss A/c			16,600
Total			1,216,600

Figure 5   *The Tudor – balance sheet*

The hotel is owned and operated by Tudor Hotels Ltd, a small private company whose main shareholders are Mr and Mrs David Evans. Mr Evans acts as General Manager and Managing Director, Mrs Evans as Company and General Secretary. The company does not own any other properties. Mr Evans had been an executive with a major manufacturing company: he bought a controlling interest in the Tudor Hotel by combining his redundancy money with a legacy and borrowing the remainder. Neither he nor his wife had any practical hotel experience, but they have been running the Tudor Hotel for fifteen years now. Both are in their fifties.

The staff consist of a Restaurant Manager, a Chef, a Housekeeper, a Head Receptionist and a Maintenance Engineer, together with their subordinates. The front office is staffed by the Head Receptionist and two part-time assistants. Mrs Evans provides cover if necessary.

The current profit and loss account and balance sheet are as shown in Figures 4 and 5.

The Pancontinental Hotel

The Pancontinental Hotel is located on the outskirts of Melcaster, a major northern city.

Greater Melcaster currently has a population of some 2.75 million, and is an important industrial and commercial centre. There is a large new national exhibition hall, and the city has been energetically promoting itself as a national venue for major sporting and other events.

Melcaster also has considerable attractions as a tourist centre. It is surrounded by moorlands, much of which is of considerable natural beauty and scientific interest, and is also well situated for a number of historical sites. The city itself has begun to develop its potential as a centre for industrial archaeology, and a thriving cultural life.

The city is well served by the transport network, with both north–south and east–west motorway connections close to hand, and excellent inter-city rail connections with London and other urban centres. In addition, there is a major international airport within eight miles of the city centre.

The Pancontinental is located on the south-western side of the city, close to the motorway ring road and within two miles of the airport. Access to the city centre is currently limited to taxis or express coach services, but a light railway link is being constructed as part of the city's new rapid transit system, and is due to commence operations within two years. The region as a whole is still relatively depressed due to the destruction of its old staple manufacturing industries, so that unemployment is currently averaging 10.2 per cent. However, this does not apply to the south-west Greater Melcaster area, which acts as a dormitory suburb for the employees of the region's commercial services and is relatively affluent. This area also has a number of flourishing industries such as computers and light engineering, so that local unemployment is only a third of the regional rate, and local hotels and restaurants have some difficulty in attracting and retaining staff.

The airport itself falls within the city boundaries, but the Pancontinental has been carefully situated just outside these, which gives it the advantage of considerably lower local rates.

There are two other airport hotels of equivalent standard to the Pancontinental, and five more in, or close to, the city centre. All these major competing hotels are owned by national or international groups. In addition, there are a considerable number of smaller two and three star establishments scattered throughout the southern Greater Melcaster area, and a larger number of bed and breakfast establishments. There are two local universities, both of which offer conference facilities at their halls of residence during the academic breaks. The city has a Tourist Information Centre operating both local and national booking services. There is also a local hotel association.

The Pancontinental stands in its own grounds, which are extensive enough to allow it to double its size should this prove advisable at some future date. At the moment much of the area is devoted to car parking space, but the remainder has been landscaped with grass, bushes and small trees. The parking areas will hold 450 cars. They are open to the weather, but there is an extensive covered porch which allows for loading and unloading. Goods are delivered at the back of the hotel out of sight of the main entrance.

The hotel was completed in 1980. The front entrance on the ground floor leads directly into the front hall and reception area and thence to a lobby running the length of the building. This is lined with a number of shops which are leased by the hotel to various operators (there is a florist, for instance, two boutiques, a souvenir shop and a newstand and bookstall). The lobby also gives access to the hotel's cocktail bar, à la carte restaurant, coffee shop-cum-buffet, discotheque, indoor swimming pool and health club.

The first floor is largely given over to conference facilities. There is one large conference area capable of accommodating up to 240 persons, four smaller seminar rooms each capable of holding fifty to sixty persons, and a dedicated lobby (used for conference registrations, morning coffees, buffet lunches, teas etc.) with separate cloakroom facilities. The main

Figure 6   *The Pancontinental Hotel (courtesy Val Slomka)*

conference hall can also be used for banqueting and has a sprung floor suitable for dancing. The remainder of the first floor is used for the hotel's own administrative offices.

There are two pairs of high-speed guest lifts which run from the ground floor to the top of the building, where there is a roof terrace garden which has proved attractive to those who like to watch aircraft landing and taking off: this area is normally glassed in for most of the year but can be left open during summer. It has its own bar and food service facilities.

The hotel is air conditioned and centrally heated throughout. Heating is based on a modern gas-fired system. All public and private rooms are fully double glazed, and aircraft noise is only noticeable outside.

The hotel's bedrooms are standardized. There are two classes – the double/double or 'DD' (equipped with two large beds) and the 'King' (a similar-sized room equipped with one large bed). Both types are capable of being used for both single or double occupancy. All rooms open directly onto the corridors but there are also interconnecting doors which are normally kept locked.

The rooms are well lit and comfortable. All have an en suite bathroom with bath and shower facilities, a washbasin with overhead strip light and razor socket and toilet. They are equipped with colour television, mini bar, telephone with direct dial facilities, electric heated trouser press and tea and coffee making facilities. All have built-in clothes hanging space, a dressing

Table 3   Arrangement of rooms

Floor	Arrangement
Sixth	30 Kings, 20 DDs
Fifth	30 Kings, 20 DDs
Fourth	30 Kings, 20 DDs
Third	30 Kings, 20 DDs
Second	30 Kings, 20 DDs

table with drawers and mirror, two chairs and a small table. The king rooms also have a two-seater settee. The furnishings are fitted with laminated surfaces and are functional but standardized, and the colour scheme used for bedspreads, curtains and upholstery does not vary from room to room.

The arrangement of rooms is as shown in Table 3.

Over the past year, the average number of occupied rooms per night in each category have been as shown in Table 4.

Table 4   The Pancontinental – average number of occupied rooms per night

	Jan	Feb	Mar	Apr	May	Jun	Jul	Aug	Sep	Oct	Nov	Dec
King (S)	93	94	94	97	99	99	94	93	99	100	99	99
King (D)	31	30	30	28	30	33	36	40	33	27	25	30
Total (150)	124	124	124	125	129	132	130	133	132	127	124	129
DD (S)	22	22	23	25	26	25	24	24	27	28	26	27
DD (D)	40	41	44	46	46	48	49	50	46	44	42	43
Total (100)	62	63	67	71	72	73	73	74	73	72	68	70

As in the Tudor, weekday (i.e. Monday to Thursday night) occupancies are higher than weekend (Friday to Sunday) ones, though the difference is not as great. The proportion throughout the year is approximately 4:3.

The hotel caters for a number of different types of business. These are:

1 *Airline business*   The hotel is used by a number of major airlines for putting up flight crews and staff during regular overnight stopovers. This business can be largely scheduled in advance and contracts are awarded annually. There are also a considerable number of travelling airline executives, in addition to frequent but unpredictable calls to put up groups of passengers delayed by unforeseen events. This category's average length of stay is one night.

2 *Business traffic*   This is mainly company executives and travelling professionals of various kinds. The hotel uses the term 'FITs' (Frequent Independent Travellers) to describe this important source of business. Most of these guests occupy kings and generally stay for one night, though since a number remain for two or three nights their average length of stay is 1.3 nights.

3 *Transit traffic*   These are people who are departing or arriving from the airport and who need overnight accommodation. They include both single and double occupancies, and

their usual length of stay is one night. A small but significant number require rooms for shorter period, giving rise to the possibility of two or more lettings within a twenty-four hour period: for this reason this category's average length of stay is actually 0.95 days.

4   *Touring business*   As with The Tudor, these are people who come to the region to stay. The hotel provides a useful base from which to explore both the city and the surrounding countryside. This business is noticeably seasonal, though there are always a certain number who come in the off-periods. Such guests provide both single and double occupancies. Their average length of stay is two nights.

5   *Groups*   These are about two-thirds conferences and one-third inclusive tours. The conference element is reasonably well spread throughout the year, while the tour business is more seasonal. Conference delegates average 2.5 nights' stay, while the tours are almost all overnight stays.

Over the past year, the average number of sleepers per night in each category have been as shown in table 5.

Table 5   The Pancontinental – average number of sleepers per night

	Jan	Feb	Mar	Apr	May	Jun	Jul	Aug	Sep	Oct	Nov	Dec
Airline	51	50	52	53	55	57	57	59	56	54	50	53
Business	110	108	107	109	111	108	107	110	115	117	113	110
Transit	37	39	40	40	42	43	43	47	42	38	37	41
Touring	22	24	26	27	29	32	35	35	29	24	23	27
Group	37	37	40	40	41	46	46	46	42	37	36	41
Total	257	258	265	269	278	286	288	297	284	270	259	272

The Pancontinental is owned and operated by Paragon Hotels plc, a medium-sized group which also owns sixteen other properties, mainly centred in the north of England. Paragon are themselves a subsidiary of Anglo-Welsh Breweries plc, a major company with important interests in the food and drink industry. Paragon's head office in Birmingham has marketing, personnel and finance departments, as well as a group reservations office.

The Pancontinental's General Manager has to submit annual budget proposals, and is required to meet agreed cost and revenue targets. However, the company policy is to allow the individual hotel managers as much freedom as possible provided that they comply with general policy directives, and the hotel's own management team has a good deal of discretion with regard to operational matters such as staffing levels and rates of pay, booking policies and even room rates.

The current General Manager is Thomas Mason, a graduate who entered the hotel industry some twenty-five years ago and has since worked his way up. He is now in his late forties. His management team consists of a Deputy Manager, a Food and Beverage Manager (whose subordinates include a Banqueting Manager, Head Chef and Restaurant Manager), an Accountant, a Sales Manager and an Accommodation Manager (whose subordinates include the Reception Manager, Head Housekeeper and Maintenance Manager). The front office is usually staffed by a Senior Receptionist and two Assistant Receptionists. Since the hotel is busy twenty-four hours a day, the desk has to be staffed throughout the night as well as during the daytime.

The Pancontinental: Profit and loss account for year ended 31.12.9–

	Rooms	Food	Bar	Other	Total
Sales	4,722,350	3,702,322	2,002,276	972,804	11,399,753
Payroll	779,188	1,517,952	676,769	246,119	3,220,029
Materials	377,788	1,443,906	800,911	270,440	2,893,044
Other expenses	45,682	67,456	52,645	48,652	214,435
Departmental income	3,519,692	673,008	471,951	407,593	5,072,245

Operating expenses		
Salaries	503,869	
Bad debts	22,800	
Fees and other expenses	125,397	
Advertising	205,196	
Entertainment etc.	91,197	
Energy costs	376,192	
Sundry expenses	85,498	1,410,149
Operating profit		3,662,096
Property expenses		
Depreciation	237,500	
Interest	312,500	
Property taxes etc.	319,193	
Repairs and maintenance	319,193	1,188,386
Net operating profit		2,473,710
Taxation		803,956
Profit and Loss b/fwd		408,162
Dividends		687,500
Profit and loss c/fwd		574,092
		2,473,710

Figure 7 *The Pancontinental – profit and loss account*

The Pancontinental's current profit and loss account for the year ended 31.12.9– is as shown in Figure 7.

The Pancontinental's apportioned share of the group's balance sheet as on 31.12.9– is as shown in Figure 8.

The Pancontinental Balance sheet as at 31.12.9–

Fixed assets:	Cost	Depreciation	Net
Land and buildings			9,500,000
Fixtures and fittings	2,968,750	1,425,000	1,543,750
Current assets:			
Stocks		239,395	
Debtors		91,198	
Cash in hand and at bank		127,446	
		458,039	
Current liabilities		216,595	241,444
Net assets:			11,285,194
Long-term liabilities			2,500,000
Total			8,785,194
Represented by:			
Share capital (150,000 8% preference and			
400,000 ordinary shares of £1 each)			5,500,000
Share premium A/c			211,102
Revaluation reserve			2,500,000
Profit and Loss A/c			574,092
Total			8,785,194

Figure 8   *The Pancontinental – balance sheet*

Assignments

1 Using the text's descriptions of the 'Tudor' and 'Pancontinental' hotels as a guide, write a descriptive account of a small country pub with letting accommodation, bringing out the nature of the facilities and type of business.
2 Write a descriptive account of a large capital city luxury hotel along similar lines to Assignment 1.
3 Discuss the differences in organization structure, management and business control between medium-sized independent hotels on the one hand and large group or chain establishments on the other.
4 Examine the role of front office in relation to those of other hotel departments.
5 Investigate and compare the different hotel classification schemes used in the United Kingdom.

'Er, I'm afraid your room isn't *quite* ready yet. Would you mind taking a seat in the lounge for a couple of days. . . ?'

Part One

Procedural Aspects

1 Advance bookings

Introduction

We shall begin our study of the work of front office with a look at its clerical functions. The first of these is dealing with advance bookings.

This is only the first part of a continuous process that runs through check-in (arrival and registration) to the guest's stay in-house and finally check-out (departure). It includes the preparation of the guest's bill and the process of settlement. We shall look at these aspects in the following chapters.

As we have already indicated, hotels use a range of methods to deal with advance bookings. Manual systems require the completion of a number of different bits of paper, whereas computerized systems rely on a smaller number of keyboard entries. We shall describe the manual systems first, then attempt to show how the computerized ones differ from them.

Whatever the method used, the system has to be able to satisfy the following aims:

1   Provide a written record of all reservations.
2   Permit the receptionist to recognize unwanted guests in time to take appropriate action.
3   Provide immediate access to room availability data on any date, thus allowing the receptionist to accept or reject requests without delay.
4   Produce a daily arrivals list.
5   Enable management to maximize occupancy and room revenue.

The actual process is set out in Figure 9. Note that this is an 'idealized' version. Many hotels omit some of the stages (consulting a black list, for instance), or deal with functions like the diary in different ways. A computerized system consolidates some of the entries, reducing the amount of copying and facilitating analysis (these are in fact some of its great advantages).

Enquiries

The process of making a booking begins with an *enquiry*. There are a number of means by which guests can contact hotels. The most common are as follows.

1   *In person*   Such guests are commonly known as 'walk ins'. They are often people who are travelling unexpectedly, or touring an area 'out of season'. Since few hotels are anything like 100 per cent full, this approach is often successful, especially if the caller has a car. Motels are particularly likely to receive many of their bookings in this way. Sometimes the caller wants to make an advance booking. This is less common, for obvious reasons, but it does occasionally happen that a traveller knows he will be coming back to a town and decides to make an advance reservation there and then. Another possibility is that the

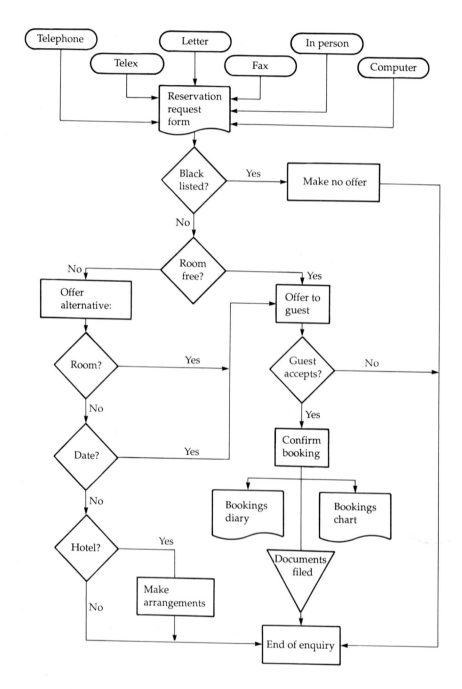

Figure 9   *Pre-arrivals procedure*

caller may want to make a reservation on behalf of someone else. This can be particularly important with regard to group bookings such as tours or conferences.

2 *Letter* In the old days, advance bookings generally took this form and were often for several months ahead. Nowadays, letter writing has gone out of fashion, but a considerable number of holiday bookings are still made in this way. Letters still offer the great advantage of being clear, unambiguous and permanent. A client may well agree on the details of a group booking face-to-face or over the telephone, but it is still good practice to set them out in the form of a follow-up letter. That way, both sides have a record of what was decided, and this helps to eliminate subsequent arguments. Letters are also useful evidence that a contract was actually agreed. Hotels suffer quite severely from people who book and then don't turn up (they are called 'no shows'). That is why you should ask for a letter of confirmation whenever possible. Written confirmation is also useful for the guest, who has a clear interest in knowing that the accommodation he has booked will actually be waiting for him when he arrives. Consequently you should also send the guest a confirmation as a matter of course.

3 *Telephone* Today, bookings are far more likely to come in the form of a telephone call. These generally request accommodation for a day or two ahead (and sometimes only a few hours). The telephone is fast and convenient, but it suffers from the major disadvantage that it does not provide a permanent record (answering machines allow messages to be left, but they do not usually record two-way conversations). This means that the speakers at either end of the line have to make their own notes of what was agreed.

4 *Telex* This overcomes the telephone's inability to provide a written record. Essentially it consists of two typewriter keyboards which can be linked together over virtually any distance, allowing the operators to 'talk' to each other. The 'conversations' are printed out at each end, thus providing a permanent record. The telex will print out any messages received even if it is left unmanned, for example overnight. This allows the hotel to receive bookings from countries in different time zones. The main problem with telex is that the equipment is relatively bulky and expensive. Consequently telex facilities are generally found only in the larger hotels.

5 *Fax (facsimile transmission)* This became very popular in the 1980s, but in fact some hotels had been using internal fax systems long before that. Fax uses modern electronic scanning techniques to send copies of documents over ordinary telephone lines to a special machine which prints out an identical copy at the other end. It can be used to send plans, diagrams and even pictures, but its main use is to transmit memos and letters. Like telex, fax will print out messages received even if it is left unmanned. Using fax, a would-be guest can send a booking instantaneously to a hotel on the other side of the world, and receive back written confirmation within a matter of hours or even minutes. The advantages are obvious, and we can expect to see all kinds of ingenious developments in the near future.

6 *Computerized communication* Written records are becoming increasingly old-fashioned, and what is called 'E-Mail' (electronic mail) is expanding. This means that a provincial travel agent's computer can 'talk' to a hotel's computer in another city, making bookings directly and leaving only an electronic record. At the moment, clients require written letters of confirmation, and these still have to be printed out, but it is possible that in the near future a would-be guest will be able to make a booking directly through his home computer, which will then retain the details in its memory. These developments are linked with various forms of group reservation systems, which are discussed more fully in Chapter 8.

No single means of communication is ideal in terms of:

1 Speed
2 Convenience
3 Economy

This means that we are likely to continue to see a mixture in use.

Reservation forms

However the booking is received, it has to be recorded. This record is generally called a *reservation form*. The actual layout will vary from hotel to hotel, but will typically include much of that shown in Figure 10.

There are several arguments in favour of using such forms:

1 They provide a permanent record. This is particularly useful with walk ins and telephone callers.
2 They summarize information in a standard format. Letters, telex and fax communications can all vary considerably in terms of form and content. Transferring the data from the original source to a standard reservation form makes it easier to check.
3 They act as a 'prompt' sheet. Would-be guests may leave out important information unless they are asked. A junior receptionist in a hurry might well forget to ask something vital unless she is prompted by having to complete a standardized form.
4 They enable management to find out who handled the booking. The practice of requiring receptionists to sign or initial every reservation form they deal with is useful in case there are any queries or errors.
5 They can provide a running check on progress. Instead of a bulky file containing the guest's original letter of enquiry, the hotel's response, the guest's booking, the hotel's confirmation and any subsequent communications, you can simply tick off a series of boxes, such as *'provisional'* and *'confirmed'*.
6 They can include information about the sources of bookings and how they are made, which is useful for marketing analysis purposes.

There is currently some disagreement about whether a computerized reservation system really requires the use of a separate reservation form. Virtually all room booking programs present the receptionist with an on-screen reservation form, and the idea of having to complete a paper version before entering the data into the computer seems like a waste of time. On the other hand, entering data via a keyboard currently suffers from two important limitations:

1 It is usually slower than using a pen because you can't 'skip' fields. Instead, you have to move through them in order, pressing *'return'* to jump to the next if you want to leave the current one blank.
2 You need to have both hands free, which means that answering the telephone requires earphones and a mouthpiece.

Reservation form

A/Date: _____ Stay Nt(s): _____ A/Time: _____

Room type: _____ No. persons: _____ Rate: _____

Name: _____ Phone no: _____

Address: _____
_____
_____
_____

Res. by: _____ Phone no: _____

Address: _____
_____
_____
_____

A/c instructions: _____

Special instructions: _____
_____
_____
_____

Guaranteed: ☐   Gtd to: _____ 6 pm: ☐

Clerk: _____ Today's date: _____

In person ☐   Phone ☐   Letter ☐   Telex ☐   Fax ☐   Computer ☐

T.B.C. ☐   By _____ Confirmed ☐   Wait list ☐

Figure 10 *Specimen reservation form*

In addition, many receptionists find that they have to concentrate on operating the computer, and this makes it harder for them to give their full attention to the caller.

Consequently, many computerized systems operate a 'two-stage' process whereby the receptionists use a reservation form while actually taking the booking, then enter the data into the computer during a later quiet period. This means that the booking records will not be completely up-to-date, but as long as the advance bookings are nowhere near full a half hour's delay is not really serious (in other words, you can take an additional booking without worrying about running out of rooms).

The black list

A black list is simply a record of people whom the hotel does not wish to accept as guests. It may be kept in book form or as a set of loose-leaf entries. There are only two essential requirements:

1   It should be easy to consult.
2   It should *not* be accessible to guests.

There are a number of ways in which individuals can find themselves on a black list:

1   They may have stayed at your hotel before and then 'skipped' (i.e. run off without paying their bill). Such a person is not very likely to come back, and even less likely to use the same name if he does, but it *can* happen, especially if he thinks that your security system is so poor that you won't spot him the second time. Alternatively, he may have tried the same trick at another hotel. Hotels commonly exchange information about suspect characters, and many black lists are compiled in cooperation with other establishments.
2   They may have shown themselves to be obnoxious in some way, perhaps by becoming violently drunk, abusive or quarrelsome, or by damaging your fixtures and fittings.
3   You may suspect them of having stolen something, either from you or another guest. Confidence tricksters and walk-in thieves find expensive hotels happy hunting grounds, and you don't want to encourage them. You may not be able to *prove* anything, but you do have an obligation to protect your other customers.
4   Finally, they may be employed by a firm whose solvency is in some doubt. Some companies are notoriously slow in paying their bills, and you may simply decide that it isn't worth the hassle and aggravation of trying to collect. This may seem unfair on the individual, but it is actually one of the more common reasons for blacklisting.

What can you say if you recognize that a would-be guest's name is on the black list? Usually you reply 'I'm sorry, we're full'. Coincidentally, you are also full the following night, the following week and even the following year. Such callers quickly get the message. You have to be careful about saying 'We don't want *you*' because of the innkeeper's duty to accept any bona fide traveller, and even more cautious about giving your reasons (after all, suspicion is not the same as proof).

In practice, the black list is more theoretical than real nowadays. In the past, a high proportion of bookings arrived in the form of letters, and the receptionist had time to consult the list before replying. Nowadays, far more of them arrive in the form of telephone calls, and many of these are made on behalf of third parties who may not even be named until much closer to the time of arrival (this is often the case with group tour bookings or company representatives). As a result, a great many are now taken without reference to any form of black list.

However, it still makes sense to ask 'Do we really want this guest?' *before* you take a booking, and advances in computer technology may well restore the black list to something like its old importance.

A final point is that a black list need not just be a list of persons whom we wish to reject. It can also be used to 'flag' VIPs or anyone whom you think might require special treatment.

Offering alternatives

If you find that you don't have a room of the type requested on the night in question, it is worth offering a series of alternatives rather than letting the guest try elsewhere. You should try to do this in the following sequence:

1 *A different type of room*   This usually means a more expensive one (e.g. single occupancy of a twin), though not always. Many guests will agree rather than face the inconvenience of hunting for accommodation somewhere else.
2 *A different date*   This won't work in most cases, but it is surprising how many would-be guests are prepared to change their travel arrangements in order to obtain a guaranteed booking. Even if you only succeed with 10 per cent, this is still 10 per cent more than you would have obtained had you not suggested the alternative. There is another advantage too. This will usually have the effect of shifting bookings from a high demand night to one for which demand is lower, thus helping to maximize occupancy.
3 *A different hotel*   Obviously, it is preferable to use one belonging to your own group. This is usually possible if the group is large and your hotel is located in a major city, because there will probably be one or two others within reasonable travelling range. Even so, there can be institutional barriers to this process. Sometimes group hotels see each other as rivals, and are reluctant to pass on customers. This is a petty attitude which can only harm everyone concerned. If you are the group's only representatives within a wide area, you will have to direct your surplus business towards a competitor. This is not necessarily as bad as it seems. Kemmons Wilson, the founder of Holiday Inns, would not allow his managers to put up 'hotel full' signs. Instead, he required them to fix up any surplus traveller at a nearby establishment. As he explained, Holiday Inns thereby made two friends. One was the traveller, who would be likely to return to Holiday Inns again, and the other was the competitor, which would be more likely to send its surplus to the local Holiday Inn in future.

The bookings diary

The bookings diary's purpose is to provide a list of arrivals on any particular night. It is not so much a specific document as a *function*, for hotels vary considerably in the way in which they obtain this information. Its importance is shown by the fact that manual systems normally produce it by means of an *additional* entry, which is inevitably expensive in terms of clerical time.

The traditional bookings diary

This was just what its name suggests: a daily diary in which receptionists listed all the arrivals due on that particular date. This diary was usually kept on a loose-leaf basis, with pages being removed from the front as the dates were reached, and new blank pages being added at the back. Page layouts varied, but typically included those shown in Figure 11.

Date of arrival...*3rd. March 199-*					
Date booked	Name	Stay	Room	Terms	Other details
27. 1. 9–	Mr/s Carter	2N	24	B & B	Arriving Late
3. 2. 9–	Mr Swann	1N	16	Room Only	—
5. 2. 9–	Miss Price	3N	12	Inclusive	—

Figure 11   *Traditional bookings diary*

Note that entries were only made for the date of arrival: the stays themselves were shown on a separate document called a bookings chart. Diary entries were made consecutively: in other words, the first booking taken for any particular date appeared on the first line, the second on the line below and so on. It was not usual to print room types or numbers down the side, though this was possible.

This traditional bookings diary was typical of the old approach to clerical operations, which required transactions to be transcribed laboriously into 'journals' or 'day books' before they were transferred to the accounts. During the 1960s and 1970s, more and more managers realized that the bookings diary could be replaced by a set of reservation forms filed in batches according to date of arrival, and then arranged in alphabetical order within the batches. This was more efficient because it involved less copying and also produced an alphabetically arranged arrivals list.

The Whitney advance booking rack

Another approach was pioneered by the American Whitney Corporation. It is known as the Whitney System. We shall be describing other aspects of the Whitney System later: at the moment we are only concerned with the advance booking rack.

The Whitney System was very widely used, especially in American or American-influenced hotels. It was particularly common in large and busy hotels, and has consequently tended to be superseded by computers nowadays. However, it is still likely to be found acting as a backup manual system in such establishments, and you need to be familiar with it.

The system is based on the use of standard sized cards or 'shannon slips'. These can be colour coded to show various kinds of reservation (group, airline, VIP etc.). It is possible to obtain sets of slips made of NCR ('no carbon required') paper which allow you to produce additional copies with no extra work.

The slips are designed to be placed in light metal carriers, which fit into vertical racks in such a way that only the top part of the slip can be seen. Because of this, it is usual to reserve the top line for the essential information and use the rest of the slip for less important details. It is possible to consult this whenever necessary because the slips and their carriers can easily be pushed upwards in the rack.

D/arrival	Name	Room type	Rate	D/departure
How received		Who by		Date received
Agency (if any)				
Account instructions			Confirmation date	

Figure 12   *Whitney slip*

A typical layout for an advance bookings slip is shown in Figure 12.

The set of racks holding the slips acts as a bookings diary. There are normally a number of these racks, arranged side by side within a framework hung vertically against a wall and capable of being moved along or lifted out if necessary. Special 'header' slips are used to divide the contents into different sections. Usually there will be a separate section for each of the next thirty or so days, one for each of the succeeding twelve months, then a single one for any bookings beyond that. As each day is reached, the rack in question is taken out and the others moved along, so that the whole mass of information is constantly being kept up to date.

Figure 13   *Whitney advance reservation rack*

The slips in their carriers can be moved around just as easily within the racks. This means that it is possible to subdivide next month's bookings into weeks as soon as they start to accumulate. The weeks themselves can be broken down into days just as easily. As we have seen, the slips can be colour coded, giving a quick 'at-a-glance' overview of the main sources of business.

Just as important is the fact that the slips can be kept in alphabetical order. This was impossible with the traditional diary, where written entries had to be made as and when the bookings came in. Using a Whitney rack, '*Aaronson*' can always be made to precede '*Barnaby*', which is a considerable help if you are trying to find the details of a booking in a hurry. Amendments don't affect this: you simply take the slip out of the rack and place it somewhere else without disturbing the order of the other slips.

The Whitney advance bookings rack offers a number of important advantages:

1   As we have seen, bookings can always be kept in date of arrival order, subdivided alphabetically.
2   The racks and the carriers can be reused, so that running expenses are limited to the cost of the paper slips.
3   The racks can be fixed vertically, which saves space (often at a premium in hotel back offices).

Room availability records

The next stage in the procedure requires us to check whether we actually have a room available. This is the most important part of the process, and involves using the room availability records, or bookings charts.

There are three alternative systems which you may find in use in different kinds of hotels:

1   The bedroom book (very small hotels).
2   The conventional chart (small to medium hotels).
3   The density chart (medium to large hotels).

In addition, some hotels used stop/go or space availability charts to supplement the main records.

The general principles on which these are constructed are the same whether they are prepared on paper or through the medium of a computer screen. If you wish to understand the latter form of presentation, it helps to follow it through on paper first. In any case, there are still strong arguments for a paper-based system in a small to medium-sized hotel. It is often much faster to operate than a computer program, since you don't have to get into 'reservation mode' and then type in the date you want to check. In the traditional system, this month's chart (the one you are most likely to need) is usually left open, and all you have to do is glance at it. Moreover, as more than one reception manager has said: 'A paper chart doesn't break down or suffer from power failures.'

1   *The bedroom book (reservations journal)*

This is derived from the bookings diary. In the normal diary, we enter the guest's name and particulars on his date of arrival only. However, we *could* write in his name for every night of his stay. If we do this, our diary becomes a bedroom book.

It is usual to have a list of the room types and numbers down the side of each page so that we can make sure we don't put a couple into a single room, or make them change rooms during their stay. The bedroom book thus looks like Figure 14.

Clearly, entering a guest's name on every night of his stay increases the amount of writing to

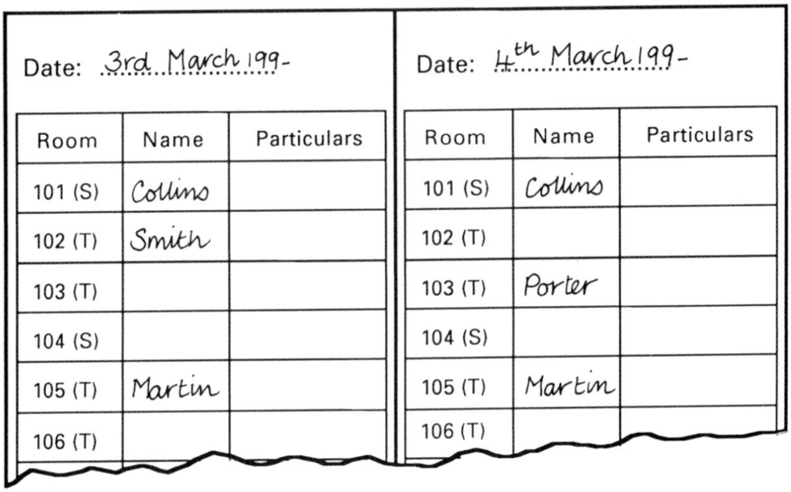

Figure 14 *Bedroom book*

be done. If he was staying for seven days, we should theoretically have to write his name out seven times, though it is usually possible to devise a simpler system, such as a horizontal line carried forward across successive pages, e.g.:

10 1 (S) BLOGGS —————————————   101 (S) ————————————————→

However, we would still have to turn several pages over to record a five night stay, which is a chore. Moreover, the page size limits the number of rooms we can book using this system. Consequently, bedroom books are really only suitable for small hotels, especially those with a high proportion of one night stays (these don't increase the amount of writing to be done because you have to enter them once anyway). Small bed and breakfast establishments in areas where there is a lot of touring would find this system perfectly satisfactory.

2 The conventional chart

This is a development of the bedroom book which is designed to be easier to read and more convenient to operate. It is laid out as shown in Figure 15.

The guests' names are written in block capitals and their arrival and departure dates are indicated by '‹' and '›' respectively. The usual convention is that the date column represents the *night* of the guest's stay, so that a guest arriving on the 1st and leaving on the morning of the 2nd would be recorded under the '1st' only. As a result, the point of the arrow is usually placed against the vertical line. However, some receptionists place it in the middle of the column to indicate that the guest is actually staying until mid morning. This is technically correct, but is harder to read and thus liable to lead to misunderstandings.

The conventional chart is simple to operate and shows most of the information the receptionist needs to know in an easy-to-read form. It is simple to enter a lengthy stay. The chart can display an entire month of bookings on one sheet of paper, and the left-hand columns can show the type of room, any interconnections, and even the rack rates if so desired.

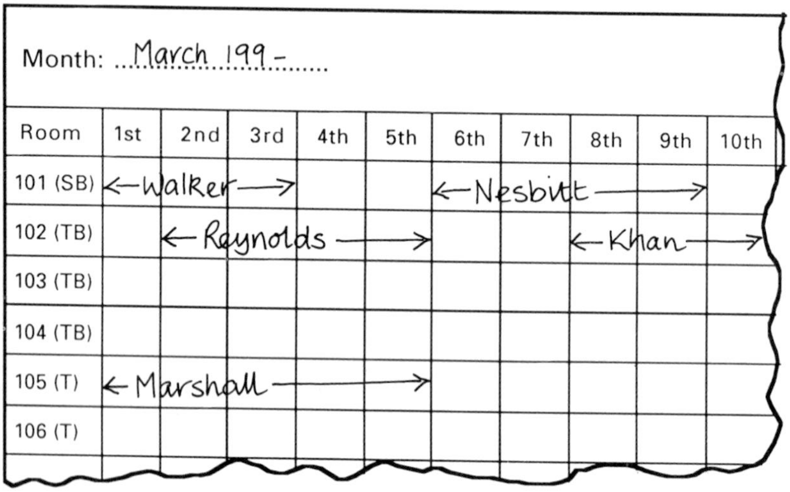

Figure 15   *Conventional chart*

Nevertheless, the conventional chart has a number of limitations. These become more serious the larger and busier the hotel is. They are (in ascending order of importance) as follows:

1   The so-called 'long name/short stay' problem. Imagine that you have someone called 'Foulkes-Fotheringham' staying for just one night. It can be difficult to fit such a name into a relatively small space, and this sometimes reduces inexperienced receptionists to panic. However, you can always abbreviate it to 'F-F' since the full details are available elsewhere.
2   The chart quickly becomes untidy because of amendments and corrections. It is usually printed on stout paper with the entries made in pencil to allow for this. Nevertheless, an extensively altered chart generally looks more than a little messy.
3   You can only get 30–60 lines on one sheet if you are going to write the names legibly, which means that this type of chart is limited to medium-sized hotels.
4   It is not easy to count the number of free rooms on any one night. If you receive a request for a group booking, you have to run your finger down the appropriate date column, counting the number of blank spaces and checking to see whether they are singles or twins. This limitation becomes important in larger hotels with a high proportion of group bookings.
5   It is difficult to overbook, since an entry on the chart is synonymous with a room reservation. You *can* make provision for overbooking by leaving a number of blank lines at the bottom of the chart, but it isn't always easy to know when you should use these since, as point 4 above indicates, the chart is not designed to show the total number of rooms let very clearly.
6   Most importantly, the conventional chart makes it necessary to allocate a room on booking rather than on arrival. In practice, most large hotels find it easier to allocate a room when the guest arrives, rather than weeks (possibly months) in advance. Rooms can then be allocated as they become ready after being serviced, rather than the housekeeping staff having to rush to prepare a particular one for an earlier arrival. Allocating rooms in

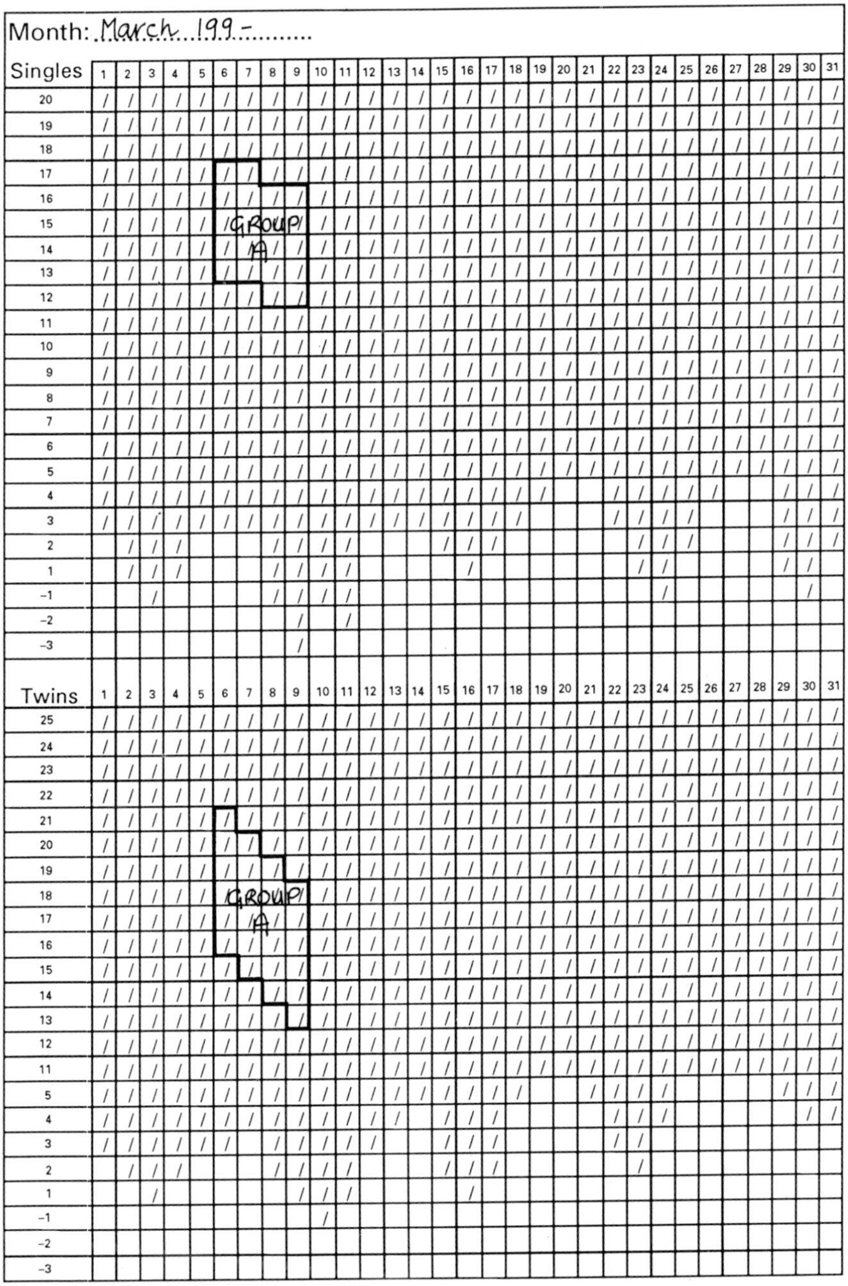

Month: March 199-

Singles

GROUP A

Twins

GROUP A

Figure 16 *Standard density chart*

advance can also lead to the creation of awkward 'gaps' which are then difficult to fill. You might find that Room 102 (a twin) is free on Monday and Room 103 (also a twin) is free on Tuesday. You have a twin available on both nights, but they are not the same rooms, which makes it difficult to accept a two-night booking without some complicated last minute alterations.

These last three factors make it difficult to maximize occupancy using the conventional chart. However, you would have to use this kind of chart if all your rooms were different and guests were likely to want one in particular. Conventional charts are thus best suited to hotels with:

1   Fewer than sixty rooms.
2   Non-standard accommodation.
3   Relatively long stays, especially of the 'end on' (everyone arriving and leaving on the same day) type.
4   Few short notice group bookings.
5   Few 'no-shows' (i.e., little need to overbook).

These features tend to be characteristic of the smaller, older type of resort hotel, though you should note that points 2 and 3 also apply to timeshare letting. However, most modern establishments find it more convenient to use the next type of chart to be discussed.

3   The density chart

This is a development of the conventional chart, designed to overcome its weaknesses. It can only be used in hotels with standardized rooms because its fundamental principle is that all rooms of a particular type are 'blocked', i.e. grouped together. The receptionist does not reserve a specific room: she only books one of the particular type requested. The actual room allocation is done on arrival. This means that the guest does not know which room he is going to occupy until he arrives, but this does not really matter since all rooms of the same type are identical.

Figure 16 shows a standard density chart for an hotel with twenty singles and twenty-five twins. These are shown as two 'blocks'. The vertical columns indicate the dates, as in the conventional chart, though they are narrower because you only put a stroke (/) instead of writing in the guest's name. However, the horizontal rows do *not* indicate room numbers as in the conventional chart. Instead, they show the total number of rooms of the specified class.

The density chart is completed as follows. New bookings are entered as strokes in the appropriate date columns. Strokes are always made in the first free space reading from the top. This means that a series of strokes representing a two or three day booking does *not* have to be on the same horizontal line. In fact, this becomes unusual once the chart has a number of previous entries on it (to check this, look at Figure 16 and try entering a three night single booking commencing on the 1st).

Newcomers to the density chart sometimes fear that this might mean guests having to change rooms during their stays. It doesn't. It would if we were using a conventional chart, because in that case each row represents a specific room. With the density chart, however, the row merely represents a room *type*. There must be a room free for any subsequent reservation, otherwise you would not be able to get the booking onto the chart (even if you use one of the minus or overbooking rows, you are simply assuming that one of the other bookings won't appear).

Group bookings can be indicated by drawing a rough circle around a group of strokes, as shown in Figure 16. The group's reference number can be added for greater clarity.

The density chart offers a number of important advantages, though there are also one or two corresponding disadvantages. These are as follows:

Density chart for 30th March 199-

Twins

96	95	94	93	92	91	90	89	88	87
86	85	84	83	82	81	80	79	78	77
76	75	74	73	72	71	70	69	68	67
66	65	64	63	62	61	60	59	58	57
56	55	54	53	52	51	50	49	48	47
46	45	44	43	42	41	40	39	38	37
36	35	34	33	32	31	30	29	28	27
26	25	24	23	22	21	20	19	18	17
16	15	14	13	12	11	10	9	8	7
6	5	4	3	2	1	-1	-2	-3	-4
-5	-6	-7	-8	-9	-10	-11	-12	-13	-14

Singles

48	47	46	45	44	43	42	41	40	39
38	37	36	35	34	33	32	31	30	29
28	27	26	25	24	23	22	21	20	19
18	17	16	15	14	13	12	11	10	9
8	7	6	5	4	3	2	1	-1	-2
-3	-4	-5	-6	-7	-8	-9	-10	-11	-12

Suites

16	15	14	13	12	11	10	9	8	7
6	5	4	3	2	1	-1	-2	-3	-4

Density chart for 31st March 199-

Twins

96	95	94	93	92	91	90	89	88	87
86	85	84	83	82	81	80	79	78	77
76	75	74	73	72	71	70	69	68	67
66	65	64	63	62	61	60	59	58	57
56	55	54	53	52	51	50	49	48	47
46	45	44	43	42	41	40	39	38	37
36	35	34	33	32	31	30	29	28	27
26	25	24	23	22	21	20	19	18	17
16	15	14	13	12	11	10	9	8	7
6	5	4	3	2	1	-1	-2	-3	-4
-5	-6	-7	-8	-9	-10	-11	-12	-13	-14

Singles

48	47	46	45	44	43	42	41	40	39
38	37	36	35	34	33	32	31	30	29
28	27	26	25	24	23	22	21	20	19
18	17	16	15	14	13	12	11	10	9
8	7	6	5	4	3	2	1	-1	-2
-3	-4	-5	-6	-7	-8	-9	-10	-11	-12

Suites

16	15	14	13	12	11	10	9	8	7
6	5	4	3	2	1	-1	-2	-3	-4

Figure 17 *Two night density chart*

1 It is easier to complete than the conventional chart, since you only have to make a stroke rather than printing the guest's name in full. The corresponding disadvantage is that it is easier to make mistakes, and more difficult to check them since you have no idea which stroke represents which guest. In practice, manual density charts in large hotels have often been as much as 5 per cent out either way, and it was common practice to check them shortly before each date of arrival.

2 You can fit more rooms onto a density chart because the 'boxes' can be much smaller than on a conventional chart. This makes the density chart particularly suitable for large hotels. Even so, it was often the case that you needed one page for each night, rather than being able to show an entire month's bookings on one sheet. The disadvantage (as we have already noted) is that you can only use it in hotels with standard rooms. Attempts to use it in older hotels where the rooms vary considerably in terms of attractiveness (even if they are all similar in theory) run up against the problem of the regular guest who begins to ask for a specific room. This is not easy to guarantee when you are using a density chart.

3 It allows you to see at a glance just how many rooms of any particular type you have left. Going back to Figure 16, you can see that on the night of the 6th we have two

singles and two twins free (all you do is run your finger down the relevant column, then across to the 'total' figure on the left). This is very useful if you are handling lots of block bookings.

4   It makes it easier to handle overbooking. You can see at a glance just where you are and control your overbooking levels by using the 'minus' rows. This helps you to maximize occupancy.

These features appeal particularly to large modern hotels, which generally have standardized rooms and cater for a lot of block bookings and business trade (the latter often characterized by a high proportion of no-shows). Nowadays, such hotels generally use computerized reservation systems, but their room availability displays are still based on density chart principles.

There are various versions of the standard manual density chart. They include the so-called 'peg board' chart, which has a solid base and uses coloured pegs instead of pencil strokes. These pegs can be colour coded, so that the chart shows the 'mix' of business for the month in question at a glance.

Hotels with a large number of rooms often find that it is only possible to fit one or two nights onto a single sheet. This permits a slightly different arrangement of the room total figures, as shown in Figure 17.

Such charts are completed by crossing out the figures in descending order, i.e. from the highest to the lowest. The basic principle remains exactly the same, however, as it does in Figure 18, which shows a chart laid out in 'blocks of five'.

Density chart for ...March 199 —..........................
Singles

100 ༄	95 ༄	90 ༄	85 ༄	80 ⑴⑴⑴	75
70	65	60	55	50	45
40	35	30	25	20	15
10	5	0	−5	−10	−15

Figure 18   *One night condensed density chart*

This is completed by what is called 'gate scoring', as shown.

4   Stop/go or space availability charts

Convenient though it is, there can only be one density chart in a hotel. This sometimes proved

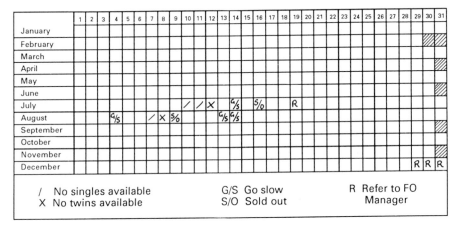

Figure 19 *'Stop/go' or space availability chart*

inconvenient in very large establishments where five or six receptionists might all find themselves taking bookings at once.

The answer was a 'stop/go' or space availability chart. This did not replace the main chart, but merely indicated the future letting position at a glance so that receptionists could tell whether it was safe to go ahead and take a booking. It commonly looked something like the chart shown in Figure 19.

The codings were written in pencil or some other erasable medium. They signalled the room availability status. If a particular date was clear, receptionists could go ahead and let rooms without worrying. 'G/S' (go slow) might mean that they could sell single rooms but had to check whether they could accept a group.

Stop/go charts were limited to large hotels, and they have now been largely superseded by computers. One of the computer's advantages is that each receptionist can see the current room availability situation on her own VDU, which eliminates the need for a stop/go chart.

Computerized reservations

Computerized reservation systems follow much the same stages as manual ones, though they *look* very different since everything appears on the screen, usually with a series of 'prompts'. The details will vary from one system to another, but in general the process is as follows:

1 Enter the advance reservations part of the program. This usually has to be done through the 'main menu'. This step is equivalent to a receptionist using a manual system turning to the chart.
2 Call up the room availability display for the night in question. This almost always means typing the required date in via the keyboard. The computer will then show you how many rooms of each type are available (this is very similar to the density chart, with the added advantage that the computer counts up the number of free rooms instead of you having to do it!). The computer will generally display up to fourteen successive nights as well in case you have to book a lengthy stay: it is usually possible to 'flip' backwards or forwards in

fourteen night increments with a simple key press. Systems generally have a 'booking horizon' of something like two years or so, which is more than sufficient for most purposes. The display will look something like that shown in Figure 20 (this assumes a hotel with 50 singles, 100 twins and 50 doubles). This display is mostly self-evident. The 'occupancy percentages' are room occupancies.

```
Jan 90  Room availability                        01 Jan 90

Room           01  02  03  04  05  06  07  08  09  10
type          Mon Tue Wed Thu Fri Sat Sun Mon Tue Wed
------------------------------------------------------------
SB             37  33  34  36  40  44  43  36  30  33
TB             67  65  66  70  78  82  82  66  63  62
DB             35  34  36  38  41  43  43  36  35  38
40
------------------------------------------------------------
Room          139 132 136 144 159 169 168 138 128 133
avail
------------------------------------------------------------
Occupancy 44% 47% 46% 42% 36% 32% 33% 45% 49% 47%
```

Figure 20   *Advance reservations screen*

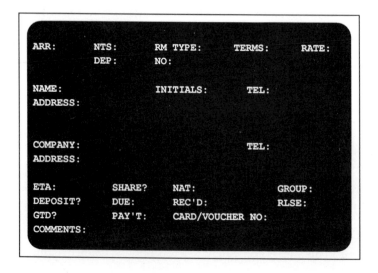

Figure 21   *Bookings screen*

3   Enter the bookings section of the program. This is really a computerized version of the reservation form. It will look something like Figure 21. The abbreviations vary from program to program but are mostly self explanatory, and soon become familiar with use. In

this example 'Arr' means arrival date, 'Nts' means the number of nights stay, 'Dep' the departure date, 'Rm Type' the type of room, 'No' the actual number of rooms being booked (remember that a family may book two or more), 'Terms' the type of package (weekend break, bed and breakfast etc.) and 'Rate' the price agreed. 'ETA' means expected time of arrival, 'Share' establishes whether or not the guest is willing to share a room (often the case with conference delegates, for instance), 'Nat' means nationality, 'Group' the particular tour or conference (these are usually given reference numbers or codes), 'Deposit' 'Due' and 'Rec'd' are self explanatory, 'Rlse' means release date (i.e. the date by which the computer will automatically cancel the booking unless a deposit has been received). 'Gtd' refers to the increasingly common practice of taking certain types of booking on the understanding that they will be charged for whether or not the guest turns up. Such bookings generally depend on the method of payment agreed so the next two 'fields' ('Pay't' and 'Card/vouchr no') relate to that. Finally, 'Comments' allows any individual requests to be noted. There may well be other 'fields'. Some programs require you to classify guests by type (e.g. regular or VIP), or allow cross-reference to a pre-existing guest history file. Virtually all will require you to identify yourself by adding your own identification code (if you don't, or the code is invalid, the program won't allow you to proceed any further). This is the equivalent of your initialling the reservation form. Programs usually allow you to 'skip' fields if these are irrelevant to that particular booking. They will also allow you to preprogram particular keys in order to save on typing time (for instance, the 'function' keys may be programmed so that 'F2' produces 'USA' in response to the 'nationality?' prompt). Finally, they will allow you to review the booking details and make any necessary corrections before you finally press the 'Return' or 'Enter' key and commit it to the computer's memory. Even then, all is not lost, for all the programs will allow you to cancel or amend bookings, though they will usually retain records for security reasons. It is thus often possible to enter, cancel, and then reinstate a booking without having to go through the lengthy business of retyping the details in through the keyboard.

4   Many systems will also allow you to book a specific room (in other words, they will double as a conventional chart).

5   Once the booking has been put into the computer's memory, a great many operations can be handled automatically. The most important of these are as follows:

(a) The room count is automatically adjusted to reduce the number of rooms available. If a specific room has been reserved, that room is 'flagged' so that it cannot be let to anyone else. In this way the program acts as both a density and a conventional chart.

(b) A list of expected arrivals is prepared for each future date. This list is always up to date, and always in alphabetical order. Many programs will also allow you to extract the names of particular types of guest (e.g. VIPs), or even to search the files for particular names (this is very useful if you receive an enquiry about a guest who has not yet arrived). In this way the computer can double as a bookings diary and an arrivals (or departures) list.

(c) Finally, the computer can provide up-to-date details of expected occupancies and room revenue figures at the press of a key. As we shall see later on, this is important when we are trying to maximize revenue through what is known as 'yield management'.

Assignments

1   Describe the type of advance booking system you would expect to find in the Tudor Hotel.

2   Describe the type of advance booking system you would expect to find in the Pancontinental Hotel.

3   Obtain specimens of the type of advance booking documents and an outline of the procedures used at a selection of local hotels, and compare these with one another, relating their characteristics to the type of hotel involved.

4   Discuss the arguments against and in favour of handwritten reservation forms in hotels with computerized advance booking systems.

5   Describe the nature and purpose of the black list. Assess its current importance, and discuss how it might develop over the next decade.

2 Check-in and related issues

Introduction

Some time normally elapses between the guest making a booking and his actual arrival. During this period the hotel may deal with scores or even hundreds of other visitors. However, it must still be ready to receive the guest. There must be a room ready for him, and there are various necessary formalities to be gone through when he arrives.

In addition, the hotel must keep track of him once he is 'in house'. It may be required to provide various services for him, and it must make sure that these are properly recorded and (if appropriate) charged for.

All this means a good deal of record keeping. Much of this is the business of front office, and it forms the subject matter of this chapter.

The process is summarized in Figure 22.

Guest action	Front office task
Arrival	Checks booking detail
Registration	Checks registration
	Allocates room and issues key
Goes to room	Directs guest or arranges escort
	Notifies other departments
	Opens bill
Uses Hotel facilities	Posts charges
	Passes mail etc.
Settles account	Checks and presents bill
Departs	Notifies other departments
	Updates records

Figure 22 *Check-in procedure*

Arrival and registration

The Arrivals list

The check-in process actually starts some time before the guest's arrival, for front office commonly makes out an arrivals list beforehand. This is, as its name indicates, a list of the arrivals expected on any specific date. Copies are circulated to the housekeeper, telephonist, head porter, food and beverage manager and possibly to the general manager (especially if any VIPs are expected) as well as being retained by reception.

The arrivals list is usually prepared twenty-four hours in advance, though group arrivals lists may be circulated up to a week beforehand (groups require rather more preparation). Although adequate for most purposes, the list will not be completely accurate because:

1 Some of the expected guests may turn out to be 'no shows'.
2 There may well be some last minute ('chance') bookings.

The arrivals list is usually prepared from the bookings diary. The entries are rearranged so that they are in alphabetical order, and a note added if a room has been allocated in advance, a late arrival is expected or if there are any special requirements. The layout is typically as shown in Figure 23.

Date: .....31st....March..199.–.....

Name	No. of guests		Room		No. of nights	Arrival time	Remarks
	Adults	Children	Type	No			
ADAMS	2	—	TB	204	2	6·00	
JONES	2	1	TB	306	3	6·30	COT REQUIRED
LACY	1	—	S	110	1	7·00	REGULAR

Figure 23   *Arrivals list*

This process is time consuming, and various short cuts have been devised. One ingenious practice has been to reproduce the appropriate Whitney advance booking rack by taking it out of its frame and laying it face downwards on the photocopier. Since the slips are already in alphabetical order with the key information visible at the top, this works well.

However, these expedients are not necessary with a computerized system. As we have seen, once the information has been entered, it can be analysed and reproduced under as many different headings as necessary. The advance bookings can be listed according to date of arrival, for instance, and displayed on a VDU or printed off on paper as an arrivals list.

Registration

When a guest arrives, he must be greeted politely and then asked to 'register'. This means requesting him to put down certain particulars in a book or on a form. Registration serves three main functions:

1 It satisfies the legal requirements.
2 It provides a record of actual arrivals as opposed to bookings. The traditional explanation of the need for some form of registration was that it provided some form of record in the case of a fire or other disaster. Since the register only shows arrivals this was never wholly convincing. However, analysis of registration records can provide a useful market analysis.
3 It helps to confirm the guest's acceptance of the hotel's terms and conditions, and is thus useful should legal proceedings be necessary.

In addition, registration gives the guest something to do while the receptionist is checking her own records and perhaps deciding which room he should be allocated. Activities of this type fulfil a very useful social purpose, not least because they help to reassure the guest that his booking really is going to be honoured.

Legal requirements

These are at present to be found in the Immigration Order of 1972, which requires the hotelier to distinguish between non-aliens and aliens. Non-aliens are currently:

- British passport holders.
- Commonwealth citizens.
- Citizens of the Republic of Ireland (Eire).
- Members of NATO armed forces serving in the UK.
- Foreign nationals serving with the UK's armed forces.
- Foreign diplomats, envoys and their staff (this is under the Diplomatic Privileges Act, 1964).

Any non-alien over sixteen years of age staying for one night or more is required to state his full name and nationality (you will notice that this exempts short-period 'day lets' from registration). The law does *not* require a non-alien guest to give his address, and it is well established (by custom and precedent) that the name he gives need not be his own, though he must not use a different one with intent to defraud.

The law does not require the guest to physically sign a register. This allows a husband to sign on behalf of his wife, or vice versa, and although both must be registered, it is permissible to do so on one line as 'Mr and Mrs . . .'. This exemption also permits a tour guide or conference organizer to sign on behalf of a group of guests, though again each one must be separately registered. If hotels *do* ask guests to sign, it is to confirm the guest's acceptance of the hotel's terms and conditions, and a signature is not compulsory, though few guests know this.

An alien is anyone who does not fall into the categories deemed to be non-alien. In addition to his name and nationality, such a guest is required to provide the following information:

- The number of his passport or registration certificate.
- Its place of issue.
- Details of his next destination, and if possible his address there.

The purpose of this last provision is to enable the immigration authorities to keep track of foreign nationals staying in this country. It is seldom used in practice, but it *does* sometimes happen that the police will contact a hotel to find out if a particular individual really has been staying there, as perhaps he said he would. Consequently this provision is important, and you should not allow yourself to be deterred by the fact that it is often difficult for the guest to answer this particular question, especially if he is simply touring 'on spec'. In such cases it is necessary to 'flag' the guest's bill so that the question can be put again when he is leaving. If all else fails, you might have to be content with the name of a town or region: at least that would show that you had done your best to get the information.

The law provides that registration particulars must be kept for a period of twelve months, and must be produced if requested by a police officer or Home Office representative.

Types of register

There are two basic types of register. The first is the registration book. It has the following advantages:

1   It is compact, relatively cheap and difficult to lose.
2   It is hard to alter without detection.
3   It records arrivals in chronological order.

On the other hand, it has certain disadvantages:

1   It is very slow if there are large numbers of guests.
2   It lacks confidentiality (guests can see who else has arrived).

The balance of the factors tends to favour its use in the smaller, 'family' type of hotel. It typically looks like Figure 24.

Date	Surname	Forenames	Address	Nationality	Room no.	Car reg no.	Passport no.	Place of issue	Next destination

Figure 24   *Registration book*

```
┌─────────────────────────────────────────────────────────────┐
│                    Registration card                         │
│                                                              │
│   Surname......................................  Arrival date................. │
│                                                              │
│   Other names...................................................  │
│                                                              │
│   Nationality...................................................  │
│                                                              │
│   Home address...................................................  │
│                 ...................................................  │
│                 ...................................................  │
│                                                              │
│   Room no....................................  Car registration............. │
│                                                              │
│                                                              │
│   For foreign visitors only:                                 │
│                                                              │
│   Passport no................................  Issued at............. │
│                                                              │
│   Next destination...................................................  │
│                                                              │
│                                                              │
│   All visitors:                                              │
│                                                              │
│   Signature...................................................  │
└─────────────────────────────────────────────────────────────┘
```

Figure 25 *Registration form*

Large hotels find the registration book's lack of flexibility a major handicap, and generally use individual forms or cards. The layout of such registration cards varies from hotel to hotel, but they will generally include the items shown in Figure 25.

The advantages and disadvantages of the looseleaf registration form 'mirror' those of the book. It is rather more expensive and a great deal easier to lose. In theory, it would be easy to remove a card and insert a substitute (though this can be made more difficult by using serially numbered forms). Cards are much more flexible, since they can be issued in batches to groups, even in advance, and you can even have different cards for different nationalities (Japanese-English, for example). Moreover, they cannot easily be read by other guests.

Preregistration

It makes sense to try to complete as much of the registration process as possible in advance because this reduces delays at reception. This can be applied to preregistered private guests. However, it is even more common with group bookings because these often arrive together and form an impatient queue at the desk.

What usually happens is that front office receives a list of group names and room preferences from the group organizer several days in advance. Staff then prepare individual registration cards showing name, group, dates of arrival and departure and any rate details.

On the day of arrival, rooms are allocated and blocked off on the room rack. The room numbers are added to the pre-prepared card, and room keys attached. The complete set can then be placed in an envelope together with the group programme and hotel promotional material.

When the group members arrive, they can be directed to a separate desk, which is often set up in another room. There they are issued with their individual envelopes and asked to sign the pre-prepared registration card. This process clearly demands the use of cards rather than a book-type register.

Computerized check-in

If the hotel is using a computerized system, it is usually possible to 'call up' the guest's booking particulars on the screen when he arrives and continue the process from there. Obviously the computer must be 'told' that the guest has arrived, and there must be provision for any last minute changes. You will probably find that the program starts with something like the original booking screen (see Chapter 1), deleting some items which are no longer necessary (like expected time of arrival) and adding one or two others, such as the room allocated, any agreement regarding 'extras' (i.e. items to be charged to and paid for separately by 'package' guests) and the guest's credit limit (i.e. the amount he will be allowed to run up on credit before being asked to settle his account).

The resulting screen may look something like Figure 26.

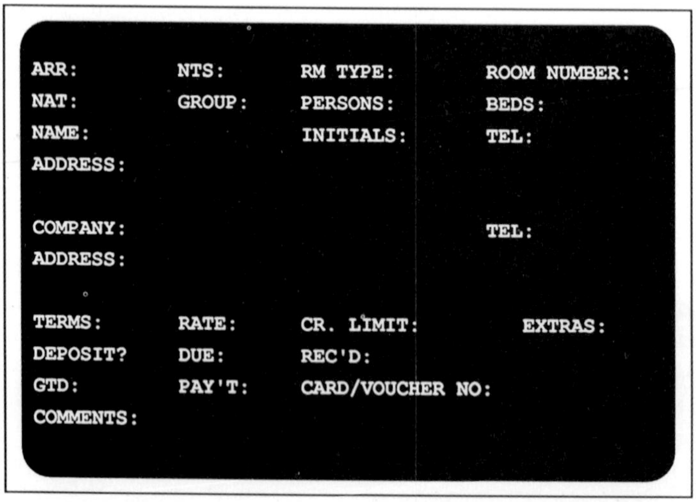

```
ARR:          NTS:        RM TYPE:          ROOM NUMBER:
NAT:          GROUP:      PERSONS:          BEDS:
NAME:                     INITIALS:         TEL:
ADDRESS:


COMPANY:                                    TEL:
ADDRESS:


TERMS:        RATE:       CR. LIMIT:        EXTRAS:
DEPOSIT?      DUE:        REC'D:
GTD:          PAY'T:      CARD/VOUCHER NO:
COMMENTS:
```

Figure 26   *Check-in screen*

Most of these fields will already have the details displayed, but they can be altered if necessary.

The procedure for checking in a 'chance' guest is very similar, except that here the fields will be empty and you will have to fill them in on the basis of the guest's responses.

Automated check-in

This is a relatively new development. It is now possible to install a machine rather like a bank cash dispenser which is able to handle late arrivals and 'chance' bookings without any staff having to be present.

Such machines are usually activated by a credit card. The customer approaches the machine and inserts his card. If he has already made an advance booking, he will have quoted his card number when he did so. The machine is able to recognize this and display details of the booking for the guest to confirm. The machine can then display a personalized welcome and issue a computer-coded room key.

If the machine does not recognize the card number, it assumes that the owner is a 'chance' guest and displays a menu showing the rooms available and their rates. The guest chooses a suitable room and the machine goes on to display its personalized welcome and issue a computer-coded room key.

Sophisticated machines can also offer a range of other services for the guest to select, such as early morning teas and calls. They can also be programmed to turn on the heating and lighting in the room selected.

Such systems offer a number of important advantages:

1 *They reduce costs* Maintaining twenty-four-hour coverage of the reception desk is expensive. Automated 'after hours' customer service is already common in other industries, and the same arguments apply to hotels. At the same time, the system reduces the number of errors caused by 'operator fatigue'.
2 *They can increase occupancy and room revenue* It is not unknown for bored or overtired night staff to simply 'shut up shop', even when there are still rooms available. Moreover, some establishments prefer to close their doors early for security reasons. The machine does not become bored, overtired or frightened.
3 *They increase security* The hotel does not have to leave its front door open or maintain cash floats in the front office area overnight in order to deal with late check-ins. Only valid credit card holders can gain access legitimately, and while this does not guarantee immunity, it undoubtedly reduces the risks.
4 *They can be moved closer to the customer* They could be placed on the street outside the hotel, for instance, or located at a distance (at the local airport for instance).

The disadvantage is a reduction in the 'hospitality' element of the check-in process. Most present-day guests still prefer to be greeted by a smiling, cheerful, pleasant receptionist. However, automated check-in systems are likely to appeal increasingly to the computer-literate guests of the future, especially if they save them time.

The full implication as far as registration is concerned are not yet clear. As we have already pointed out, there is no legal requirement for a signature, and an electronic check-in record of the type we have just described would probably be sufficient as long as all the questions required by law were answered. The records would have to be retained for the required twelve-month period.

At the moment, however, 'computer-assisted' registration is the furthest most British hotels have been prepared to go in this direction. This involves printing a computer-generated registration form prior to the guest's arrival. The details are taken from the original booking, as earlier, with additional information such as the room number added. The form is checked by the guest on arrival. Until it is clear whether electronically stored records actually do satisfy the legal requirements, it is probably safer to run off a copy of the registration particulars in this way.

Room status records

It is necessary for a hotel to keep track of the current status of each room so that it can tell:

1 If occupied, by whom, for how long, and for how much.
2 If unoccupied, whether it is available for letting, or not yet ready, or unavailable because it has been taken out of service for repairs or redecoration.

Bed sheets

Some hotels have handled these requirements by keeping a looseleaf record known as a 'bed sheet'. This had preprinted pages which showed the rooms and their current letting position. A typical layout was as shown in Figure 27.

Day....................		Date...........................										
	Departures				Stays				Arrivals			
Room	Name	Sleepers	Rate	D/D'ture	Name	Sleepers	Rate	D/D'ture	Name	Sleepers	Rate	D/D'ture
101 SB												
102 TB												
103 DB												

Figure 27   *Bed sheet*

The previous day's stays and arrivals were brought forward into the appropriate columns on the following day's sheet, using the 'date of departure' entry as a guide. Expected arrivals were added from the advance booking records, leaving the remainder available for letting. 'Chance' arrivals were added to the sheet so that it provided an accurate record of the night's occupancy. Rooms out of service for various reasons could be noted as such.

This provided a written record of both occupancies and room revenue, but was labour intensive. It was thus only suitable for small to medium-sized hotels. In fact, all that a manager really needs is a *summary* of the occupancy and revenue figures, and this can be extracted easily enough from a much more flexible aid which serves much the same purpose and is found in most medium-sized hotels operating manual systems.

Room racks

The 'room rack' or 'reception board' is simply a means of displaying the current letting position of every room in the hotel. Its relationship to the advance bookings chart must be clearly understood. The chart shows *future* bookings. Most of these will eventually become arrivals, but the chart will still be inaccurate because of 'no shows' and 'chance' arrivals. The room rack shows the situation *now*. It is the rack which acts as the basis for reports on occupancy and letting revenue. Consequently, unlike the chart, it *must* be kept up to date and be completely accurate.

Room racks differ in detail from hotel to hotel, but the basic principle is always the same. There is some form of slot for each room, into which is placed a card or slip showing the current occupancy situation. Each slot is marked with the room number, and may carry other information as well, such as the current rack rate or a summary of its facilities.

Layouts vary, but the most common divides the accommodation up into floors, with adjacent rooms side by side to show any interconnections. The rack has to be located where the receptionists can consult it easily, but not where it is visible to guests.

The old-fashioned guest card was filled in with the basic details of the booking, as shown in Figure 28.

Name	
Date of arrival	Date of departure
No. of guests	Terms

Figure 28 *Room rack card*

Other cards in different colours could be used to indicate:

- Staff use
- Being cleaned
- Out of service

Providing this display was kept up to date, front office staff were able to tell the current occupancy situation at a glance.

Another variation on this theme was provided by the Whitney Corporation. The Whitney room rack consists of a 'ladder' of metal slots, each exactly the right size to take a standard sized Whitney slip. Each slot is labelled with the appropriate room number.

Some of these Whitney racks have an ingenious 'window' in the centre of each slot with a transparent perspex sleeve which can be slid backwards and forwards over a card insert. The card is used to indicate details such as the type of room or its current rate. The left-hand part of the sleeve is tinted red, the centre is clear, and the right-hand side is tinted yellow.

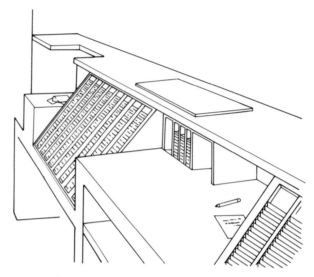

Figure 29   *Whitney room status rack*

The slips and sleeves are used in combination to indicate room status. Typically, the sequence is as follows:

1   No occupant or booking   No slip, sleeve set at clear
2   Room reserved for expected arrival   No slip, sleeve set at red
3   Room allocated to arrival   Slip inserted, sleeve covered
4   Departure   Slip removed, sleeve set at yellow
5   Room cleaned   Sleeve changed to clear

The similarity to this system and a set of traffic lights is obvious. Red means 'stop', yellow means 'on change' and clear means 'go'.

This 'traffic light' parallel was taken even further by some large hotels, which fitted their room racks with coloured signal lights controlled jointly from front office and the house-keeper's office. The exact sequence and colours of the lights could vary, but the general principle was much the same in all these installations. When a room was allocated, the receptionist would switch its light to red to stop anyone else from letting that particular room. When the guest checked out, she would change it to yellow to signal that it was now ready for cleaning. As soon as the housekeeping staff had finished making it ready, they would use their terminal to switch it to 'clear' (sometimes green), thus telling front office that it was available for letting again. Sometimes this had to be done from the housekeeper's office, but there were installations which allowed it to be done from the room itself.

Computerized room status displays

The elaborate systems we have just described are now becoming obsolete. They were only used in very large hotels, which were among the first to install computers. A computerized system does the same job as the manual room rack, but the information is stored in an electronic memory rather than on a board or rack physically located in the front office. This

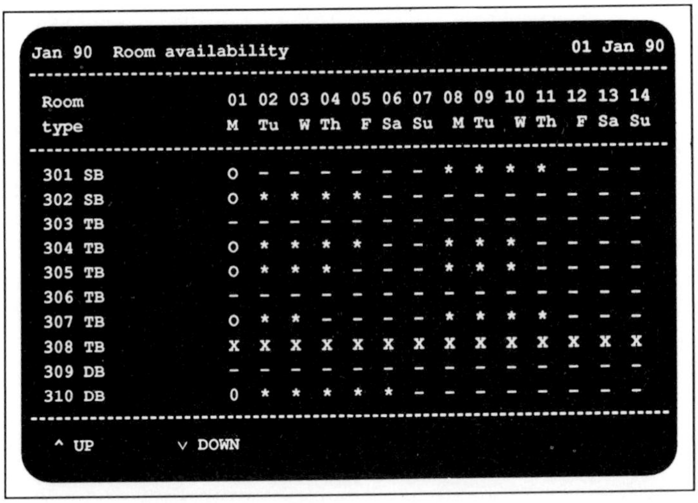

Jan 90 Room availability														01 Jan 90
Room	01	02	03	04	05	06	07	08	09	10	11	12	13	14
type	M	Tu	W	Th	F	Sa	Su	M	Tu	W	Th	F	Sa	Su
301 SB	O	–	–	–	–	–	–	*	*	*	*	–	–	–
302 SB	O	*	*	*	*	–	–	–	–	–	–	–	–	–
303 TB	–	–	–	–	–	–	–	–	–	–	–	–	–	–
304 TB	O	*	*	*	*	–	–	*	*	*	–	–	–	–
305 TB	O	*	*	*	–	–	–	*	*	*	–	–	–	–
306 TB	–	–	–	–	–	–	–	–	–	–	–	–	–	–
307 TB	O	*	*	–	–	–	–	*	*	*	*	–	–	–
308 TB	X	X	X	X	X	X	X	X	X	X	X	X	X	X
309 DB	–	–	–	–	–	–	–	–	–	–	–	–	–	–
310 DB	O	*	*	*	*	*	–	–	–	–	–	–	–	–

^ UP   v DOWN

Figure 30 *Room availability display*

means that it can be consulted by anyone with access to a keyboard and VDU, and changes can be made in the same way.

The computer keeps track of room allocations through the registration process. It notes the rooms allocated, and removes them from the list of those available for letting. When the guest checks out, this fact is also entered into the computer, which then adds the room to the list of those to be cleaned. Once this has been done, the housekeeper enters in the fact, and the computer immediately adds that room to the list of those available for letting. All this is done without the need to prepare separate cards or slips, which represents a considerable saving in clerical time.

The computer will usually combine current room availability with an advance booking display so that you can see whether a particular room is likely to be needed over the next few days. In large hotels it will show blocks of rooms on a floor by floor basis with the facility to move 'up' or 'down'. Typically, the display may look like that shown in Figure 30.

The conventions used may vary, but in Figure 30 'O' means occupied, '*' means allocated, 'X' means out of order and '–' vacant. Movement 'up' or 'down' is by cursor key.

Guest indexes

Manual indexes

The room rack shows who is in any particular room, but it is not always easy to find a particular guest's name, especially in very large hotels with high occupancies and a high turnover of visitors (imagine having to scan 500 slots, most of them filled with slips bearing guests' names). This makes it necessary to maintain an 'alphabetical guest index' of current guests with their accompanying room numbers. It is particularly useful to the telephonists, who have to know which room a guest has been allotted in order to put calls through to him.

The Whitney system is ideally suited for this purpose, since (as we have seen) it allows slips to be inserted or removed at any point without disturbing the order of the other slips. The switchboard section in large non-computerized hotels commonly have their own alphabetically arranged Whitney rack. The slips are generally duplicates of those inserted in the room rack. In fact, front office staff usually makes three or four copies, one for the room rack, another for the switchboard and a third and fourth for other departments. These last act as arrivals notifications.

When the guest leaves, the room rack slip is removed and marked with a large 'X'. This is then passed on to the switchboard as a departure notification. The switchboard operators then remove *their* slip from the rack. Of course, switchboard need to supplement their guest index with other documents. Sometimes they receive calls for guests who are expected but who have not yet arrived, or who have already left. This means that the telephonists also need to have arrivals and departure lists to hand.

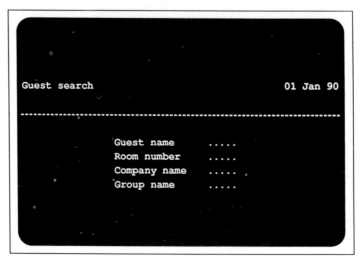

Figure 31   *Guest search screen*

Computerized guest name search facilities

By now it will hardly be necessary to point out that a computer can handle two types of query without any need for additional entries. It can tell you which guest is in any room, and it can also 'search' its memory for the whereabouts of any particular guest. Some programs are very sophisticated in this respect, and can find near equivalents to the name you have typed in. This is very useful if you haven't heard the caller distinctly or are not quite sure how the guest's name is spelled.

Typically, a program will present you with the alternatives shown in Figure 31. This offers more chances of finding a particular guest than simply looking through a set of manual index slips. The program will normally print out full details of all guests who meet the criteria selected, including their date of arrival, departure date, credit status and whether there are any messages waiting for them.

Room allocation

The room rack (or its computerized equivalent) is the basis for room allocation. It shows if there are rooms available, and whether they are actually ready for occupation. This applies even in hotels using conventional charts. Although these allocate rooms when the booking is made, it is still necessary to check room status on arrival. The room might have been taken out of service unexpectedly or the current occupant may want to stay on for another night or so.

Even in modern, standardized hotels, some rooms are usually better than others. They might have a better view, for instance, or be further away from the lift. Guest preferences should be respected whenever possible, and room allocation should be conducted along the following lines:

1 VIPs should be allocated whatever room they want. If they express no preference in advance, they should be given one of the best available. A note may have to be placed in the room rack to make sure that the room selected is not let to someone else.
2 Guests with special requirements (e.g. the disabled) should be treated in the same way.
3 Regulars, early bookings and long stays should be given priority in respect of the better rooms.

Some compromises will have to be made when applying these principles, but an experienced receptionist will quickly learn to 'hold back' a proportion of the better rooms for such arrivals.

This process can lead to problems. Many receptionists have been found to 'favour' certain rooms over others, often quite unconsciously. This means that some rooms can get far more usage than others, which makes any planned maintenance programme difficult to execute.

Because of this, some hotels have tried to equalize room usage over the course of a year, either by instructing receptionists to maintain a room letting record, or by requiring them to let them in strict rotation. These attempts have not proved particularly successful.

However, it is perfectly feasible to assign room allocation to a computer, which will maintain its own record of room usage and make sure that all the rooms are used equally. This is clearly a good idea as long as it does not conflict with the guest's wishes. You would have to make sure that there was an 'override' facility allowing you to substitute your own choice for the computer's.

Guest in residence

Your responsibilities towards the guest do not end when he has been registered and allocated a room. Your main ongoing task is to make sure that his bill is kept up to date. This subject is dealt with in Chapter 4. However, there are a variety of other services which you may be required to perform. Individually these do not involve any particularly complicated procedures, but they still add up to a very important part of front office work.

```
┌──────────────────────────────────────────────────────────────┐
│                 Room and rate change                          │
│                                                                │
│                                    No. ..................      │
│                                                                │
│  Name................................   Date...........................  │
│                                                                │
│  From room.........................   To room........................  │
│                                                                │
│  From rate..........................   To rate..........................  │
│                                                                │
│  Reason.....................................................................  │
│                                                                │
│  Receptionist...............................................................  │
└──────────────────────────────────────────────────────────────┘
```

Figure 32   *Room or rate change notification*

Room changes

Sometimes a guest will want to change rooms during his stay. The hotel should try to accommodate such changes wherever possible, because the guest's wishes must always come first. However, such alterations are potentially disruptive as far as the records are concerned, and they must be properly recorded.

The same principle applies to any rate changes (you might decide to make a reduction because of some deficiency in the facilities, for instance).

It is common to prepare a 'room or rate change' slip in such cases. This might be laid out as shown in Figure 32.

Copies would have to go to any department which had been notified of the original room or rate allocation (e.g. switchboard and the bill office). A copy would be retained as a record and added to the guest's file.

Most computerized systems will allow you to do this electronically, but there would still be advantages in having a written record.

Key control

Traditionally, one of reception's main jobs was to issue room keys to guests and then take them back for safe keeping when the guests went out. The keys had large and heavy tags attached to them to stop guests from walking off with them. The tags were numbered so that the key could be hung on a 'key rack' when not in use. The key rack was usually situated behind the desk.

The old-fashioned metal key was a security risk. Guests often lost or mislaid them, necessitating much rushing about with pass keys. Worse still, thieves could abuse the system by walking up to the desk during a busy period and asking for 'Room 105's key, please' in a confident tone. Receptionists in large hotels with a high turnover of visitors were not able to

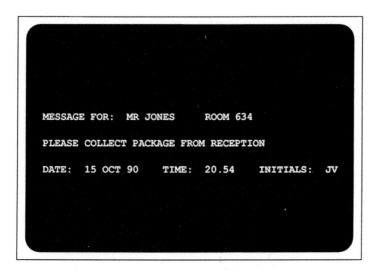

```
MESSAGE FOR:  MR JONES      ROOM 634

PLEASE COLLECT PACKAGE FROM RECEPTION

DATE:  15 OCT 90    TIME:  20.54    INITIALS:  JV
```

Figure 33 *Guest message display*

remember every single guest, so this often worked. In order to guard against this, bona fide guests had to be issued with 'key cards' which showed that they were entitled to a particular key.

Modern hotels now use electronic key cards. These have magnetic strips which can be 'imprinted' with a randomly selected code on issue. The room lock is simultaneously programmed to accept only that code, which is changed every time the room is let. It can even be changed during the guest's stay should he lose his card. The key cards themselves are relatively cheap, so their loss does not matter very much.

Such key cards have cut down the number of thefts from rooms by a significant amount. Just as important from the procedural point of view, they have eliminated the time-wasting process of taking keys in and handing them out again, allowing the receptionists to concentrate on more productive contacts with guests.

Mail

In the past, handling mail addressed to guests was one of front office's more important duties. The older form of key rack was usually combined with a set of pigeon holes, one for each room, so that the receptionist could hand over any waiting mail whenever she issued or took back the key. Packages too large to go into the rack were dealt with by a simple 'mail advice slip'.

With shorter stays and increased use of the telephone, such mail has decreased dramatically in volume. Many modern hotels (especially those using electronic keys) have discontinued the traditional key/mail rack. Nevertheless, guest mail still arrives, and must be dealt with promptly. The following steps represent 'good practice':

1 Guest mail is date and time stamped on arrival. This eliminates disputes about delivery times.

2   It is either placed in the key/mail rack, or, if this has been discontinued, delivered to the guest's room or held in front office. In the later case, a message must be sent to the guest. It used to be common to use a standard 'message slip' which asked the guest to call at front office to pick up a telegram, letter, parcel or whatever. Nowadays he is usually contacted via the telephone. Most guest room phones have a 'message light' controlled from the switchboard: this flashes until the guest answers it. Computerized systems will normally contain a message facility. This allows front office to enter a message against a room number or guest name. The telephone light is then turned on and the message is held until the guest replies. The guest's name and room number are 'flagged' so that anyone with access to a terminal can see that there is a message waiting and deliver it if necessary. These computer-held messages are automatically timed and dated. The text might appear as shown in Figure 33.

Current messages can be scanned periodically to see whether any further action is necessary. They are logged off when delivered, but remain on the guest file with the fact that they have been delivered noted.

3   Messages for guests who are expected but who have not yet arrived are dealt with in much the same way. The advance booking file or arrivals list can be 'flagged' in the same way as the current occupancy records, and the message delivered on arrival.

4   Messages for guests who have already left require different treatment. The address can usually be recovered from the registration card, but it is not practicable to readdress letters for overseas customers. Such letters may have to be forwarded under separate cover and the cost borne by the hotel. Security mail (e.g. a registered letter) is best dealt with by sending a notification and request for instructions. In all cases, the hotel should keep a list of any mail forwarded in order to avoid disputes.

Security mail inevitably creates special problems. Once a member of the hotel's staff has signed for such mail, responsibility passes from the Post Office to the hotel. It is therefore very important that only trustworthy employees be authorized to sign, and that the Post Office be informed of their identity.

Incoming telephone calls

These are now more important than mail. Ideally, they should be put straight through to the guest. Switchboard thus needs to know every guest's room number. As we have seen, manual systems had to employ an alphabetical guest index for this purpose. Computer systems allow name searches.

Guests are not always in their rooms. Sometimes they have left the hotel's premises, but often they are in the restaurant, or bar, or perhaps the pool. One solution is the 'message light', which ensures that the guest gets the message as soon as he returns to his room. However, this may not happen soon enough for urgent calls.

This problem has traditionally been dealt with by 'paging'. A uniformed employee used to be sent round the public areas calling 'Paging Mr Jones . . . paging Mr Jones . . .' until Mr Jones was finally located. A modern alternative is the loudspeaker public address system. The trouble with both these systems is that they disrupt other guests' conversations.

Some modern hotels issue guests with 'bleepers' on request. If a guest knows that he is likely to receive an important call out of normal business hours (perhaps because it originates from a country in a different time zone) it makes sense to let him have one. A note should be attached to his bill or file to ensure that the 'bleeper' is recovered before he leaves, since these useful items are relatively expensive.

Outgoing telephone calls

Guests are making an increasing number of calls on their own account. In the past technical limitations meant that these had to be dialled by the hotel's own switchboard operators and then logged by hand. Nowadays, direct dialling and automatic metering systems are almost universal, except in the very smallest hotels.

This has helped to reduce the number of disputes, especially since the time of the call and the number dialled are recorded (in the past, guests sometimes claimed that calls had been made by hotel staff using their pass keys while the guest himself was out).

The main area still open to argument lies in the basis on which the calls are charged. Hotels do not have to restrict themselves to just recovering the cost of the call; indeed, since the guest is making use of the hotel's own expensive equipment, an element of 'mark up' is justified. However, this sometimes arouses resentment, and the basis upon which calls are charged out should be made clear beforehand.

Safe custody

The Hotel Proprietors Act of 1956 lays down that a hotel proprietor may be liable for any loss or damage to a guest's property even though this was not due to any fault of the proprietor or his staff. This liability is limited to £50 in respect of any one article and £100 for any one guest, unless the property in question has been deposited or offered for deposit for safe custody. This only applies if a notice has been displayed, warning the guest of these limitations and effectively advising him to use the safe deposit provision for anything of value.

This places the responsibility for looking after valuable articles directly on the hotel and means that it has a duty to accept such articles for safe keeping. It is no use claiming that you do not have proper facilities or enough staff to look after them. In practice, most hotels install a safe in the front office area, and make this part of the receptionist's responsibilities.

Safe custody routines are simple, but important.

1 When a guest brings an article in for safe keeping, he should be asked to place it in a strong envelope. This prevents different items from becoming mixed up, and also allows him to keep whatever he is depositing confidential. He seals it and then signs over the seal. The receptionist makes sure that the envelope is marked with the guest's name and room number, and then issues a receipt. The receipt simply specifies 'one sealed envelope'. The approximate value may be added in order to avoid possible disagreements later.
2 When the guest wishes to reclaim the article, he must produce the receipt. If he has lost or mislaid this, the hotel *must* satisfy itself that it is really his property, and would be well advised to obtain a signed waiver discharging it from any further liability (it is possible, albeit unlikely, that the guest might later 'find' the missing receipt and then demand that the hotel produce the property he had already withdrawn). The receipt should be retained as proof that the item was reclaimed.

This process can seem somewhat irksome, especially if the property consists of jewellery which may be deposited, reclaimed and then redeposited more than once during the guest's stay, but it is the only safe way.

An alternative method is to provide safe deposit boxes. These require the use of two keys – one held by front office, the second issued to the guest against a signature. The guest has to sign a receipt every time he wishes to open his box, which allows the receptionist to compare signatures. The receipt should be countersigned by the receptionist.

Information

One of the receptionist's most important duties is the provision of information about the hotel and the locality. It goes without saying that they ought to know everything about the hotel itself, including details of any special functions which might interest guests. The information-giving process ought to be two-way: in other words, management must ensure that front office staff are told about what is happening elsewhere in the establishment.

Many managers assume that because most receptionists live locally they are, therefore, familiar with all the local features. This is simply not true. Ask yourself, for instance, whether you could direct a guest to the nearest Greek Orthodox Church or antiquarian bookshop. There are bound to be lots of specialist queries of this kind, and all you can do is know *how* to find the necessary information. You should have all the necessary reference material (the local *Yellow Pages*, for instance) ready to hand in the front office.

Nevertheless, many of the queries will be relatively straightforward. Management should be able to anticipate these and train new staff to answer them. This is important as far as the hotel's own 'image' is concerned. A busy executive is not likely to form a very high opinion of a hotel whose receptionist can't tell him how long it is likely to take to get by taxi to the local airport.

Some of the facts that guests may want remain unchanged for long periods. These can be dealt with by various kinds of 'static' displays, such as maps, guides, brochures or timetables which can be made part of guest information packs, picked up from the desk, or read off from a permanent display in the Lobby (this often gives guests something to look at while they are waiting).

Other information may change from day to day, or week to week. This can be brought to guests' attention through attractive noticeboards in the lobby.

Early morning wake-up calls

This used to be an important front office function, but has become much less important with the spread of personal alarms and automated hotel wake-up systems. Nevertheless, you may still receive requests from the older and more nervous type of visitor, and you ought to know how the old procedure worked just in case your electronic system goes 'down'.

An analysed call sheet was laid out as shown in Figure 34.

The intervals could be five or ten minutes if necessary. As the example shows, the name and room number were written in the appropriate column, together with any special requests. In

Call sheet	Date: ....31st....March...199=							
6.00	6.15	6.30	6.45	7.00	7.15	7.30	7.45	8.00
	604		310 (EMT)	516 (COFFEE e 'TIMES)				

Figure 34 *Analysed call sheet*

the morning the receptionist (or switchboard operator) worked from left to right, ticking off each alarm call as it was answered.

Departures

The procedures required on departure are very much a mirror image of those used to record arrivals. The main operation is the presentation and settlement of the bill, which will be dealt with in Chapter 4. However, there are certain other procedures to consider.

One point which is often overlooked is that departure is a good time to do some selling. Another and more obvious one is security. We shall look at these aspects in more detail later. At the moment we will confine ourselves to the procedural aspects.

Confirming departures

In theory, the hotel knows when the guest is going to leave. In practice this is not always so. Guests sometimes change their plans at the last minute, and expect to be able to stay on without having given you anything like enough notice. It is good practice, therefore, to confirm departures the night before if at all possible.

Additional services

The guest may require:

1   An alarm call.
2   Assistance with luggage.
3   Help with onward travel.

These form part of the service 'package', and the hotel should try to anticipate any such need rather than waiting to be asked.

Departure notifications

The hotel's other departments may need to know about departures. The switchboard will want to know which guests will be leaving, the housekeeper what rooms have to be prepared for reletting, and the bar and restaurant may need to be told not to extend any further credit.

This information is often communicated by means of a departure list, which is prepared and circulated in the same way as the arrivals list (indeed, the two can be combined). However, the departure list only shows *planned* departures, and it was common for large hotels to circulate actual departure notifications as well. These were used to update the departure list. Such hotels now use computerized systems, which handle these notifications automatically.

Updating the immediate records

In a manual system it is vital to keep the Room Rack up to date. If a card is inadvertently left in a slot after the guest has gone, that room will not appear to be available for reletting. Accordingly, an essential part of the check-out process consists of taking the card or slip out of the rack and disposing of it in some way. Cards normally have the date of departure on them in order to allow them to be checked for overstays.

The alphabetical guest index must be updated in the same way. In a manual system this was accomplished by sending a departure notification to the switchboard.

In a computerized system both operations are carried out automatically as part of the check-out entry.

Guest history records

These are intended to provide continuity in the treatment of regular guests. It is often difficult to ensure this because there will be long intervals between visits and the front office staff may have changed in the meantime. Nevertheless, it is very nice to be greeted with something like 'Hello, Mr Hamilton. Better weather than when you were here last, isn't it? Would you like the same room again. . . ?', and the guest history card used in some manual systems was designed to allow this to happen.

Typically, such cards record:

1   Dates of stays.
2   Rooms used.
3   Total bills.
4   Any special likes or dislikes.

Since such cards have to be made out or updated every time a guest stays at a hotel, they are very expensive in terms of clerical time. Nowadays they are generally only found in the kind of luxury hotel which offers a very high standard of service. Such hotels try to 'personalize' their services by keeping records of their guests' preferences in terms of flowers, food, drinks and even furniture. Most medium-class hotels can no longer afford to keep such records, except possibly for regular guests.

However, the guest history is making a comeback through computerization. A computerized system can prepare or update guest histories automatically as part of the check-out procedure. Whether it does this or not depends very much on the available memory. As the cost of information storage has come down in real terms, so the availability and usage of guest history modules has increased, and you can expect these to be a standard feature of most systems.

One of the main advantages of computerized guest history files is that they can be linked with the advance bookings section, so that the computer 'searches' its records to see whether a new booking has ever stayed at the hotel before. It can then 'prompt' the receptionist via the VDU screen, allowing her to respond appropriately.

Room record cards

These were another optional part of a manual system. They provided particulars of actual occupancies, together with details of any periods during which the room was out of service for repairs or redecoration. They were useful for planned maintenance purposes, but the process of entering the name of every guest who had ever stayed in the room was time consuming, and added little to the information already obtainable from the conventional chart or the registration cards (which, as you will recall, have to be kept for twelve months). Consequently, such cards are now obsolete, though some form of room record is still desirable.

Filing

We need to add a brief word about the filing of the various documents, because these can amount to a considerable stack. There will probably be a reservation form, possibly with an initial letter of enquiry, a confirmation and possibly amendment. There may also be a registration card (unless you are using a book type register) and perhaps a copy of the bill.

Although particulars of the booking are transferred to easily-consulted sources like the diary and chart, the primary documents need to be kept within reach in case there is any dispute about the terms. The critical time is likely to be on check-in, though the presentation of the bill on departure may also lead to problems. The documents thus need to be available for reference at these periods.

The logical way to file advance booking documents is by date of arrival.

That way, they can move along as if on a conveyer belt, so that you constantly have today's arrivals to hand. Once the guests are in the hotel, you should rearrange the documents so that they are in date of departure order. That way you will have tomorrow's departures to hand as well.

It is probably most convenient to retain the documents in date of departure order. If there *are* any queries, this is likely to be the date quoted. It also allows you to operate a twelve-month retention period, after which the records are disposed of.

The documents should be arranged in alphabetical order within the date sections. However, there is no need to be too obsessive about maintaining this system in absolutely perfect order. Generally, only a very small number of primary documents ever need to be looked at again, and it is usually enough to know their approximate whereabouts.

Assignments

1 Describe the type of check-in system you would expect to find in the Tudor Hotel.

2 Describe the type of check-in system you would expect to find in the Pancontinental Hotel.

3 Obtain specimens of the type of registration documents and an outline of the check-in procedures used at a selection of local hotels, and compare these with one another, relating their characteristics to the type of hotel involved.

4 What reference sources would you expect a well-equipped front office to possess in order to answer guest enquiries?

5 Discuss various methods of filing guest documentation. To what extent are these systems likely to be affected by developments in computerization?

3 Guest accounting

Introduction

It is front office's responsibility to prepare the guest's bill, present it, and ensure that it is paid. This is an important function, and one which involves a good deal of record keeping. Guests only arrive and depart once during their stay, but they may incur a large number of separate charges during it, from the price of the room and the cost of various meals through to telephone, laundry and entertainment charges.

Dealing with these transactions would be relatively easy if they could be put on a simple cash basis, but the tradition in the hotel industry is one of giving credit during the stay. The amounts involved can be quite substantial: a room for one night coupled with an evening's business entertaining in a top city centre hotel can come to several hundred pounds. In contrast to many other businesses, this credit often has to be extended to relative unknowns at short notice.

There is also the question of speed. Details of the various transactions must be collected from different departments of the hotel and put on to the guest's bill before he leaves, which is often quite early in the morning. An item omitted is very difficult to recover afterwards, not least because the guest may well live in another country, which means a different legal jurisdiction.

Guest accounting is thus an area which is both complex and sensitive. In large hotels it is usually the responsibility of a separate bills or accounting section, with the settlement process being the responsibility of a cashier. In smaller hotels the duties generally have to be combined. Wherever you work, you are likely to find yourself undertaking them at some time, and you need to understand the principles involved.

The objectives of the guest accounting procedures are as follows:

1   To maintain accurate and up-to-date guest accounts.
2   To ensure that payment is received promptly and in full.
3   To provide management with accurate and up-to-date financial reports.

We shall be looking at the third objective later on in this book. This chapter is therefore divided into two parts.

Guest accounting

There are three main methods of preparing guest bills:

1   The tabular ledger.
2   Electro-mechanical or electronic billing machines.

Day.WED...				Date.31st...MARCH 199–						
Room	Name	Slprs	Rate	B/fwd	Accom.	B'fst	Lunch	Dinner	Emts etc.	B.
6	BLAKE	1	22·50	30·20	20·00	2·50	✓	✓	✓	.
8	ROSS	2	35·00	48·20	30·00	5·00	12·00			1·
12	PLATT	2	35·00	—	30·00	5·00	✓	18·70	1·40	.
14	DAVIS	1	22·50	—	20·00	2·50		8·00		0
Totals				78·40	100·00	15·00	12·00	26·70	1·40	1

Figure 35   *Horizontal tabular ledger*

3   Computerized guest accounting systems.

We shall look at each in turn.

The tabular ledger

This is the oldest and most labour intensive of the methods. It is typical of smaller hotels which are still dependent on manual systems.

The tabular ledger is based on the conventional sales day book. It provides a record of all charges incurred by guests during a twenty-four hour period, analysed according to their nature. Figure 35 shows a typical layout.

The tab produces:

1   A record of all charges, credits, payments and outstanding balances.
2   A separate total for each guest's bill.
3   A separate total for each category of item.

You complete it as follows:

1   You start by entering all the guests staying over from the previous day. Each individual or family unit requires a separate row. 'Name' and 'Room' should be self explanatory. 'Slprs' means 'sleepers'. It is important to note this on the tab sheet because some charges may be on a 'per person' rather than a 'per room' basis. The 'Rate' agreed should be noted because this helps to prevent over or undercharging. The entries are usually made in room number order. This helps you to find the correct row when entering charges from the departmental vouchers, most of which are marked with the room number rather than the guest's name.
2   Bring forward any outstanding charges from the preceding day, and enter these under the heading 'B/fwd'. Remember that each tab sheet covers one day only, and that guests in the third or fourth nights of their stay will already have incurred a number of such charges.

Wines	Sprts	Minrls	Phone	VPOs	Total	Credit	Cash	Ledgr	C/fwd
✓	✓	✓	✓	✓	52·70			52·70	
			0·80	1·10	101·30		101·30		
6·50	2·20	✓	1·60	✓	65·40				65·40
					32·60		25·00		7·60
6·50	2·20		2·40	1·10	252·00		126·30	52·70	73·00

These items will be found on the preceding day's tab sheet. As we have already noted, it is customary to rearrange the b/fwds so that they are in room number order.

3   Next, enter all the room charges under '*Accom.*'. They may not be the same as the figure in the '*rate*' column, because many hotels offer inclusive packages (i.e. one charge to cover both room and table d'hôte meals). However, this charge needs to be split up for accounting purposes. '*Accom.*' thus means the room rate component of the overall charge. Room charges for guests in residence are normally entered at a set time, such as 6 pm.

4   Enter the various other charges as they come through. This spreads the work out and keeps the bill and tab up to date. In manual systems, all such charges are recorded on 'checks' or 'vouchers', which originate in the department providing the service and are then passed to the bill office to be 'posted' to the tab. It is essential that this be done systematically, and that the vouchers are cancelled as soon as the entries have been made. Charges such as '*Breakfast*', '*Lunch*' and '*Dinner*' are self-explanatory. Meals included in inclusive rates should be detailed here. '*Bar*' and '*Phone*' are also self-explanatory. Remember, however, that there may be more than one entry per guest against these headings, so try to leave room for them. Some tab layouts allow two or more lines for such items. Others also provide one or more blank columns. These allow you to detail any unusual items. 'VPOS' ('visitor paid outs' or 'disbursements') cover any payments made by the hotel on behalf of the guest. You may have to send someone out for toiletries, for instance, or pay for a COD (cash on delivery) package. These payments have to be recovered from the guest before he leaves.

5   When a new guest arrives, you should begin a new row. As we have indicated, this means the room numbers may not be in the correct order any more. This is unfortunate, but it cannot be helped. You should begin a new row even if the guest is occupying a room vacated earlier. This means that you might have two rows with the same room number on the tab sheet. The room charge is entered as the account is opened, and any other charges are added as the vouchers come through.

6   Enter any '*credits*' (often called '*allowances*') as and when they arise. This heading allows you to make the adjustments which are probably inevitable given the volume of transactions to be recorded. If a breakfast charge is wrongly posted to Room 105 instead of Room 150, for example, it will have to be cancelled. It is good practice to maintain an allowances book, in which full details of every such entry must be recorded. This should be inspected by management regularly.

7   When a guest checks out, he will settle his bill. The *'cash'* column records any payments he makes. 'Cash' means all the 'bankable' forms of payment such as cash itself, cheques, travellers' cheques or those credit cards issued by banks (e.g. Access or Visa). *'Ledger'* covers any arrangement whereby the hotel claims back the amount of the guest's bill from someone else. Many group bookings are settled in this way. Obviously, some form of authorization is necessary before an account is transferred to ledger. *'Ledger'* also covers what are called 'travel and entertainment company' credit card payments (e.g. American Express or Diners) and travel agent coupons, because these require you to send a statement to the card company or agent in order to obtain payment. It is customary to put a line through any unused portion of the row relating to a guest who has checked out. This prevents any further charges being mistakenly entered in that space.

8   Not all guests will be leaving. The *'c/fwd'* column allows you to 'carry forward' the total of all charges incurred to date. The total will be identical to the *'b/fwd'* figure for the following day, though the items will not be in exactly the same order because (as we have seen) you will be rearranging the stopover guests in room number order.

9   The tab sheet must be 'balanced' before it can be accepted as correct. You have to add up all the vertical columns and the horizontal rows. These must all come to the same total, thus providing a check on the arithmetical accuracy of the records. Balancing will normally be done during a quiet period. The hotel's 'day' really ends about 12.00 noon, after all the departing guests have left and before any new arrivals appear. However, the usual time for balancing the tab is some time after 11 pm, during what is sometimes known as 'the graveyard shift'. This allows you to check the rows for any guests departing the following morning and to make sure that their *'totals'* are correct. If the nightly rate is inclusive of breakfast, no further entries should be necessary unless the guest has papers or an early morning tea. These would have to be added before the bill was presented.

It should be obvious that the 'guest' row on the tab sheet contains exactly the same items as the guest's own bill. In very old-fashioned systems these two documents were produced separately, mainly because it was easier to add up both vertically in the days before hand calculators became common. This could obviously lead to errors.

Because the bill duplicated the tab entries, a number of patent systems were introduced to allow both to be completed simultaneously, thus reducing the number of entries required and the possibility of transcription errors. These systems required the bill to be superimposed over the tab, with the duplication being achieved by the use of carbon or NCR (no carbon required) paper.

Since bills almost invariably show the items in columnar form (making it easier for the guest to check that the total is correct), this required an alternative 'vertical' method of presentation for the tab sheet. The horizontal rows were now used for the different categories of bill item. These had to be added across before the tab could be balanced, but this process became easier after the introduction of calculators.

Figure 36 shows a 'vertical' tab with superimposed bill. Various ingenious methods were devised to make sure that the bill could be placed over the correct column. This particular bill has two 'date' columns, allowing a two-day stay to be recorded. The previous night's stay would have been duplicated on the preceding day's tab sheet.

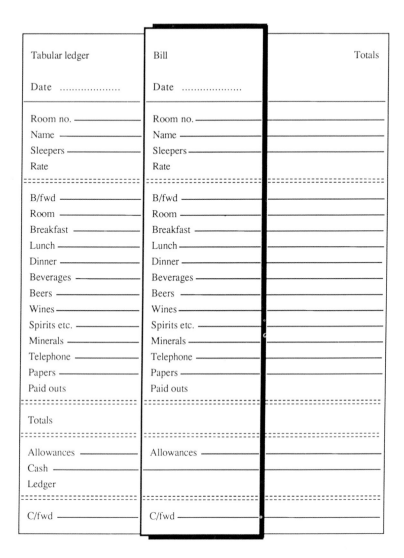

Tabular ledger	Bill		Totals
Date	Date		
Room no. ————————	Room no. ————————		————————
Name ————————	Name ————————		————————
Sleepers ————————	Sleepers ————————		————————
Rate	Rate		
B/fwd ————————	B/fwd ————————		————————
Room ————————	Room ————————		————————
Breakfast ————————	Breakfast ————————		————————
Lunch ————————	Lunch ————————		————————
Dinner ————————	Dinner ————————		————————
Beverages ————————	Beverages ————————		————————
Beers ————————	Beers ————————		————————
Wines ————————	Wines ————————		————————
Spirits etc. ————————	Spirits etc. ————————		————————
Minerals ————————	Minerals ————————		————————
Telephone ————————	Telephone ————————		————————
Papers ————————	Papers ————————		————————
Paid outs	Paid outs		
Totals			
Allowances ————————	Allowances ————————		————————
Cash ————————			————————
Ledger			
C/fwd ————————	C/fwd ————————		

Figure 36   *Vertical tabular ledger with bill superimposed*

Electro-mechanical or electronic billing machines

The handwritten tab remains suitable for small hotels. However, the need to handle large numbers of postings in larger establishments led to the introduction of various models of billing machines from the 1930s onwards. Most of these machines have now been replaced by computerized guest accounting systems, but you may still find them in operation, or standing by ready for use as back-up systems (one of the advantages of an electro-mechanical machine is that it can always be operated by turning a handle even if the power goes off).

The billing machine does exactly the same job as the patent bill and tabular ledger combinations we looked at in the last section, but it handles the tab function by 'storing' the

Rack Hotel
Melcaster

Room no. 121   Name Matthews   Date 01.0.9-   Rate £45.00

No. of persons 1

Key		Line	Date	Reference	Amount	Misc
		1	01JAN90	Dbal	000.00	
Dbal	Debit balance	2	01JAN90	Room	045.00	
Cbal	Credit	3	01JAN90	Dinn	012.50	
Room	balance	4	01JAN90	Bar	003.25	
Bfst	Room charge	5	01JAN90	Pout	001.25	
Lnch	Breakfast	6	01JAN90	Totl	062.00	
Dinn	Luncheon	7	02JAN90	Dbal	062.00	
Bar	Dinner	8	02JAN90	Bfst	005.50	
Bvgs	Bar	9	02JAN90	Papr	000.30	
Rmsv	Beverages	10	02JAN90	Totl	067.80	
Lndr	Room service	11	02JAN90	Serv	006.78	
Papr	Laundry	12	02JAN90	Totl	074.58	
Pout	Papers	13	02JAN90	Paid	074.58	
Misc	Paid out	14	02JAN90	Dbal	000.00	
Adjt	Miscellaneous	15				
Serv	Adjustment	16				
VAT	Service	17				
Paid	charge	18				
Totl	VAT charge	19				
	Paid					
	Total					
		33				
		34				
		35				
		36				

Cash ☐   CHARGE TO ....

Cheque ☐   ADDRESS ....

Credit card ☐   CO.................   ....

NO.................   SIGNATURE ....

Figure 37   *Guest bill produced by billing machine*

various charges in 'registers' (memories) and printing out totals as required. In other words, the guest bill remains much the same, but the tab is replaced by a 'summary sheet' which simply shows the totals for the various types of charges and allowances. Since the transactions are also listed on an 'audit roll', it is possible to check these in detail should this be necessary.

Billing machines offer the following advantages:

1   All bill entries are simultaneously recorded in the machine's memory, so that bill and ledger totals are always in agreement.
2   All the calculations are handled automatically, which reduces the number of errors significantly (it is still possible to enter a charge incorrectly, of course, but at least the bill will be arithmetically correct).
3   Bills are printed rather than handwritten. In theory, this makes them more legible, though

not everyone would agree, especially customers trying to puzzle out a bill containing a lot of cryptic abbreviations and produced on a machine which badly needs to have its ribbon renewed.

4   Charge vouchers are automatically cancelled. This cuts down the risk of vouchers being posted twice (or not posted at all).
5   Control is easier. Since the billing machine is always 'in balance' (in other words, bill and ledger totals are always in agreement), the control procedures at the end of a shift are considerably simplified.

There are certain corresponding disadvantages, mainly centred on the training time necessary to produce a competent operator, which is likely to be about a week. Of course, learning how to complete a manual tab also takes time.

The guest bill produced by a billing machine is usually known as the 'guest folio'. The most common layout is the columnar one shown in Figure 37.

Other billing machines produced folios with four columns, namely:

Code   Charges   Credits   Balance

The particular style of layout does not matter: the important thing is that the folio shows all the charges, adjustments, payments and closing balances clearly.

Guest folios are normally completed in duplicate. The upper portion is the guest bill, while the lower portion is the hotel's duplicate record. This lower portion is usually made of thin card rather than paper. This enables the folio as whole to stand upright in a guest folio rack (often called the 'bucket') which is kept beside the billing machine. The room number is usually shown prominently at the top of the folio, which helps the machine operator to keep the folios in room number order.

The procedures for dealing with a guest folio vary in detail from machine to machine, but will generally follow the following sequence:

1   When a guest arrives, the operator opens a new account by taking a blank folio card and *typing* the guest's name, address, room number, date of arrival, rate and number of persons on it (few billing machines have full alphabetic keyboards, so this step has to be done separately).
2   The folio is then placed on the billing machine's 'platform' (a kind of horizontal tray projecting from the front). Once inserted, the folio cannot be removed until the sequence of entries has been completed. This acts as a safeguard when (as often happens) the operator is interrupted halfway through the posting process.
3   The folio is opened by entering the room number and the opening balance. This last will be zero unless a deposit has been paid. Some systems will allocate a reference number at this point: this will remain in force for that room number until cancelled by a final payment or transfer to ledger.
4   The first charge posted will usually be the room rate. The others will be entered from vouchers, just as with the tab. The billing machine offers an improvement over the manual system, however, in that it can automatically cancel the voucher by overprinting it. All postings are made in the same way. The folio and the voucher are placed side by side on the 'platform'. The operator enters the room number and the previous balance, if any. This 'pick up' figure is always the last balance to be shown on the folio: you can see that in Figure 37 the balance at the end of 1 January was £62.00, and that this has been 'picked up' again on the following morning. Once the entry has been made, the billing machine:

(a) Prints the item on the folio.

(b) Prints the same item (with the relevant room number) on an 'audit roll', which can be checked back against the vouchers if necessary.

(c) Calculates a new balance, which it can print on demand.

(d) Cancels the voucher by overprinting it.

It should be obvious that if you push a folio which already contains a number of items into the billing machine, it will simply overprint the existing entries. This is why most such folios contain something like the 'line' column shown in Figure 37. This allows the operator to select the line at which new printing will commence. Voucher posting is usually carried out in room number batches as far as possible. This cuts the time involved in locating a folio, making the entry and then returning the folio to the bucket, to a minimum.

5   At the end of the shift, the billing machine is balanced. This is usually done by inserting a special key known as the 'X key' into the machine and putting a summary sheet on the 'platform'. The calculation is then as follows:

- Balances brought forward (entered from last summary sheet).
- Plus total debits (maintained by machine).
- Less total credits (also maintained by machine).
- Equals total balances carried forward.

The last figure is obtained by add-listing the last figures shown in all the folios. Since all the calculations are done automatically, the balancing process should take less time than with the manual tab. However, there are still likely to be errors, especially those caused by 'picking up' an incorrect balance, which is why the process is necessary. Even this does not guard against certain common types of mistake, such as posting the right amount to the wrong folio, or the wrong amount to the right folio, or labelling a charge wrongly, or omitting it altogether.

6   Once all the transactions for the shift have been balanced, the operator prints out a summary on the summary card. This shows the totals of all the 'registers', in other words, the different kinds of charges, allowances and receipts. Once this has been done, the machine's memory is 'cleared' and it is reset to zero. This is done by inserting another special key known as the 'Z key', which is usually held by a senior employee. Once the machine has been cleared, the operator starts a new audit roll and resets the date (some machines do this automatically).

7   When the guest is about to leave, the operator puts the appropriate folio onto the 'platform' and enters any last-minute charges. Then she enters the amount and method of payment, if any, or alternatively makes an entry to show that the outstanding account has been transferred to a ledger account. Many machines will automatically print a receipt on the top (guest's) copy of the folio at this point.

Billing machine keyboards vary in detail, but the basic layout is usually as follows:

Guest	Figure	Register
Keys	Keys	Keys

The 'guest keys' correspond to the 'key' shown on the bill itself. Pressing one of these will print 'room', 'bfast', 'lnch' and so on. They show the type of transaction to the level of detail required by the guest.

The 'figure keys' are simply numerical keys used to enter the room number or the amount of the charge or credit.

The 'register keys' enter transactions into the machine's memory. The 'registers' may group a number of items together: for example, *'bfst'*, *'lnch'* and *'dinn'* charges may all be posted to the 'restaurant' register.

There are also a set of special keys used for various purposes, such as 'pick up debit balance', 'pick up credit balance', 'enter line' etc. The initial impression produced by all these different keys can be somewhat overpowering, but their use soon quickly becomes familiar with experience.

Computerized guest accounting systems

These represent a further major advance in terms of speed and efficiency. Computers offer all the advantages of billing machines, with a number of additional ones, as follows:

1 *A further reduction in the number of entries* Whereas the billing machine is able to store all the transactions arising in a single *shift*, the computer can store them throughout the duration of a guest's *stay*. This means that the tedious process of looking for the correct folio, inserting it in the billing machine, picking up the old balance, entering a batch of transactions and then replacing the folio in the bucket can be eliminated. Since the guest's account is maintained electronically in the computer's memory, all that you have to do is call it up on-screen and add whatever details are necessary. In addition, computers have full alphanumeric keyboards rather than the more limited 'cash register' type characteristic of billing machines. This means that all the necessary entries can be handled through the same keyboard (you will recall that guest folio headings had to be prepared on a typewriter before they could be used in a billing machine). In fact, the billing entries on a computer are just a continuation of the registration entries: there is no need to retype guest particulars such as name, room number etc.
2 *Reductions in the number of vouchers* It is possible to connect the central computer to any number of point of sale (POS) terminals, so that charges can be 'input' directly by the departments concerned, rather than having to be entered on vouchers which must then be physically transferred to the bill office before being entered on the guest's folio.
3 *Easier access to bills* Although machines maintain up-to-date bills, it is still necessary for guests to call at front office in order to obtain these. With a computerized system, it is possible for them to see their bill anywhere and at any time, as long as they have access to a TV screen, such as the one in their room. This allows guests to check their bills the evening before they leave, thus permitting 'fast check-outs' and helping to reduce the post-breakfast bottleneck so characteristic of large and busy hotels.
4 *Greater detail* It is possible for a computerized bill to show the precise times at which various charges were incurred. This helps to reduce disputes.
5 *Even greater accuracy* Arithmetical accuracy can be taken for granted, but computers can also be programmed to check whether various entries are within sensible ranges. They can be made to charge the normal rack rate for a room unless instructed otherwise, and to do so automatically on room allocation. They can also 'pick up' deposits automatically. All these facilities help to reduce the kinds of operator errors which still afflicted machine-produced guest accounts.

Nevertheless, computers are not yet perfect. They are much more complex than the simple handwritten tab or the relatively primitive billing machine, and this leads to two disadvantages:

1   The operators need more training time.
2   The systems are more prone to breakdowns.

This second drawback means that it is still necessary to produce a written 'audit trail' so that the accounts can be recreated from scratch in the event of a computer failure. This in turn implies that there should be a back-up system of some kind.

An 'audit trail' is also necessary because computer operators are still liable to make incorrect entries, such as charging an item to the wrong room. We shall look at this point again when we consider control.

There are many different types of computerized system available, and we can expect to see more coming onto the market. These systems vary in detail, and it would be absurd to single out just one, or to attempt to describe all the features it might include. The manuals tend to be a hundred or more pages long, and the typical training period a week to ten days.

However, most systems will have certain features in common:

1   There will generally be a *'cashier'* or *'billing'* module available from the main menu. Once you enter this, the system will prompt you to enter the appropriate room number. In many cases you can use the guest's name as an alternative. In either case the system will display the other item to allow you to cross check.
2   The system will prompt you to tell it whether you are making a posting, an adjustment or a transfer (postings are bill entries, adjustments are corrections of various kinds, while a transfer facility is necessary because bill items or accounts are sometimes paid by other guests). The computer has to be 'told' this because it can't read your mind. It is the equivalent of your choosing the appropriate row or column on the tab.
3   The system will then prompt you for the type of item to be entered. Most will simplify this process as far as possible by using numerical codes or the function keys (the ones at the left on a standard IBM keyboard). Their use quickly becomes automatic, but the system will generally display the available codes for reference, or at least contain a *'help'* function so that you can consult them.
4   Many postings will be made automatically. The computer will have asked you for the room rate when you registered the guest. If you 'skipped' this field, it will automatically post the standard rack rate, and it will continue to update this automatically for every additional night (no more forgetting to post room charges on the tab or billing machine folio!). These automatic postings may be known as 'system' entries or some similar term. If you discover that the rate is in fact wrong, you can always correct it by an adjustment, though this entry will remain on the record in order to provide the necessary 'audit trail'.
5   You will usually find that you are required to enter an ID (identification) code at some point in the process. This is equivalent to your initialling a form or voucher, and is desirable for control purposes.
6   The system may or may not display the guest's folio at this point. If it doesn't, it will still check that the guest's credit limit has not been exceeded, and display a warning message if it has. Even if the folio is not displayed, you can always call it up from the main or submenu. As Figure 38 shows, it will generally look very much like the printed version.

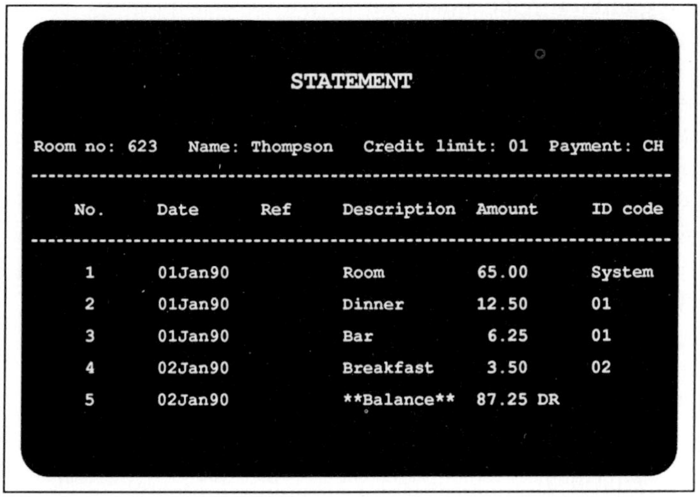

STATEMENT

Room no: 623 Name: Thompson Credit limit: 01 Payment: CH

No.	Date	Ref	Description	Amount	ID code
1	01Jan90		Room	65.00	System
2	01Jan90		Dinner	12.50	01
3	01Jan90		Bar	6.25	01
4	02Jan90		Breakfast	3.50	02
5	02Jan90		**Balance**	87.25 DR	

Figure 38 *On-screen display of guest statement*

Petty cash

Although they are not strictly speaking part of guest accounting procedures, front office staff commonly find themselves having to deal with petty cash transactions, and they therefore require mention.

Petty cash is almost always dealt with by the 'imprest system'. This means that the cashier is given a fixed sum by way of a float or imprest. Small incidental payments are made out of this imprest. If possible a receipt should be obtained for each payment, but this is not always practicable and a 'petty cash voucher' may be accepted instead as long as this is countersigned by a senior member of staff (Figure 39).

Petty cash voucher

Details	Amount	£	p

Date Signature

Approved by

Figure 39 *Petty cash voucher*

Some of the payments will be made on behalf of guests (a visitor may send out for toothpaste, possibly, or borrow some change to pay for a taxi). These 'VPOs' (visitor paid outs) must be recorded as quickly as possible in the guest's account and the petty cash voucher endorsed accordingly. However, the imprest will still have been reduced by the amount of the payment, so the voucher will be kept with the petty cash until this is reconciled.

Reconciliation is carried out at regular intervals (often daily, sometimes once a week). The total of the various vouchers plus the remaining cash should always equal the original imprest. Once this has been confirmed, the imprest is made up to its original amount.

Petty cash records are not usually computerized. Instead, an analysed petty cash book is maintained by hand (Figure 40). The principle is similar to that of the 'tab'.

Petty Cash Book

Imprest	Date	Details	Ref	Total	Postage	Stationery	Travel	Gratuities	Donations	VPOs	Sundries
25.00	4 Apr	Cheque									
	5 "	Post		1.50	1.50						
	6 "	Pencils		1.60		1.60					
	"	Taxi		3.50			3.50				
	7 "	106 (Razors)		2.60						2.60	
	8 "	Tip		1.00				1.00			
	9 "	Paper		.30							.30
	10 "	Taxi		2.00			2.00				
				12.50	1.50	1.60	5.50	1.00	—	2.60	.30
		Balance C/D		12.50							
25.00				25.00							
12.50	11 Apr	Balance B/D									
12.50	"	Cheque									

Figure 40   *Analysed petty cash book*

Methods of payment

Guests can settle their accounts in a variety of ways. The most common are:

1 Cash
2 Cheque

3 Eurocheque
4 Foreign currency
5 Travellers' cheque
6 Credit card
7 'Smart' card
8 Travel agents' voucher
9 Transfers to ledger account

Point 9 will be discussed in Part Three, and the remaining points will each be considered in turn.

Cash

Although travellers no longer carry purses full of gold coins to pay their reckonings with, cash is still the only 'legal tender', and a hotelier *could* insist on payment in notes and coin if he so wished. In fact, cash has long been obsolete as a means of payment, partly because the amounts involved can be quite considerable, and partly because of the inconvenience of having to make the payment long before the banks open. In fact, any hotel insisting on cash payments would probably lose a lot of business.

Nevertheless, some guests *do* make payments by cash, and the cashier must be prepared for these. This means that the hotel must provide a 'cash float' to allow the cashier to give change, and the cash received must be stored safely until it can be banked. All this means that there must be adequate accounting records, and the cashier's section must be properly secured.

The bill should be receipted 'paid by cash'. The issue of a receipt is particularly important in this case because the guest will have no other record of the payment.

Cheques

Most travellers now have bank accounts, and the use of cheques has grown enormously over the past few decades. Cheques are very convenient, since they can be made out there and then for any amount desired, but they have certain disadvantages as far as hotels are concerned.

The obvious ones are the fact that there will be a delay before the amount is credited to the hotel's account, and a small handling charge when it is. These are common to all businesses, and are bearable. The real problem is one that hotels share with most retail businesses, namely, the fact that guests are often complete strangers whose cheques may turn out to be 'dud'.

In the past, this problem had to be dealt with by imposing a clause in the contract for accommodation to the effect that three days' notice was required before the hotel would accept a cheque in settlement (this was usually long enough to allow the hotel to confirm the guest's creditworthiness). Nowadays most guests carry cheque guarantee cards, which guarantee anyone who accepts a cheque payment provided that:

- Only one cheque is used per transaction.
- The cheque is signed in the presence of the cashier.

- The bank code and signature on the cheque and guarantee card agree.
- The guarantee card is not past its expiry date.
- The card number is noted on the back of the cheque.

Unfortunately, most guarantees are currently limited to amounts of £50 or less, and the banks are reluctant to increase this amount because of the increasing incidence of cheque fraud. This limits the value of cheque guarantee cards as far as many hotels are concerned. Although they could ask for a series of separate cheque payments on the grounds that each night's stay was a separate 'transaction', a great many bills would still come to more than £50 per night, and current trends suggest that they are likely to stay ahead of any foreseeable rise in cheque card limits.

If payment is made during normal banking hours, the hotel can verify that a cheque will be paid by telephoning its own bank, which will then ring the drawer's bank. This involves a charge, which will have to be borne by the hotel unless it passes it on to the guest. Needless to say, such guests are likely to resent the implied slur on their truthfulness, as well as the extra cost involved.

Even perfectly honest guests can make silly mistakes which will invalidate their cheques, and there are certain simple rules which should be followed whenever you accept one. You should check:

- That the date and year are correct. In particular, watch out for 'postdated cheques' (i.e. those with future dates) since these will not become payable until the date shown (by which time the account may have nothing in it) or 'stale' cheques (i.e. those made out over six months ago).
- That the cheque has been made out to the correct payee.
- That the amounts shown in words and figures agree.
- That any corrections have been properly signed.
- That the signature is the same as that on the cheque guarantee card. If in doubt ask for some other form of identification such as a passport or driver's licence.

Eurocheques

Eurocheques are a relatively recent development which allows customers to make payments in a variety of currencies. They are written in the local currency (i.e. pounds, francs, Deutschmarks etc.) but are debited to the customer's account in his own currency at whatever the rate of exchange was when the cheque was presented for payment.

Eurocheques are accompanied by a special cheque guarantee card known as a Eurocard. The rules are exactly the same as for ordinary cheque cards except that the amount guaranteed is higher (£100), and any number of Eurocheques can be made out for one transaction.

This means that Eurocheques are preferable to ordinary cheques as far as hotels are concerned. If one £100 cheque does not cover the full amount of the bill, the guest can write out a second, a third or a fourth. Providing that the various security checks reveal no inconsistencies, such cheques are as good as cash. The security checks themselves are the same as for an ordinary cheque guarantee card.

09-01-26

19

ABBEY NATIONAL

Abbey National plc, P.O. Box 382, Prescot Street, London E1 8RP

Pay _____   Or Order

SPECIMEN   £

MR. A. COLLINS

⑂100 299⑂ 09⑁0126⑉ 12345678⑂

(a)

£100 CHEQUE CARD
For conditions see over

ABBEY NATIONAL BUILDING SOCIETY

SPECIMEN

5603 0922 1234 5618

MR A COLLINS
12345678

090126 1234567890 -- JAN 90

CODE NUMBER   CARD NUMBER   ISSUE   EXPIRY DATE

(b)

Figure 41   *(a) Sample cheque; (b) Sample cheque card (courtesy Abbey National)*

eurocheque

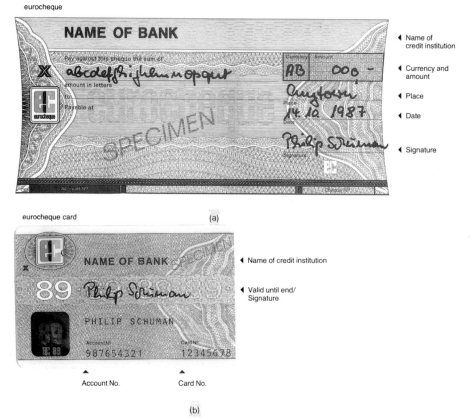

Figure 42   *(a) Sample Eurocheque; (b) Sample Eurocheque card (courtesy* **Eurocheque** *International)*

Foreign currency

This is sometimes offered by foreign visitors, especially if they come from a country with a strong currency (indeed, there are stories of American visitors who simply didn't know that the dollar was not a universal currency). Such currencies present no problem, but others may be very difficult to convert into cash except at a substantial discount, and cashiers need to be careful about which to accept.

There is no obligation to accept *any* foreign currency since it is not legal tender, but there is an obvious goodwill aspect. Apart from this, hotels can often make a profit by doing so, especially if their rate of exchange is less favourable to the guest than that offered by the local banks. This is in fact normal. There is no legal obligation to follow the current bank rates, and the hotel is free to offer lower ones if it wishes. The justification is that the unfavourable rates cover the extra cost of providing the service and guard against the risk of a sudden fall in the exchange rate (hotels are not expert foreign exchange dealers, after all). If a guest objects, he should be told that he is perfectly free to exchange his currency somewhere else.

Some large hotels apply for registration as authorized foreign exchange dealers. This imposes certain obligations on them, but they do it in order to be able to provide an additional service for their international clientele. Cashiers in such hotels have to observe currency regulations and must be aware of current rates of exchange, which may change daily or even hourly.

If a hotel is *not* registered as a foreign exchange dealer, it can only *receive* foreign currency, not sell it. This means that it would be illegal to give change in a foreign currency, even if the guest requested this.

Cashiers need to be able to recognize the major foreign currency notes in order to avoid the risk of being tricked by relatively crude forgeries (it is not normal practice to accept foreign coins). In larger hotels there should be a noticeboard showing the current exchange rates as set by head office or the chief cashier. Smaller hotels can deal with this problem on the 'exception principle' namely by checking with their bank or even a daily newspaper whenever the need arises.

Foreign currency accepted in payment of a guest's bill should be recorded at the value set on it by the hotel. This may be either higher or lower than the amount finally credited to the hotel's account by the bank when it is paid in (though it will usually be higher for the reasons already given). This 'profit or loss on foreign exchange' is shown as a separate item in the hotel's accounts: in other words, it is treated as a purely financial transaction and not credited or debited to the guest's account.

Travellers' cheques

Travellers' cheques are issued by major banks and financial institutions in different currencies and in fixed denominations, such as £10, £20 and £50, or $10, $20 and $50. Customers buy them in their own currencies, then exchange them in the currencies of the countries they are visiting.

Customers have to sign their travellers' cheques when and where they are issued, but they do not become valid until they are signed a *second* time in the presence of the receiving cashier. Once properly signed, the cheque becomes the equivalent of cash and is treated as such in the accounts.

Travellers' cheques bear a service charge which is used to defray the cost of administration and to cover additional insurance against accidental loss or theft. This charge is paid by the customer. As far as the hotel is concerned, travellers' cheques only incur the same handling charges as ordinary cheques, though they offer greater security.

Since travellers' cheques bear the original bearer's signature, a skilful forger can easily convert them to his own use, so it is common to ask for additional documentary evidence of identity, such as a passport. Lists of lost or stolen travellers' cheques are circulated regularly to hotels, and cashiers should check these before accepting any such cheques.

Cashiers receiving travellers' cheques in payment should observe certain simple rules:

* Check the denomination and work out the exchange value, if any.
* Check that the date and payee entries are correct.
* Insist that the travellers' cheque is signed in your presence, and then compare the two signatures on its face.
* Check the cheque number against the current stop list.

It is also common practice to note the room number on the reverse side, just in case there are any queries later.

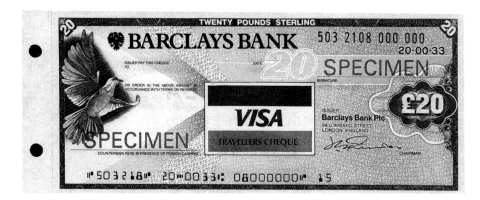

Figure 43   *Sample travellers' cheque (courtesy Barclays Bank Travellers Cheques)*

Credit cards

Credit cards now represent one of the main methods by which bills are settled (so much so, indeed, that many American hotels now regard guests offering to pay by cash with some suspicion).

Credit cards are issued by the major banks, who are affiliated to either the Access (Mastercard) or Visa networks, or else by major travel and entertainment organizations such as American Express (Amex) and Diners Club International (Diners). The terms and conditions upon which they are issued vary somewhat, but this need not concern the cashier. What is important is that the issuing organization issues a franchise to the hotel, entitling it to accept card payments in exchange for services offered.

This franchise includes a 'floor limit', which restricts the amount the hotel can accept on any one card for without special authorization. This floor limit will be greater for large hotels than for smaller ones. It is quite independent of the cardholder's credit limit. If a bill exceeds the floor limit, the cashier must obtain authorization from the credit card company by calling a toll-free number.

The issuing organizations guarantee payment of all bills run up by the holder up to his credit limit. This limit is almost always much higher than the cheque card limit, which makes the credit card a very useful means for settling hotel bills.

Unfortunately, credit card fraud is widespread, and cashiers have to be vigilant, since 'payments' made on the basis of an invalid card will not be honoured by the issuing company. Rewards are paid for recovery of lost or stolen cards.

The procedure for dealing with credit card payments is as follows:

1   The customer hands over his card and the cashier checks that it bears the correct name and a valid expiry date.
2   The cashier also checks the card against the card company's current 'stop' list.
3   The cashier checks that the amount is not over the floor limit.

4 The cashier makes out a sales voucher, usually in triplicate, and enters the authorization number (if any).
5 The cashier then uses a special machine (called an 'imprinter') to make an imprint of the card on the sales voucher.
6 This done, the customer signs the voucher with a ballpoint pen. The signature must be checked against that on the card. This done, the customer is given a copy of the voucher plus his card back.
7 Finally, the cashier should offer to destroy any carbon paper used in the preparation of the voucher (this is because it bears both the card number and a copy of the signature and could be passed on to a third party by an unscrupulous cashier).

All credit card companies operate on a commission basis. In other words, they deduct commission before final payment is made. However, the procedures for dealing with them differ. Vouchers for bank-issued cards like Access and Visa are simply paid into the hotel's bank and are cleared like ordinary cheques. The only difference is that you have to use a separate paying-in slip, and your bank deducts the card company's commission before crediting the hotel's account. Travel and entertainment card vouchers such as Diners or American Express are collected together and sent off in batches to the respective companies for payment. This process takes longer than with the bank-issued cards, though the companies claim that the delay is seldom more than two or three days.

Figure 44 *Sample credit card (courtesy Eurocard International)*

'Smart' cards

These can be expected to increase in importance over the next decade. They resemble cash cards in that they allow holders to make payments directly from their current accounts to establishments equipped with appropriate terminals. Hotels thus equipped can have the money paid directly into their own accounts without delay. The advantages are obvious, though card holders will still have to sign a sales voucher and this will still have to be forwarded in some way to their bank to provide a written record.

'Smart' cards are likely to be used in other ways, too. One possibility is that they might replace the present computerized room key (receptionists would pass the card through a reader which would automatically programme the door lock to respond to that particular magnetically coded number), or be used to record and pay for hotel mini bar purchases.

Travel agents' voucher

Many guests present travel agents' vouchers in whole or part payment. These vary much more than the other forms of payment we have been considering, and need to be examined carefully.

Travel agents' vouchers arise when the guest pays the agency for his food and accommodation in advance. The agency then prepares two copies of the voucher. One copy goes to the hotel to confirm the booking, and the other is given to the guest for him to present to the hotel when he registers.

The cashier should have the first copy of the voucher as part of the reservation documents. When the guest arrives and presents his copy, she should compare the two to make sure that there have been no alterations. She should also make sure that she knows exactly what the voucher covers, and whether there are likely to be any 'extras' (laundry, for instance, or bar bills). If there are, she should open an 'extras' bill and make sure that the guest understands the arrangement. Guests are normally asked to sign their bills to show that they have actually stayed at the hotel and incurred the charges stated.

Not all vouchers actually show the price agreed, so this may have to be established from other documents. The vouchers are then collected and sent off to the various travel agents for payment. The accompanying statement usually deducts the agreed discount from the total, and it is this net figure that the agency eventually pays.

Special problems arise when dealing with overseas travel agents. Since payment will be delayed, there may be a loss on foreign exchange. It is sensible practice to require that payment be made in sterling. This means that it is the travel agent who has to accept the risk.

Group tours organized by travel agents are often paid for by group vouchers. The principle is exactly the same, but the tour courier is generally expected to agree the number of persons, meals and so forth prior to departure. Individual 'extras' bills are likely with this kind of business, and it is front office's task to make sure that these are presented and paid by the guests.

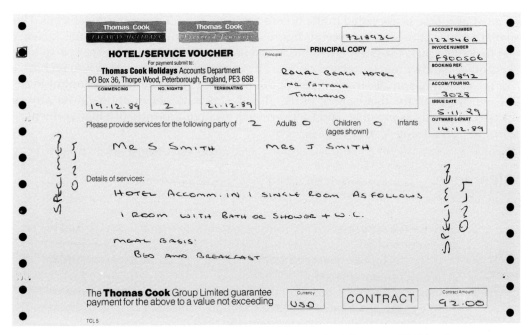

Figure 45   *Sample travel agent's voucher (courtesy Thomas Cook Faraway Holidays)*

Disputed bills, discounts and refunds

There may be occasions on which a guest objects to a bill, either because the amount is not what he agreed to pay, or because he has not received one or more of the items charged, or simply because he feels he has not had adequate service.

In all such cases, the first thing to do is to take the guest aside and ask him (very politely) to wait while his complaint is investigated. If possible, this task should be handled by a senior member of staff. Unfortunately, the nature of the hotel business being what it is, this is not always possible. It may be early in the morning, with the guest in a hurry to leave and the dispute centring upon items on a restaurant bill from the night before. In these circumstances, some hotels give their receptionists discretion to strike off the contested item or items. The theory is that it is better to avoid creating an unfavourable impression in the minds of other guests by having a noisy argument with a guest at a busy period. In theory, the hotel could always write to the guest asking for payment if it found that it had been right all along. In practice, this hardly ever happens and the amount is simply written off.

Another possible cause for complaint is disturbance or inconvenience. Not all hotel rooms are ideally located, and by no means all guests are well behaved. A noisy party in a bar may keep some guests awake, while boisterous revellers staggering along a corridor at two o'clock in the morning may disturb others. While a guest must accept that he is sharing the hotel with others, some cases of disturbance can be so extreme that he is prevented from enjoying what he is paying for. In such circumstances the hotel should be prepared to make a reduction.

Such reductions or discounts are classed as 'adjustments', 'allowances' or 'refunds', and they must of course be recorded in the hotel's accounts as well as on the guest's bill. This is essential because otherwise the receipts figure will not agree with the amount due: it is easy to forget to do it because the guest is in a hurry and the most important thing may seem to be to make a quick handwritten correction on his copy of the bill and then speed him on his way.

The tab usually has an 'allowances' row or column, while computerized accounting systems will have provision for this type of entry. It is desirable to obtain approval for any such reduction as quickly as possible, and some systems may require entry of a management code number to prove authorization.

Assignments

1 Describe the type of guest accounting system you would expect to find in the Tudor Hotel.
2 Describe the type of guest accounting system you would expect to find in the Pancontinental Hotel.
3 Obtain specimens of the type of guest accounting documents and an outline of the procedures used at a selection of local hotels, and compare these, relating their characteristics to the type of hotel involved.
4 Outline a training scheme for cashiers in a 100 bedroom hotel converting from a manual guest accounting system to a computerized one.
5 Prepare tabular ledger entries for the guests currently in residence, enter all the following transactions, and close and balance the 'tab' as at the end of the day's business, adding and reconciling all totals.

Tariff:

Room and breakfast	£25.50 (inclusive of breakfast £4.50) per person
Inclusive rate	£41.00 (inclusive of all meals £20.00) per person
Table d'hôte lunch	£4.75
Table d'hôte dinner	£10.75
Coffees/teas	60p per person

Guests in residence:

Room	Type	Name	Terms	B/forward
102	Double	Mr/s Hughes	Inc	£106.80
111	Single	Mr Booth	R&B	£ 30.25
205	Double	Mr/s Sykes	Inc	£ 86.50
206	Single	Dr Haines	R&B	£ 35.00

Transactions:

07.30 Early morning teas to all residents
         Newspapers: 205 (35p), 111 (40p), 206 (35p)
07.40 Telephone calls: 205 (£1.50), 206 (£85p), 111 (£6.50)
07.45 Disbursements: 102 Laundry (£2.50), 206 Ticket (£12.50)
08.00 Breakfasts served to all residents
09.00 Mr/s Sykes out and pay in full by cash

	Dr Haines checks out: account transferred to ledger
	Mr/s Hughes pay £50 on account by cheque
10.00	Mr Booth moves to Room 202 on R&B terms
11.00	Morning coffees for 102 (2 persons) and 202 (1 person)
13.00	102 2 lunches plus cigar (£1.75)
	202 1 lunch plus beer (£1.20)
15.30	Adjustment: Mr Booth wrongly charged for Lunch yesterday
17.30	Arrival: Mr/s Cummings, Room 208 (double), inclusive terms
18.45	Arrival: Mr/s Jones, Room 100 (double), R&B Terms
21.30	100: 2 dinners plus wine (£9.50), spirits (£6.25)
	102: 2 dinners plus wine (£7.75), cigar (£1.75)
	202: 1 dinner plus beer (£1.60)
	208: 2 dinners plus wine (£9.95), cigar (£3.70)
23.00	Arrival: Mr Power, Room 103 (single), inclusive terms
23.30	Adjustment: morning paper (35p) should be charged to 102 and not 206 as noted earlier

4 Security

Introduction

We make no apology for devoting a chapter to this topic. Security is the business of every employee, not just that of the security officer and his assistants, and since front office staff are closely involved with the guests, they must be constantly on the alert.

There are two kinds of threat that you need to be concerned about:

1 Anything that might affect a guest's health, comfort or well-being. This must be given priority. The hotel exists to provide a service for guests, and if it ever starts to put its own interests or convenience first, it will quickly go out of business.
2 Anything that may affect the hotel, in particular its fixtures and fittings, its revenues or its reputation.

Strictly speaking, there is also a third major area, that of possible risks to the hotel's staff. However, this 'health and safety at work' aspect falls outside the scope of this book, which is concerned primarily with the guest–front office relationship, and we shall simply note it here for the record.

Not all guests are honest, and the hotel must protect both its guests and itself against the occasional dubious customer. This may involve taking some form of legally-sanctioned action to exclude him, to obtain payment from him, or to prosecute him. You should consult a specialist law textbook for the full particulars, but a preliminary look at the relevant provisions may be of help:

1 *Contracts for accommodation* When a hotel accepts a booking from a guest, it enters into a binding contract. The guest is expected to turn up, and the hotel must provide the agreed accommodation. If either party fails to honour its side of the bargain, it must compensate the other for any loss suffered. However, the guest is also expected to behave reasonably, and if he turns up in a drunken or verminous state, or behaves in a violent and quarrelsome fashion, he may be deemed to have broken the contract and the hotel may require him to leave. Just what kind of behaviour would constitute breach of contract is a matter for the courts.
2 *The Hotel Proprietor's Act, 1956* Under this, a hotel has an obligation to accept bona fide travellers who 'appear able and willing to pay a reasonable sum for the services and facilities provided, and who are in a fit state to be received'. This excludes would-be guests in the kind of state we have described above. It also excludes guests who are *known* to be dishonest. The hotel cannot refuse to accept such guests merely on the grounds that it *suspects* their honesty. It may put a guest on its black list if it has previously had an unfavourable experience with him, but the question of whether it can do so on the basis of some other hotel's report does not seem to have been tested.

3 *The Sex Discrimination Act, 1975* This prohibits a hotel from discriminating against women as far as the provision of goods, facilities or services are concerned.

4 *The Race Relations Act, 1976* This prohibits a hotel from discriminating against any person on the grounds of colour, nationality, race or ethnic origin, again as far as the provision of goods, facilities or services are concerned.

5 *Payment in advance* Nothing in the above provisions prevents the hotel from demanding payment in advance. This is in fact one of your main lines of defence against dubious customers, so long as you do not use it as a concealed form of discrimination. You may also request interim payments at any time.

6 *Trespass* Normally, a property owner can stop anyone else from coming onto his property without permission. The intruder is a 'trespasser' and can be required to leave. He can also be sued if he causes any damage, though he cannot be *prosecuted* since trespass is a civil law matter. The obligation to accept bona fide travellers imposed by the Hotel Proprietors Act limits this right as far as hotel operators are concerned, but it certainly does not give travellers the right to wander all over the hotel. One who has merely called in for refreshment would be entitled to enter public rooms such as the bar or restaurant, but not the accommodation block, and even a guest who is staying the night has no right to explore corridors other than his own. No guest has any right to enter areas which are clearly marked 'staff'. These limitations are important because they allow hotel staff to challenge suspicious characters, though of course this should always be done tactfully ('May I help you Madam? Which room are you looking for?')

7 *The right of lien* This old common law right was codified in the Innkeepers' Act of 1878. It allows a hotel to seize a guest's belongings and sell them to defray its costs if his bill is not paid. It is hedged around with a number of restrictions, and in any case the professional swindler normally takes care not to bring much that is worth seizing.

8 *The Theft Acts* Section 1 of the Theft Act, 1968 defines theft as follows:

> A person is guilty of theft if he dishonestly appropriates property belonging to another with the intention of permanently depriving the other of it.

It goes on to add:

> A person is guilty of burglary if he enters any building . . . as a trespasser and with intent to commit any such offence. . . .

These provisions cover the thief who enters hotel premises in order to steal property belonging either to the hotel or its guests, but the position regarding the person who simply leaves a hotel or restaurant without paying remained obscure until the Theft Act of 1978, which added:

> Any person who by any deception dishonestly obtains services from another shall be guilty of an offence.

and:

> Any person who knowing that payment on the spot for any goods supplied or services done is required or expected from him, dishonestly makes off without paying as required and with intent to avoid payment shall be guilty of an offence.

Note however, that as with all serious criminal offences, you have to prove not only the facts (that the defendant stayed the night and then made off without paying, for instance), but also that he did so 'with intent'. The difficulties this can cause are illustrated by *R. v. Allen* (1985). In this case, the defendant did indeed stay at a hotel but then left without paying his bill. He came back later to collect his belongings, saying that he intended to pay the bill as soon as he received the proceeds from certain outstanding business transactions. He was arrested and convicted under the Theft Act, 1978, but the Court of Appeal quashed the conviction and the House of Lords upheld its decision on the grounds that intent to avoid payment required an intention to avoid payment permanently, and not merely an intention to delay such payment. Any serious criminal charge must be proved 'beyond all reasonable doubt', and *R. v. Allen* shows how difficult this can be.

9 *Right of arrest*   Serious criminal offences such as theft carry the right of arrest as far as private persons are concerned. According to the Criminal Law Act, 1967, you may arrest without warrant anyone who is committing an arrestable offence, or who has committed such an offence, or whom you have reasonable cause to suspect of committing or having committed such an offence. However, you need to be very sure of what you are doing. Indeed, any such action is highly dangerous, legally speaking, because it can form the basis for a number of torts. Stopping a guest without good cause may amount to false arrest, and detaining him against his will to wrongful imprisonment, while grabbing his suitcases without his consent may constitute conversion. Threatening him is likely to be assault, while holding him back by force is probably battery as well. Finally, wrongly accusing him in the presence of witnesses could well amount to slander. The risks are serious, and you would be well advised *not* to commit yourself to any of these actions unless you are absolutely sure of your facts.

Protecting the guest

There are a variety of possible threats to a guest's comfort and well-being, but the most serious is any threat to his physical safety.

Threats to the guest's life or limb can arise from internal or external sources. The melancholy fact is that more guests are injured as a result of a hotel's carelessness than as a result of the action of external agencies. Since we hold that security is *everybody's* business, we ought to consider this first.

Internal threats to the guest's person

The major threat is of fire. Fire puts everyone in the hotel at risk, not just the careless individual who may have started the blaze in the first place. The real hazard, as you should know, is not the fire itself but the smoke and fumes, which generally suffocate victims long before the flames actually reach them.

The chief responsibility for ensuring that fire risks are adequately guarded against belongs to management as a whole, acting on the specialist advice of the local fire officers, who are empowered to issue a fire certificate provided that their requirements are met.

However, occasional fire inspections can be undermined by slack or inefficient working practices. Since we believe that all front office staff have a responsibility to protect the guests in their charge, we maintain that *you* ought to satisfy *yourself* with regard to the following key areas:

1 *Fire detection systems* A high proportion of hotel fires begin at night, when most guests and staff are asleep. It is essential that the hotel should be protected by appropriate detectors (smoke, heat or flame, depending on location) and that these be properly maintained and tested regularly.
2 *Fire containment provisions* A good deal of time and money has been spent on the installation of fire doors and adequate fire escape facilities, but all too often these are not maintained as they should be. Doors are left propped open, windows are allowed to become unopenable. Such practices are not in the guests' long-term interests.
3 *Escape procedures* Clear and unambiguous instructions must be displayed in every room so that guests know which way to go in the event of an emergency.
4 *Fire-fighting equipment* Hotels should be properly equipped with fire extinguishers. These must be serviced regularly, and staff should be trained in their use.

If you *aren't* satisfied with respect to all or any of these, then say so, tactfully but firmly. After all, you don't want to work in a death trap.

There are plenty of other possible hazards to guests, such as worn carpets, slippery tiles, insecure handrails, faulty electrical wiring or unreliable lifts. Your management will be aware of the dangers involved should the guest be able to prove negligence or breach of occupier's liability, but it may still need to have specific threats brought to its notice. If a guest says on checking out 'Oh, by the way, you ought to get that electric kettle in my room seen to; I got a slight shock when I plugged it in . . .', then get it checked out: the next occupant may not be so lucky.

Terrorist threats

Unfortunately, the world does not seem to be growing noticeably safer, and hotels which cater for VIPs need to take bomb threats and other forms of terrorism very seriously indeed.

Such hotels will normally liaise closely with their local police forces, who will advise them regarding security precautions and take over whenever visitors particularly at risk are staying. The most dramatic threat is that of some kind of assassination attempt: fortunately this is very unlikely and even if it did happen nobody would expect front office staff to 'have a go' or do anything other than take cover.

The police will expect cooperation in other respects, however. Hotels are by their very nature vulnerable to the infiltration of terrorists masquerading as innocent guests. In particular, staff would be expected to keep their eyes open and to report anything suspicious, from a visitor who does not seem to 'fit' to an unattended piece of luggage.

In other respects, front office staff are likely to remain 'in the front line', and need to conduct themselves accordingly. The chief threat is the telephoned bomb warning. The vast majority of these are likely to be hoaxes, but they cannot be taken lightly. Staff liable to take such calls (usually one of the switchboard operators) need to be trained to handle them correctly. There are two essential requirements;

1 The caller should not be interrupted , and his words must be written down *exactly*.
2 As soon as he is finished, you should write down as many details as you can remember about the caller's voice, mannerisms etc. It is essential to do this as quickly as possible

---

Bomb threat form

Date .... Time call began .... Time call ended ....

Caller's *exact* words ....

....

....

Questions to ask:

- When is bomb due to explode? ....
- Where have you put it? ....
- What does it look like? ....
- Why have you done this? ....
- Who do you represent? ....

Details of caller (complete as soon as call ended)

    Sex ....

    Age ....

    Voice: Fast ☐ Slow ☐ Coherent ☐ Incoherent ☐ Loud ☐ Quiet ☐

    Manner: Calm ☐ Angry ☐ Amused ☐ Emotional ☐

    Accent: Local ☐ Educated ☐ Foreign ☐ Country?............

    Can you imitate voice? Yes ☐ No ☐

    Was voice familiar? Yes ☐ No ☐

    Was call long distance or local? ....

    Any background noises? ....

Further action:

    Manager notified .... Time ....

    Police notified .... Time ....

Signed   .... Date

.... Time ....

Figure 46 *Bomb threat form*

because it is then that the facts are freshest in your mind. Bear in mind that there is an almost irresistible temptation to 'decorate' the facts with each retelling.

It would be a good idea to have a standard form ready to hand for this purpose (Figure 46).

Another related threat arises from letter bombs. Again, the police will normally advise you on these, but it is not always possible to foresee exactly where and when a deranged terrorist may decide to strike.

Staff responsible for dealing with mail should be given some instruction in the recognition and handling of suspect packages. As a general rule, such packages are safe enough as long as they are not opened, but this may not apply if they arrive in a damaged state. Moreover, there is a slight but genuine risk that the detonator might be affected by radio transmissions, so all packages should be kept separate from any radio paging equipment being operated by the hotel.

Threats to privacy

Again, this is most likely to be a problem as far as VIPs are concerned. It is very tempting to tell one's friends all about a well-known pop star who might be staying at the hotel, but such friends tend to pass the information on to *their* friends, and it soon becomes public property.

The risk is not limited to casual gossip. The activities of the famous make good 'copy', and there are always reporters who are on the look out for spicy stories. Such reporters may try to get you to give them information by using flattery or even a little low-level bribery. You should resist being used in this way.

Famous guests might also be pestered by fans and autograph hunters. It is part of your job to prevent this from happening.

There is yet another way in which you might breach your duty of confidentiality. Let us suppose that an earring is found in a room after a couple have left. The room maid reports it to the housekeeper, who tells you. Wishing to be helpful, you check the couple's home telephone number on the registration form and ring them up. A woman's voice answers. 'Hello, Mrs Smith,' you say, 'I'm sure you'll be pleased to hear that we've found your earring.' 'What earring?', she asks, clearly puzzled. 'The one you left at our hotel,' you reply. 'What hotel?', she asks. 'The one you've just been staying at with Mr Smith . . .', you answer. Only then does it become clear that whoever Mr Smith had been staying with, it wasn't the lady you are now talking to. . . .

In this instance you may be inclined to argue that 'Mr Smith' deserves all he is likely to get, but that is none of your business. A guest is entitled to privacy, whoever he or she is, and you should regard confidentiality as a major duty.

Threats to guests' property

Hotel guests often carry considerable amounts of money or other valuables around with them, and this makes them obvious targets for a variety of unscrupulous characters. The threat comes from a variety of sources:

1 *Muggings* A hotel room offers a quiet and secure location for an assault if the criminal can persuade the unsuspecting guest to open the door. Hotels do not offer easy getaway routes, but this is only a problem if the assailant leaves the victim able to raise the alarm afterwards. Fortunately, few British criminals are quite as ruthless as this, but hotel muggings *have* become a serious problem in some particularly violent urban areas in other countries.
2 *Sneak thieves* Large and busy hotels offer happy hunting grounds for certain kinds of professional thieves. There are pickpockets and bag snatchers who might work the bars, the lobby or the pool, or well-dressed, confident-looking room thieves. The latter can wander around the corridors undisturbed, testing bedroom doors to see whether they have been securely locked, or even trying out their armoury of skeleton keys. Should they, by chance, find themselves faced with a genuine guest they can always apologize and withdraw: mistakes over rooms are easy enough to make, after all. Obviously, it is even better from the thief's point of view if he *is* a genuine guest, because then he has a perfect right to walk around the hotel. Some thieves do check in as legitimate guests: their aim is to steal enough to cover their expenses.

3   *Confidence tricksters*   Expensive hotels offer the perfect background for con-men. Their guests are generally well off, and often surprisingly lonely and gullible. Confidence tricksters book in as legitimate guests and then move in on likely-looking targets. Their 'scams' vary, but are almost always based on some character weakness on the part of the 'mark', or victim. The result is that the victim is often too embarrassed to complain afterwards, which makes prevention particularly difficult. Confidence tricksters generally pay their bills in a perfectly normal manner (from their point of view, these are legitimate business expenses).

Prostitutes   These present hotels with something of the same problem as confidence tricksters in that guests seldom complain if they end up on the losing side. Prevention is made even more difficult by the fact that the guest will deliberately conspire to smuggle the prostitute into his room, evading whatever security routines you may have introduced to prevent this from happening. Prostitution itself involves taking money for sexual services, and many prostitutes are honest enough in their way. However, they often live in a shadowy borderland between the legal and the illegal (although prostitution itself is not illegal, 'pimping' most certainly is, and some prostitutes are in fact drug addicts). It would be unreasonable not to expect some to take advantage of situations where they might find themselves alone in a room with a guest who has just dropped off to sleep for a moment, carelessly leaving his wallet in plain view. Some years ago the Metropolitan Police felt justified in launching a campaign based on the slogan 'prostitutes are thieves'. There are other reasons why hotels should do everything they can to discourage prostitution, and we will look at them later. For the moment, we will just add that a guest who has just lost all his money and credit cards to an anonymous prostitute will have to offer *some* kind of explanation to his wife or bank manager, and he is hardly likely to tell the truth. In these circumstances, guests have been known to accuse hotel staff of theft, causing considerable embarrassment to all concerned.

For the sake of completeness, we ought to note two further possible sources of risk:

5   *Staff*   The contrast between staff and guest incomes is often marked, and guests are not always either very tactful or very careful. It can be very tempting to come across a bulging wallet lying on a dressing table, especially when the guest's behaviour leads you to suspect that he does not know exactly how much was in it when he put it there. There are far fewer staff thefts than one might suppose, but they *do* occasionally happen.

6   *The guests themselves*   Some guests are tempted to level accusations against the hotel when it is really their own carelessness that is the cause of the loss. Others may do so rather than admit to having lost the money in some more embarrassing way, such as to a prostitute, or gambling. Finally, there are a few wholly dishonest guests who will deliberately claim to have lost something they never had in the first place, hoping that the hotel will agree to compensate them rather than mount an embarrassing investigation.

Clearly, all these threats should be avoided as far as possible. There are several lines of defence:

1   The hotel must do its best to ensure that casual undesirables such as thieves and prostitutes do not obtain access to public areas such as bars and pools. This can be difficult, since visitors are constantly going in and out, but a hotel is private property and you have every right to require trespassers to leave.

2   Deterring known con-men and 'gentleman thieves' is mainly a matter of putting them on your black list and then refusing to allow them to make a booking. Hotels can, and do, exchange information about such individuals.

3   The prevention of casual theft might also involve the installation of discrete surveillance equipment in the public areas. This is not so common as in department stores because there is not the same amount of pilferable stock on display, but it might be necessary in certain crowded sectors where pickpockets could otherwise work with impunity (such as a casino). .

4   Guest rooms must be made as secure as possible. Wide-angle viewing lenses can be built into bedroom doors, and adequate door chains provided at relatively little cost. If mugging is a serious risk, guests may have to be warned not to open their doors unless they are sure who is outside. This might sound alarmist, but it is better to be safe than sorry. In fact, muggings are much more likely to take place outside the hotel. The guest may be unfamiliar with the immediate environment, and may have to be warned if he proposes to go out late at night on foot. This ought to be as much a part of your job as key control. The whole question of locks and key control has been revolutionized over the past two decades or so. The old metal key has now been largely superseded by the new computerized key card, which:

- Allows front office to change the combination (in effect, the lock) every time a room is relet, or even any time the guest loses his key.
- Allows *selective* room access. Maintenance staff, for instance, can be given keys which allow access to a specified room or group of rooms only, and these can be automatically cancelled after use.
- Produces a complete record of all room entries, showing both the exact time of entry *and* the type of key used (guest, room staff, maintenance, management etc.). The systems do not as yet show *who* used the key in question, but this may well come about in the near future.

The disadvantage of these electronic systems is that they tend to be relatively expensive, though the cost can be offset by lower running expenses such as insurance premiums and key and lock replacements. A compromise approach developed in America allows for removable 'lock cores' which can be replaced quickly and then reprogrammed and used elsewhere.

5   Guests' property must be safeguarded. We have already discussed the hotel's obligation to accept valuables for safe keeping, and looked at the routines involved. However, depositing cash and jewellery can be inconvenient, and many guests would prefer to use a room safe. There are a variety of different products available, ranging from a full-blown, permanently installed safe down to a portable safe box which can be rented out from front office and attached to one of the fixtures in the room. Such safe boxes come in various sizes, from small versions which are only large enough to hold cash, jewellery and a camera, up to larger models which can take documents. They do not provide the same amount of security as a wall safe, but they are usually sufficient to deter the casual, hurried sneak thief. The question of whether the provision of a room safe affects a hotelkeeper's legal liability is an interesting one which does not yet seem to have come before the courts. Normally, if a guest elects to leave valuables in his room, he is deemed to have accepted the risk involved, and thus bears the responsibility for any resulting loss unless the hotel can be shown to have been negligent. It might be argued that if the hotel provides a room safe it is by implication offering an alternative to its 'deposit for safe keeping' obligation, and

should thus be liable in full should the safe prove to be insecure. However, we think that there is an important difference in that the front office safe is (or should be) under constant guard, whereas the room safe is bound to be unwatched for considerable periods (i.e. while the guest is out of the room). Consequently, we do not think that such safes affect the general legal position regarding the hotelkeeper's liability. The hotelier is still obliged to accept valuable articles for safe keeping, and remains fully liable for them. Should a guest decide to entrust such articles to a safe in his room, that remains *his* decision, and he must accept responsibility.

Other threats to the guest's enjoyment

The main problem is likely to be drunken, quarrelsome or noisy behaviour on the part of other guests. Inconsiderate behaviour of this type has probably ruined more holidays than fire or theft ever did.

If a traveller turns up in a drunken state and asks for a room, you are entitled to refuse him on the grounds that he is not in a fit state to be received. This is true even if he already has a booking, because he has broken one of the implied conditions of the contract.

The same applies to a guest who misbehaves during his stay. The fact that he was fit to be received when he arrived does not mean that the hotel is obliged to let him stay if he subsequently alters his behaviour.

Drunken guests are a threat to your possession of a liquor licence, because permitting drunkenness is grounds for removal of that licence. You must therefore take steps to persuade them to leave the bar and go to their rooms.

Normally, what they do there is their own business, as long as they do not damage your property or inconvenience any other guests. If they persist in singing, shouting or behaving in a noisy and boisterous fashion, then someone will have to go up and try to quieten them down. In the last resort, they can be asked to leave.

Obviously, this process requires considerable tact, but then so does dealing with complaints from your other guests. Always remember that if a guest rings down to reception to complain about being kept awake, that guest has probably spent a sleepless hour or so nerving himself up to do it. Most people don't really *like* to complain (there are always exceptions, of course), so if you get two or three such calls it is definitely time for action!

Protecting the hotel

Threats to the hotel's property

Guests can be careless, and your furniture, fixtures or fitting may suffer damage as a result. Some degree of fair wear and tear is only to be expected, and it would be unreasonable to hold a guest to account for normal domestic accidents such as broken glasses or spilled coffee. However, furniture smashed as a result of boisterous horseplay or a drunken quarrel is a different matter. A hotel is entitled to expect that its guests will behave at least as carefully as they do at home, and there is thus an implied condition in the contract that they will compensate the hotel for any loss or damage if they don't. In such circumstances the hotel could add a reasonable amount to the guest's bill to cover the cost of repairs or replacement. Whether it does so or not is a question of policy, and would probably depend on the seriousness of the damage.

The real security problem, however, lies with guests who steal things. As any hotelier will confirm, virtually anything that isn't securely fastened down is liable to vanish from a hotel bedroom. Soap, towels, mats, sheets, blankets, coathangers, lamps, trouser presses, electric kettles, TV sets and even plumbing fixtures have been known to disappear. Motels are particularly vulnerable, because their guests are often able to park their cars conveniently close to the accommodation and commonly pay in advance so that they can make an early (and unobserved) departure. There are stories of couples who have arrived in a van or station wagon and then spent the night removing every fixture and fitting in sight with a view to installing them in their own homes.

The only answer lies in having housekeeping staff inspect the room as quickly as possible, and preferably before the guest checks out. This is much easier to recommend than to organize. However, let us assume that rooms staff *have* checked the room and that you have just received a report that certain items are missing. What do you do now?

As we have seen, a direct challenge may have awkward legal consequences. However, a more tactful approach sometimes works. You might ask the guest to step to one side and then say, very politely 'I'm sorry to bother you, but the room maid says she can't find all the towels. Guests occasionally pack one or two hotel items when they're in a hurry, quite accidentally of course. I wonder if you mind very much just checking before you leave?' At which point the guest usually says 'No, of course not,' opens his suitcase, turning slightly pink as he does so, and lo! there are your towels. If instead he elects to brazen it out, saying something like 'I'm sorry, I don't have time. If I *do* find anything, I'll return it, of course . . .' then you are probably best advised to accept his statement and write off the items.

Expensive items of equipment can be protected to some extent by fixing them to the furniture or walls. Another useful idea is security marking: a permanent and visible mark will make it more difficult to sell the item and more embarrassing to use it at home, while 'invisible' marking is helpful in tracing stolen items. Nowadays such items can also be linked to a computerized alarm system.

Remember that not all such thefts are committed by guests. One of the thief's simplest and most effective methods is to don a pair of overalls and then walk into a busy establishment with a nonchalant air, trusting (generally correctly) that anyone who sees him will assume that he has a legitimate reason for being there. Many a piece of electrical equipment has been brazenly removed under the eyes of a dozen or so staff.

'Walk-outs', 'skippers' or 'runners'

Guests who leave without paying are known as 'walk-outs', 'skippers' or 'runners'. They can be divided into three groups:

1   *The 'accidentals'*   Although it sounds unlikely, there *are* guests who simply forget to pay. They may be confused over who was due to settle the account, or a conference delegate may genuinely forget an 'extras' bill. Forgetfulness is a real possibility, so you should

always be tactful when contacting a walk-out. Genuine 'accidentals' will normally be highly embarrassed and pay up immediately.

2   *The 'opportunists'*   These are people who had every intention of paying their bills when they first checked in, but who subsequently realized that they could get away without doing so. Hotels whose design allows guests to reach the car park without passing reception could well find a number of their guests yielding to this kind of temptation. Opportunists also take advantage of slip-ups in the hotel's billing procedures. In the days before POS (point of sale) computer terminals became common, cashiers often had to ask a guest whether he had consumed breakfast. A surprising number said 'No' and left before their breakfast voucher could come through. This is still likely to be a problem in a non-computerized hotel. The same problem often occurs with 'extras' bills.

3   *The 'premeditators'*   These are people who never have any intention of paying in the first place, and who sometimes go to considerable lengths in order to avoid doing so (in one case, a guest booked by means of a telex purporting to come from a well-known company with whom the hotel had an account. He stayed for four nights, eating three full meals a day, then signed the bill and left. Only when the account was queried by the company did the hotel notice that the telex confirmation number was that of a telex agency and not the company). There will always be someone trying this on for the first time, of course, but 'premeditators' are often found repeating the same offence at hotel after hotel around the country. This underlines the need for some kind of information exchange. This is an odd crime inasmuch as the 'skipper' is seldom destitute. Indeed, if he were, he could not be sufficiently well dressed and groomed to carry off the pretence. He cannot guarantee that he will not be stopped and made to pay, and yet he gets no permanent benefit from his crime even if he gets away with it. In other words, his motivation is often a kind of cheeky desire to put one over on the establishment. This helps to explain why experienced reception staff can claim that they have a 'nose' for walk-outs. There are various subtle indicators which help the skilled receptionist to 'smell a wrong 'un'. They include an absence of luggage and a lack of corroborative evidence of identity. Evident nervousness and a reluctance to provide registration particulars may betray the inexperienced 'first timer' planning a walk-out. On the other hand, a high degree of self-confidence and a very plausible but hard-to-check explanation to account for his missing luggage is likely to mark the practised 'skipper'. As one security officer said 'It's the little inconsistencies I look for, especially between the things he can get on credit and the things he can't, like an expensive suit and a cheap haircut for instance.' Experienced room staff can often detect 'premeditated' walk-outs in much the same way. They are in a better position to check whether the guest has unpacked very many personal belongings: a minimum of toiletries and a locked suitcase are strong grounds for suspicion. In a well-run hotel the first department to have its suspicions aroused will communicate these to all the others, and the establishment will begin to operate like a top class intelligence-gathering machine, with the doubtful guest being reported on wherever he goes, while the security department tries to establish his bona fides.

Walk-outs do not really cost the hotel very much (you may not have been able to let that room to anyone else anyway, and the real cost of the food and drink is much lower than the selling price), but they are annoying, and you should be on your guard against them. The biggest problem you face is that the 'professional walk-out' is usually very plausible (this plausibility is his stock-in-trade). In addition, he will generally pick on the most inexperienced-looking member of staff available, and choose the busiest time of the day to make his approach.

Hotels use, or have used, a number of security measures to reduce the incidence of 'walkouts':

1   *Credit status checks*   It may be possible to confirm a guest's credit status from his registration particulars by checking with a commercial credit agency. This is the job of the security officer, but he needs the cooperation of the receptionists, who should refer *any* 'chance' or otherwise doubtful customers to him for clearance.
2   *Payment in advance*   As we have seen, a hotel is entitled to demand this, and receptionists should always do so if they have any doubts about the guest's reliability. It should be normal practice in the case of a 'chance' guest, for example.
3   *Interim payments*   An alternative approach is to establish a credit limit, and to ask for an interim payment as soon as the guest's account reaches it. Computerized billing programs almost always allow you to enter this limit, and will 'flag' the account as soon as it is reached. This practice prevents the guest from running up a very large bill. The process of approaching the guest and asking for the interim payment requires considerable tact, but most customers do understand the problems caused by the dishonest minority and cooperate willingly enough, especially if it is explained to them as 'hotel policy'.
4   *'Guaranteed' bookings*   This is a term used in connection with credit card bookings. If a would-be guest has given a credit card number at the time of booking, and does not then cancel the booking within a reasonable time, the hotel can simply make out a credit card voucher in the usual way and the company will pay it and debit the guest's account. This is obviously a considerable improvement from the hotel's point of view, and helps to explain why credit card bookings may be preferred to cash ones. Naturally enough, the hotel is expected to have gone through all the usual security routines, such as checking the card number against the stop list, ensuring that it does not exceed the floor limit and so on.
5   *Luggage passes*   These used to be common in the days when guests commonly travelled with large amounts of baggage requiring armies of porters to move them. Such baggage used to be taken down to a luggage room on the day of departure, and not released until the cashier issued a luggage pass confirming that the bill had been paid. Air travel has made these obsolete.
6   *Lien*   As we have seen, this is the right to retain possession of a guest's luggage until he has paid his bill.

Cash frauds

Guests may stop at front office, ostensibly to pay their bills, but in fact to practise various kinds of sleight of hand.

1   Credit card or travellers' cheque fraud. Lost or stolen cards or cheques are often presented as 'payment'. Cashiers should follow the normal security checks.
2   'Confusion cash' frauds are attempted quite frequently in some major centres. In these, the fraudster offers a variety of notes of different denominations, then appears to change his mind, offers a different combination, and ends up by so confusing the cashier that she accepts his word regarding the amount of change due and hands over more money than the fraudster started with. Set down in black and white this practice sounds unlikely, but some people are very clever at such sleight of hand.

3　Foreign currency frauds are also quite common. The fraudster may obtain some out-of-date foreign notes (countries sometimes call in their old currency and replace it with new notes as part of their financial control process, or as a result of revolutions) and pass these off on an unsuspecting cashier in a small hotel. Alternatively, they may try substituting a little-known currency with a lower value than its better known cousin (for years, the Eastern Caribbean dollar was worth half the American one, and the Icelandic krona was worth an eighth of the Swedish one). The answer is to equip cashiers with a display showing all the current foreign currency notes accepted by the hotel.

Bad debts

Bad debts are not the same as 'walk-outs'. A bad debt is a bill which the hotel has transferred to the ledger in good faith, but which simply does not get paid for one reason or another.

One possible source of bad debts is the 'guaranteed' booking. Not all of these arise as a result of credit card bookings. Sometimes companies or travel agencies handling large volumes of business may make arrangements whereby rooms will be kept beyond the normal check-in time, and that bills will be honoured even if the guest does not turn up. This type of arrangement is a fruitful source of misunderstanding. The guest involved may dispute the bill, saying 'I telephoned and cancelled the booking in plenty of time,' or 'I arrived late and was told they were full so I had to go elsewhere. . . .' Hotels are often reluctant to press the guaranteeing company for payment because they represent important sources of business.

One of the main sources of bad debts, however, is the insolvent company. The fact that an organization has paid its accounts reasonably promptly until now does not mean that it will go on doing so. One of the standard responses to a cash flow crisis is to slow down payments. Any money available will tend to go to wages and to major trade creditors, and hotels come pretty far down the list. Again, hotels are often reluctant to press companies with whom they may have been doing good business for years.

Responsibility for controlling bad debts rests on the accountant, who must keep a wary eye on the current financial situation of the hotel's major clients. However, front office staff can find themselves in the front line when they have to explain to a well-liked regular that they can't take his booking unless he pays cash.

If a company fails to pay an account, the services of a commercial debt collecting agency may be called upon. This will involve certain expenses, and the hotel may adopt a policy of writing off amounts below a certain figure.

Immorality

This is a serious problem. As we indicated in our introduction, guests who find themselves removed from the constraints of their home environments sometimes turn to call girls or rent boys for consolation. Similarly, business travellers have been known to take temporary companions along with them on their trips, and hotels sometimes find themselves acting as houses of assignation where lovers can meet in comparative secrecy.

Immorality as such is not unlawful, and even prostitution is not illegal. Nevertheless, a hotel is well advised to restrict its incidence as far as possible, for a number of reasons:

1   As far as civil law is concerned, it may affect the validity of the contract for accommodation. You should be familiar with the definition of a contract, namely, that it is an agreement which will be enforced by the law. You should be familiar, too, with the various elements which must be shown to be present, such as intention, capacity, consideration etc. One such element is legality, and certain contracts are held to be void because they are illegal. These include contracts based on sexual immorality (see *Pearce* v. *Brookes* (1866) in which a man hired a carriage to a prostitute, knowing that it was to be used for the purposes of her trade, and was not subsequently allowed to recover the hire fee). This rule might apply if you knowingly let a double room to a couple for immoral purposes. In such circumstances, you would not be able to sue the couple if they walked off without paying. Whether or not ordinary cohabitation implies immorality in these days of live-in partners is open to question, but the risk was still serious enough in the 1980s to cause many hotels to prefer not to let double rooms to unmarried couples. If a couple were to book a room and register as 'Mr and Mrs' you would normally have no reason to suppose that they were not married, and the contract would thus not be an illegal one (unless you knew one partner to be a prostitute who made a practice of masquerading as the 'wife' of a variety of partners).

2   Although prostitution itself is not illegal, English criminal law does penalize any third party who tries to profit from it. Living off immoral earnings and being concerned in the ownership or management of a brothel are both serious offences. It is possible that the management of a hotel which could be shown to have regularly let rooms to known prostitutes might be prosecuted for one or other of these offences. Such practices *have* been known: sometimes a hotel gets a reputation among local barmen and taxi drivers for being sympathetic and accommodating in this respect. That reputation is also likely to reach the ears of the local police eventually. However, prosecutions of this kind seem to be very rare, presumably because the police have a much more effective weapon to hand.

3   Under the Licensing Act, 1964, it is an offence to allow licensed premises to be the habitual resort or place of meeting of reputed prostitutes. The police may also oppose the renewal of the licence on these grounds. The importance of this provision is that the power to grant a licence is *discretionary*: in other words, the justices do not require the same high standard of proof as is needed to prove a criminal case. The effect is that the police find it easier to take action by opposing the renewal of the licence: a hotel soon finds that it loses more by not being allowed to sell liquor than it gains by tolerating prostitution.

Quite apart from these legal considerations, a hotel would be well advised to discourage prostitution for other reasons. It tends to upset other guests and, as we have seen, is associated with a higher level of theft from rooms. Prostitution thus bring the hotel into disrepute and eventually leads to a decline in occupancies.

How do you discourage prostitution? Well, as we have already pointed out, you have a duty to prevent prostitutes from using your bars as a place to meet their clients, and you have the right to prevent anyone other than a guest from entering your sleeping accommodation.

Matters become more difficult if a genuine guest claims that a prostitute is *his* guest, because the presumption is that he is entitled to entertain his own friends as if he were in his own home. However, the hotel is also entitled to charge for the use of its accommodation, and a guest who is paying the single rate for a room with two beds in it can hardly complain if he is charged extra for double occupancy, providing this can be proved.

This particular situation calls for very tactful and delicate handling. One possible ploy if you suspect that a guest has actually taken a prostitute up to a room is to call his extension, announce that you have to check the (say) hot water system, and ask (very politely) whether he would mind very much if someone came in and did so in five minutes or so. This is said to have led to some very hurried departures down the back stairs.

Other forms of illegality

There are a whole host of illegal activities which guests might indulge in within the hotel's premises. It would be impossible to detail them all but it might be helpful to have some general guidelines.

It used to be the case that you had a legal duty to report any 'felonies' (serious criminal offences), and could be prosecuted if you didn't. This no longer applies. You would still be expected to cooperate with the police in connection with really serious crimes, but you can exercise your discretion as far as 'lesser' crimes are concerned.

Awkward situations can arise in connection with illegal drugs, especially because it is not always easy to distinguish these from legitimate medication. The smuggling or consumption of hard drugs should always be regarded as serious offences, especially if they involve third parties. On the other hand, many hoteliers would hesitate before reporting a guest's private use of a soft drug, though legally they should.

A guest who can be shown to have engaged in criminal activities on your premises is in breach of his contract of accommodation and can be asked to leave. This is another of those situations which requires great tact, and should really be handled by an experienced manager. However, there is always a first time for everyone, and *you* might find yourself having to do it some day. A common approach (not that this is a common situation) is to tell the guest, politely but firmly, that you are very sorry but you require the accommodation for another guest and must request that he leaves. Most guests are quite able to perceive the real message and will pack and go without too much argument. Those who try to bluster it out can be offered the choice between departing quietly or waiting for the police.

Death

The death of a guest does not constitute a threat in the usual sense of the word. However, it does cast a pall over the remaining guests' enjoyment, and some may be so affected that they leave early, while other customers may cancel their reservations.

There is a widespread belief that hotels try to suppress any evidence of a guest's death, even to the extent of smuggling the body out in laundry basket and bribing the ambulance drivers to report that he died on his way to the hospital rather than in the hotel. This is not true.

However, there is no point in drawing attention to the fact if this can be avoided. If a body is discovered in a room, the windows should be closed, the heating turned off, and the room double locked. The management should call a doctor, who is the best person to decide whether or not there are any suspicious circumstances. In most cases, death will be found to have been due to natural causes, and the police will not have to conduct an investigation. The body will be discreetly removed via a service lift.

You may well find yourself having to deal with a deceased guest's wife or husband. It would be unbelievably inconsiderate to expect the surviving partner to stay on in the same room, and you should make every effort to move him or her somewhere else. This situation calls for great tact and discretion on the part of all staff concerned. The same applies if you have to make arrangements for the next of kin. It is not a time to press for payment of the bill, either. Some hoteliers would quietly forget this, and most others would put it to one side, to be sent to the executors at a later date.

Assignments

1 Compare the nature, extent and seriousness of the security problems you would expect to find in the Tudor and Pancontinental Hotels.

2 The 'Cranford' is a medium-sized hotel falling within the scope of the Hotel Proprietors Act, 1956 and displaying the appropriate notice. A guest wishes to deposit jewellery at front office but is advised that the safe is thought to be insecure and is currently being replaced. The manager offers to lock the jewellery in his office, but she refuses. That evening, she strikes up an acquaintanceship with another guest who steals the jewellery and disappears. The guest in question was a 'chance' arrival who had been asked for, and had paid, the first night's rack rate in advance, being subsequently given two further night's stay on credit. Advise the management of the 'Cranford'.

3 Outline the advantages and disadvantages of the different kinds of room key currently available.

4 Imagine that you are a would-be walk-out. How would you go about obtaining a night's accommodation at a prestigious local hotel without paying for it? (*Note*: we are not trying to *encourage* anyone to try this, merely to help you to anticipate the more obvious 'ploys' used by dishonest guests.)

5 How do you think security routines might develop over the next decade?

'I know we insist on you being courteous, Fosdyke, but don't you think you're taking it a little *too* far. . . ?'

Part Two

Psychological Aspects

5 Hospitality

Introduction

Up to now we have been concentrating on the procedures involved in ensuring that the guest is allocated a room, enjoys undisturbed possession until he is ready to depart, and (to quote the Hotel Proprietors Act, 1956 again) 'pays a reasonable sum for the services and facilities provided'. These procedures are important, but we must now turn our attention to what lies behind them.

In reality, complaints about booking errors or incorrect bills only account for a small proportion of guests' criticisms of hotels. If you think about it, you will realize that the majority of hotels have accommodation to spare on all but the very busiest of nights. If you have made a mistake over a booking and the guest arrives unexpectedly you can usually room him, if necessary with an apology and perhaps a reduction in price. A mistake in a bill can quickly be corrected, again with a polite apology. In most cases, prompt and courteous remedial action will disarm criticism, and can even leave a favourable impression.

So what *do* guests complain about? Well, their main criticism has to do with lack of friendliness (and sometimes the downright incivility) on the part of the staff. One British survey found that the larger hotels, particularly the chains, were 'rather cold' in their attitudes towards their customers.

Recently, one of the authors of this book overheard a guest who was staying at a small private hotel explaining why to his dinner companion. 'I'm fed up with paying £50 a night in a _____group hotel,' he said, 'Only to be made to feel that I'm interrupting the staff's tea break any time I want something.' The converse of this is that one of the things most appreciated by guests is that extra touch of personal service.

You will hear a lot about 'hospitality' and 'service'. They are vitally important. They are also elusive concepts which are very difficult to turn into a straightforward checklist of do's and don'ts for new staff. However, they must be considered, and that is what the next two chapters are about.

It may be helpful if we began by summarizing the argument in this chapter:

1   If 'hospitality' means anything at all, it must be the concept of anticipating and satisfying *all* a guest's needs. We should; therefore, start by establishing what these needs are. We will find that although they include obvious material requirements such as a reasonably comfortable bed, they also include important psychological benefits as well.
2   'Service' is closely linked with hospitality, but we have chosen to define it as the actual process of satisfying the guest's needs. We will find that the authorities stress that it is not just what is done but how it is done that is important. This links up with our recognition that hospitality involves catering for guests' psychological needs. We will also see that the customer's perception of 'service quality' depends very much on his current state of mind and his prior expectations.

3   Recognition of the importance of prior expectations brings in the question of 'roles'. We are conditioned to perform our social duties in particular ways, and we expect others to do the same. There is a 'receptionist' role, just as there is a 'guest' role, and these help to determine whether we think a person is a 'good' receptionist or a 'good' guest. We must therefore look at role theory.
4   Finally, 'service' inevitably involves staff–guest communication. Communication is an essential element of front office operations as a whole, but face-to-face communication is of particular importance. There are close links between it and the perception of 'service quality', and we shall try to bring these out.

The argument as a whole will lead us to emphasize the importance of the behavioural aspects of face-to-face communications. It therefore acts as a bridge into 'social skills', which we will go on to cover in Chapter 6.

Guest needs

Just what *are* the guest's needs? We might start by looking at the range of possible 'service transactions' between the guest and the hotel. According to Nightingale the guest:

1   Must decide where to stay and make a reservation. Clearly the way in which the reception staff deal with the initial query is going to contribute to his overall impression.
2   Must be registered and taken or directed to his room on arrival.
3   May require ancillary services or information.
4   Will almost certainly want to have a bath or shower, to shave or to put on make-up.
5   Will require a drink and a meal or at least some form of snack.
6   May wish to relax in his room, perhaps reading or watching TV.
7   May want to work in his room, and possibly even to hold a meeting there or elsewhere.
8   May also want to contact or be contacted by people outside the hotel by means of the telephone or some other means of communication.
9   May wish to meet people for purely social reasons.
10 May want to exercise in some way, by going to a sauna or gymnasium, swimming or by playing tennis or golf.
11 May want some form of group or social entertainment, such as a disco, floor show or folklore group performance.
12 Will want to keep his clothing fit to wear, which implies some kind of wardrobe space and shoe cleaning facilities.
13 Will want a good, undisturbed night's sleep.
14 May require some kind of wake-up call in the morning, and will almost certainly want some kind of breakfast and possibly a paper as well.
15 Finally, will want to settle his account and leave the hotel with as little fuss and bother as possible.

Not all guests require all the services on offer. In fact, each is likely to choose a slightly different selection. However, each service transaction chosen contributes to the guest's overall 'service experience', and clearly the extent to which his specific needs are met will affect his view of the hotel as a whole.

This analysis tends to lead to a 'facilities orientated' approach, whereby hotels are assessed largely on the basis of their physical features, such as whether or not they have bathrooms en suite, colour TVs in their rooms, discos, saunas or swimming pools. These are legitimate considerations. However, these physical facilities are only a part of the total service product, which according to Sasser, Olsen and Wyckoff (1978) is actually a 'bundle' or 'package' made up of three distinct elements:

1 Certain 'facilitating goods', such as food and drink, or temporary occupancy rights to tangible items like a bed.
2 Sensory benefits, such as the quietness of the room, the softness of the bed and the warmth of the bathwater. These have the effect of increasing the guest's comfort.
3 Psychological benefits such as the opportunity to meet acquaintances, join in conversations and make new friends as a customer in good standing.

Jones and Lockwood (1989) make much the same point. They divide the hotel 'package' into a matrix as shown in Figure 47.

		Contact	
		Social	Material
Aspects	Tangible		
	Intangible		

Figure 47

The four quadrants (or 'boxes') represent the different kinds of experience that the guest may have when he stays at the hotel. The quadrants are not intended to be rigid, mutually exclusive categories, but they do offer a useful way of thinking about the elements of the 'package' as a whole. Let us consider them in more detail.

1 The 'tangible/material' sector represents the physical aspects of the hotel's facilities. It covers the size of the room and the bed, the amount of wardrobe space available, the provision or otherwise of effective heating and/or air conditioning, the extent to which the room is insulated from external noise, and a whole host of possible facilities such as telephones, TVs, tea-makers, drink dispensers and 'external' features such as swimming

pools, saunas and the like. These relate to both the 'tangible' and the 'sensory' elements of the services package, and clearly cover a large number of the items on Nightingale's list.

2 The 'intangible/material' concept is subtler, since it covers things like style and decor and their psychological effects on the guest. One can imagine a large room equipped with every possible facility which is nevertheless painted in dull, monotonous colours and whose view is restricted to the local gasworks. A guest could be physically very comfortable in such a room, but that might not prevent him from feeling depressed, even suicidal. Even Nightingale found that business guests placed a high value on accommodation which was 'comfortable, pleasant and relaxing'. While comfort has a 'sensory' dimension, the other two requirements clearly fall within the psychological sphere.

3 The 'tangible/social' sector relates to what the staff do for the guest in a physical sense. It covers such things as the carrying of bags and the provision of room service, the frequency with which rooms are cleaned and linen changed, and general standards of hygiene maintained. As far as front office is concerned, it would cover the availability of reception services (a desk manned twenty-four hours per day, for instance) and the speed and accuracy with which bills are produced. Many of these considerations reflect the extent to which the hotel is able to satisfy the kind of guest needs itemized in Nightingale's list.

4 The 'intangible/social' sector relates to the psychological effect that contacts with the staff have on the guest. It is (sadly) not too hard to envisage a receptionist checking in a guest quickly and efficiently, but unsmilingly, and it is just as easy to imagine a porter carrying the guest's luggage up to his room in such an ungracious manner as to totally destroy any favourable impression that the physical act itself might have created.

What these analyses indicate is that guests have psychological needs which require to be satisfied just as much as the physical ones. But just what are these?

Maslow (1945) argues that human beings have a number of different needs, and that the basic ones must be satisfied before the higher level ones. This may well oversimplify the psychological reality, but it provides us with a commonsense conceptual framework which we can all recognize every time we go out for a (basic need) drink in preference to opening our (higher level need) textbook. It also helps us to understand just how psychologically complex the hotel 'product' really is, and why the same guest can appear to have different needs at different times. Let us try to follow it through.

1 Maslow's first need is for 'survival', by which he means the basic essentials of life. Travellers require (in the words of the Hotel Proprietors Act, 1956) 'food, drink, and if so required sleeping accommodation', and it is the hotel's function to provide these. At its most basic, this set of needs is met by the more primitive form of hostel. Someone caught in wild, inhospitable terrain at nightfall would be very relieved to find a rudimentary mountain refuge, especially if it contained a little firewood and a tin or two of food, and we doubt whether such a traveller would worry overmuch about the lack of clean towels or room service. Under normal circumstances, however, the basic physiological needs include something to eat and drink, somewhere to wash and change, somewhere to hang one's clothes during the night, and somewhere to sleep in reasonable comfort. In cold climates that 'somewhere' has to be warmed to a reasonable temperature: in hot climates it needs to be cooled down or at least ventilated. Standards change over time. A century ago it was possible to find examples of very cheap lodging houses offering nothing but the opportunity to sleep propped up against a rope stretched across a room, and even half a century ago it was common to put single guests together in the same room (and frequently

the same bed). En suite toilet facilities were restricted to the more expensive rooms, and married couples (and sometimes their families as well) were expected to occupy double beds. Standards are also relative. A country hotel miles from anywhere else needs to be able to provide some sort of meal for late arrivals, whereas a hotel located in a city centre and surrounded by catering establishments of all types only has to offer some kind of breakfast facilities and need not have a restaurant at all.

2   Maslow's second need is security. The hotel's job is not just to satisfy the guest's basic survival needs. It must also attempt to provide what Kotas (1975) has called 'a surrogate home'. This is difficult, because the concept of 'home' involves all kinds of subtle elements which the hotel can't supply. 'Home' is familiar territory: we generally have our own chair, our own room and our own shelf of books or records. Most hotels can't offer anything like this. The dining area is public territory where most of us feel we have to watch our manners and our general behaviour, the bedroom lacks the cosy familiarity that only comes with long use, and guests can't even enjoy undisturbed possession of it because the housekeeping staff will want daily access to clean and tidy it. 'Home' also usually means family, and here again the hotel situation suffers by comparison. Many business travellers have left their families at their real homes, and while this may seem fun for a night or two, it rapidly loses its attraction. Even families travelling together are placed in an unusual and sometimes stressful situation inasmuch as they are thrown together much more than they would be at home, without the support or refuge of their studies, workshops or gardens. It is difficult to feel secure in a strange environment, especially when one is also surrounded by strangers. The fact that many of those strangers are hotel employees who are there to assist the guest doesn't necessarily help as much as it should: hotel staff are not employed by the guest but by the hotel, and many people feel diffident about commanding their services under these circumstances. This feeling of insecurity on the part of the guest needs to be appreciated. It is, obviously, at its most intense when he enters the hotel for the first time. In addition to uncertainty as to whether the booking has been made properly, the guest is likely to have been travelling for some time and will be tired, hungry and in urgent need of a wash and change of clothes. Entering a strange environment under these circumstances is a strain, and such guests are in need of reassurance. They need to be:

(a)   *Recognized*   If *they* have to catch *your* eye, you are already off to a bad start. They also have to be recognized as individuals. 'Sir' or 'Madam' are all very well, but all good hoteliers know that it is the use of the guest's own name which really conveys this impression.

(b)   *Persuaded that you are there to help them*   'Can I help you?' says it all quickly and economically.

(c)   *Convinced that they are welcome*   A smile is one of the quickest and most effective methods of reassuring anyone.

(d)   *Assisted into their own personal 'back area' as quickly as possible*   The term 'back area' was coined by the sociologist Erving Goffman (1959) and stands for that private space which we all need from time to time: a place where we can relax, let our guards down, conduct running repairs to our make-up and generally prepare for our next foray into the public gaze.

The registration process offers a good illustration of the way that a simple procedure operates at more than one level at once. There are a number of good practical reasons why the guest should begin his stay by approaching the desk, confirming his reservation, signing the register and obtaining a key. But this process also allows the hotel to offer a whole series of reassurances. Yes, we recognize you as a guest; yes, we confirm you have a reservation; yes, we are allocating you exclusive use of Room 407; and yes, we recognize that you would like to get into that room as quickly as possible. As part of this process, the hotel hands over a visible symbol of the guest's occupancy rights in the form of a room key. Consider the traditional room key for a moment. It is normally a large, solid object, made more so by a massive tag emblazoned with the hotel's name and address in some permanent form. It is bulky and inconvenient. The traditional explanation for this is that otherwise the guest will carry it around with him and forget to deposit it with reception when he leaves the premises, as he is supposed to. But this begs the question of *why* guests behave like this. In fact, keys are potent symbols (they have a long history as central elements in important ceremonies) and you should ask yourself just what the room key might stand for as far as the hotel guest is concerned. Perhaps it is the outward symbol of exclusive occupancy rights to *his* room? If so, you would expect him to be reluctant to surrender it to anyone during his stay, which is what experience suggests is the case.

3   Maslow's third need is 'belongingness'. This recognizes the fact that man is a social animal with a strong need for companionship. Let us see how this applies to our imaginary hotel guest. Once he has checked in, washed, changed and had something to eat and drink, how does he then spend the remainder of the evening? He may of course simply read or watch the room's TV for a while, or even go to bed, but a great many come down to the bar and try to strike up a conversation with any other guests who happen to be there (or failing that, the long-suffering barperson). This used to be an attractive feature of the old-fashioned inn. Dickens and other writers have drawn vivid pictures for us of how travellers would congregate in the 'common room' to exchange news and gossip and to entertain each other with stories and songs. They would often be joined by 'mine host', who would not only make sure that they were supplied with drink but also perform any necessary introductions. This need for companionship is basic, but it can conflict with the need for privacy (i.e. the desire to retreat into a 'back area'), which will take priority under certain circumstances. Maslow helps us to understand why guests are unlikely to feel very sociable when they first arrive. It follows, therefore, that satisfying the guests' need for 'belongingness' is more likely to be a feature of longer-stay establishments, which experience suggests is broadly true. Many successful holiday packages such as holiday camps or cruises provide a whole series of opportunities for the guests to get to know each other, and the organizers employ staff to make sure that the mixing process actually does take place. A guest can also 'belong' to a hotel in the sense of being a well-liked regular, on good terms with the permanent staff. It is relatively easy to create this feeling in a small family hotel, but much more difficult in a large one with high staff turnover. One way in which chains can create some kind of 'family' link is by issuing special privilege cards to regular customers: as well as entitling such guests to various extra services and discounts, they also perform the valuable role of identifying the guest as a regular entitled to special consideration. This is perhaps not as good as a totally spontaneous welcome based on genuine recognition, but it does go some way towards meeting a need.

4   Maslow's fourth need is 'esteem'. You might say that this follows on logically from the third, because when we make new acquaintances we want them to think well of us. Unfortunately, guests are (by definition) away from their own home environments, and they sometimes take the opportunity to present their backgrounds in a more favourable light than is really justified (this is a well-known cause of embarrassment when holiday acquaintances take up your reckless invitation to visit you at home). Traditionally, many hotels cultivated an image of social exclusiveness, so that the very act of staying at them

enhanced a guest's own self esteem. Although the more extreme forms of snobbery are now much less evident, guests still expect to be treated with respect, if not outright deference. We still say 'Sir' and 'Madam', for instance, and we still offer to carry the bags of perfectly fit and healthy visitors. This exclusiveness is often reflected in high prices. To some extent this is inevitable, because high-quality, twenty-four hour service is very labour intensive. However, the link between costs and prices is only a loose one, and it is well known that a price increase unaccompanied by any change in the tangible features of the 'package' can sometimes actually improve occupancies dramatically. The usual explanation for this phenomenon is that guests are unable to discern 'quality' in advance and so use the quoted price as an indicator, arguing: 'It's very expensive so it *must* be good!' This may be true enough as far as new guests are concerned, but it hardly explains why such hotels continue to attract repeat customers. It seems more likely that the hotel is actually providing something extra in return for its high prices, over and above the obvious features of five star service. We suggest that there are really two elements:

(a) First, the fact that the guest can afford the price asked demonstrates his relatively high economic (and thus social) status, and consequently satisfies his need for 'esteem'.
(b) Second, the high prices effectively keep out persons of lower economic standing, thus underpinning the hotel's image of social exclusiveness and also satisfying the guests' need for 'esteem'.

This exclusiveness can be thought of as an important element of the total 'package', and the high prices necessary to maintain it are both its cause and its justification.

5 Maslow's final need is for 'self-actualization'. By this he means the typical human being's desire to improve himself in some way or other, physically, mentally or spiritually. You might ask what this has to do with the receptionist. In fact, it is the basis for a number of extra services that hotels offer, and it is even the reason for a lot of 'tourist' bookings. Take the guest's desire for physical improvement. This is why hotels have long found it profitable to provide swimming pools, and are increasingly finding it necessary to have saunas, gymnasiums and other such facilities. As people become more and more health conscious they are becoming increasingly aware of the need for exercise, and receptionists need to be able to advise them where and when they might obtain it (by jogging, for instance). Mental improvement is another need which can lead to all manner of unexpected enquiries. Tourists travel in order to 'see the sights', and while they may have guide books with them, a friendly word of advice is almost always welcome. Since receptionists are usually local they are well placed to provide a 'bridge' into the regional culture. They are often called upon to advise guests about when best to visit the local museums, for example, or to bring other attractions to their notice. The same is true about spiritual improvement. Leaving aside the question of whether tourism is a quasi-spiritual exercise, guests may need some guidance in respect of religious facilities. You may not know the answer to 'Where is the nearest Greek Orthodox church?', but it is the kind of question you might get, and you ought to know how to *find* the answer. In a much broader sense, 'self-actualization' means enlarging one's whole range of experiences. The longer the guest's stay, the more likely this need is to come to the fore. Satisfying it involves the inclusion of local dishes in the menu, the provision of local folk music and dancing as part of the entertainments offered, and the arrangement of guided tours to local attractions. Meeting these 'self-actualizing' needs has to be carefully balanced against the guest's 'security' needs. It has been said that tourist hotels located in exotic tropical locations provide a kind of Western sanctuary where the guests can be sure of the water, the food

and the plumbing: in other words, a 'back area' into which the guests can retreat after their expeditions into the local culture. Of course, these 'self-actualizing' needs are not always respectable. We cannot ignore the fact that guests away from their homes and families are not subject to the usual constraints. It is hardly surprising, then, that they occasionally ask hotel staff to introduce them to call-girls or to provide other dubious services. We have already considered the problems this can create when we looked at Security.

Maslow maintains that these needs form a hierarchy, with each coming to the fore in turn as soon as its predecessor is satisfied. Our hypothetical traveller lost in the wilds at nightfall would be pleased to come across even the most villainous of inns. Once lodged, however, he would start to worry about the safety of his belongings. Reassured on that score, he might well begin to join in the general conversation, and, having done so, would try to earn the respect and perhaps liking of his companions. At length, having spent an unexpectedly pleasant evening, he might take a last turn outside in order to admire the grandeur of the scenery and reflect a little on the infinite. . . .

Of course, Maslow's needs don't usually pop up to be satisfied one after another in this neat and tidy fashion. They are seldom so clearly identifiable or arranged in such strict sequence, but rather merge into each other so that it is sometimes difficult to say just which one is uppermost at any one time. When a receptionist says 'Hello, Mr Jenkinson, nice to see you again. How have you been? We've put you into Room 402 as usual,' she may well be satisfying several of Mr Jenkinson's needs at once: reassuring him that he is expected (security), initiating a conversation (belongingness), and making it clear that he is welcome (esteem). Satisfying three out of five human needs in one short exchange isn't bad: no wonder this kind of approach wins repeat business!

Service

Service involves the satisfaction of the customer's needs. It is generally accepted that this includes a 'personal' element which distinguishes it from merely producing the appropriate kind of goods.

Services are generally agreed to differ from material goods in that they are:

1 *Much less tangible*   As we have seen, the service 'package' is largely made up of sensory and psychological experiences rather than things the guest can take home and add to his permanent possessions.
2 *Much more perishable*   Goods can be stockpiled, but services can't. As virtually every commentator on the hotel industry points out, an unoccupied room can never be resold on that particular night.
3 *Simultaneous*   The presence of the customer is usually an essential element. This is obviously true in the case of the hotel guest, without whose physical presence the whole concept of a hotel experience becomes meaningless. It is quite different from a manufacturing industry, where the factory makes the product long before the customer buys it.
4 *Heterogeneous*   The product is hard to standardize. Different customers have different needs, and they are likely to be dealt with differently by different staff members. It is thus

very difficult to establish output standards for a service firm, and even more difficult to ensure that they are always met.

All this means that the 'service product' depends very much on the way the staff behave while they are providing the service elements which make up the total package. This is not true of manufacturing industries. One can admire a finished artefact without worrying about whether there might have been a bitter strike during the manufacturing process, but a comparable event would probably destroy a customer's weekend at a hotel.

How can we measure service quality? There are certain criteria which appear to be common to all service 'packages', though to varying degrees. According to Berry, Zeithaml and Parasuraman (1985) they are as follows:

1   *Reliability*   This means consistency and dependability. It covers all the processes involved in getting the bookings right, allocating only clean and tidy rooms, having the bill ready when the guest wants to check out, and making sure that it is correct.
2   *Responsiveness*   This means that it should be available as and when the guest wants it, and not when it happens to suit the staff. It thus covers the time dimension. In front office terms it means promptness in answering the telephone and not keeping the guest waiting at the desk while you finish your tea, your conversation with a colleague or whatever.
3   *Competence*   This is closely linked with reliability, but puts the emphasis on the front office staff, who must have the necessary skills and knowledge (about the rooms, the rates and the procedures) in order to do the job to the customer's satisfaction.
4   *Accessibility*   This is closely linked with responsiveness, but covers management's responsibility to make it easy for the customers to contact the staff, by ensuring that the desk is conveniently situated, for example, or that customer waiting time is reduced through sensible staff scheduling.
5   *Courteousness*   This is very much a staff responsibility. It means being polite and respectful, even when the guest is overbearing, inconsiderate or even downright offensive. It can conflict with other requirements, such as responsiveness, for it can mean being willing to explain things clearly and patiently even if there is a queue waiting. It can also mean being friendly, though it is sometimes difficult to draw the line between being coldly polite on the one hand, and too familiar on the other.
6   *Communication*   This covers the establishment's obligation to keep the guests informed. It means explaining the nature of the facilities (e.g. how to control the air conditioning) and how much they will cost, especially the reasons for any unexpected charges. It also implies two-way communication: in other words, not just telling the guests but listening to them as well.
7   *Credibility*   This really means being seen to be customer-orientated and covers the whole issue of whether the establishment is putting itself or the customer first. 'Service' means the latter. Any suspicion on the part of the guest that it is the other way round (for example, as a result of becoming the target for hard selling techniques) is likely to be counterproductive.
8   *Safety*   This means the avoidance of any tangible risk to the customer. It covers not only the more obvious physical and financial threats, but also any risk to the guest's privacy. Confidentiality is thus very much a staff responsibility. It may be very tempting to gossip about what went on in a VIP's suite the night before, but a hotel which permits this is *not* providing good service.
9   *Understanding*   This means that staff should make every effort to appreciate the

individual guest's needs. As we have seen, these may differ from other people's, and may even change from hour to hour, but appreciating them is a key feature of the service concept. Guests don't like to be treated as if they were all identical, and you need to ring the changes. It is this need to combine individuality of treatment with the maintenance of a consistent overall standard which provides much of the challenge in hospitality work.

10   *Consistency in terms of its tangible aspects*   The hotel must live up to its own claims. It must maintain its physical facilities, the equipment and even its staff's own appearance in an appropriately clean and tidy state. These are very important because customers often base their expectations of the establishment on such easily-read visual 'cues'. You can be as prompt, courteous and efficient as you like, but if the lobby is shabby and you yourself are unkempt and untidy, then the odds are that the customer will interpret every nuance of the service transaction in an unfavourable light.

Berry, Zeithaml and Parasuraman emphasize the enormously important role played by the interpersonal behaviour of the service provider. They say: 'The manner in which the service is performed can be a crucial component of the service from the consumer's point of view,' and they quote 'politeness, willingness to help (and) trustworthiness' as examples. However, if you look at the service quality determinants listed previously you will see that most of them depend very much on how the staff behave in the face-to-face encounters.

Most writers agree that the customer's perception of service quality is the result of a comparison between his prior expectations and his actual experience. Since individual expectations vary, this implies that there is no absolute standard of 'good' service, but rather one set by what the customer expects at the time of his visit. This will vary according to:

1   The class of establishment. A visitor checking into a remote fishing inn for a leisurely weekend will not expect the same standard of facilities as in a city centre business hotel. He would certainly expect to find a comparable degree of competence and courtesy, but it would be of a different nature. He wouldn't expect the desk to be answered with quite the same promptness, and he would probably look for a slower, more familiar and easy-going kind of courtesy in keeping with the nature of his weekend.

2   The personality, mood and circumstances of the individual customer. Some people need a high level of attention, while others don't. Some may want to be flattered and fawned over, while others may not want attention at all, preferring to slip in quietly with the minimum of fuss and bother. Basic personalities may also be affected by specific circumstances. A customer who has just had a bad day will react differently in a service situation from one who has just received a promotion. The first may well lose his temper over a minute's delay, the second is likely to smile tolerantly.

Roles

One of the things which determines a guest's level of satisfaction is his idea of how a receptionist *ought* to behave. This brings up the question of 'roles'.

A role can be defined as the pattern of behaviour expected of a person in a particular position. Roles are important in social life, because they offer us models for our own behaviour in given situations, and allow us to anticipate other people's behaviour. We expect ticket collectors to collect tickets, for instance, just as we expect grandparents to be indulgent and parents to be relatively stricter. In so doing, they are consciously or unconsciously imitating behaviour patterns which have been laid down by others (whom we call 'role models').

Roles do not exist in isolation. Although each may have a 'solo' element performed in isolation (like a receptionist checking an arrivals list before any guests appear, for instance) they only acquire real meaning in relation to other people. Indeed, as Goffman has pointed out, slipping through the door leading to the staff quarters offers you the opportunity to step 'out of role' for a minute or two. This is often necessary, especially if you have been dealing with a particularly difficult customer.

Because roles involve an 'audience' as well as a 'player', it is important that both parties should be in broad agreement as to what the roles involve. This is called 'role consensus'. In theatrical performances roles are carefully scripted and painstakingly directed, so that any unplanned variations (an actor 'drying up' for instance, or ad libbing wildly) have a disastrous effect. Real life roles offer more room for extemporization, but you still can't step too far out of character without causing severe problems. A receptionist who is either too distant or too familiar is doing just that, and the guest is liable to be taken aback.

Although we are chiefly concerned with the receptionist's role, you should not forget that customers are also playing a role of their own, that of the 'hotel guest'. Few people spend a lot of their time staying in hotels (though there are always exceptions, of course), so this particular role is not as familiar to them as some others. Even if they *do* stay at hotels frequently, they may not be familiar with yours: sometimes their previous experiences may lead them to expect something quite different from what you actually provide. They may not be quite sure whose chair 'belongs' to whom in a residential hotel, for instance, or which channel is preferred on a communal TV. The relationship with the hotel staff is one of particular difficulty, since very few people these days have any experience of dealing with household servants, and find it correspondingly awkward to strike the right note with staff who are there to provide comparable services. They may thus be slightly ill at ease, and it is part of the receptionist's job to 'lead' the customer if necessary.

Roles which involve a lot of customer contact are called 'boundary roles', and it is generally agreed that they involve particular stresses. The problem comes not so much from the need to satisfy conflicting demands (we all face this in one form or another, as members of different family, social and working groups) but in having to deal with a number of simultaneous demands while in a particularly exposed position. Just imagine the dilemma faced by a receptionist trying to cope single-handed with a group of boisterous sportsmen trying to check in, a shy foreigner unfamiliar with the requirements of the registration form, and a rather domineering lady who has come down to complain about the room she has been allocated.

The receptionist's role is determined first of all by the management, which lays down the basic 'script'. It is also influenced by the customers, who provide a kind of interactive audience, and who will soon tell you if they don't like the way you are playing it. It is quite possible that management's and customers' views might diverge: many managers grew up in the industry and still model their behaviour on the pattern they learned in their youth, possibly with an entirely different set of customers. Roles are also profoundly influenced by colleagues, because they are generally learned on the job, usually by imitating an older and more experienced receptionist. Normally this 'role model' will be reasonably successful, but there is always the possibility that the learner will pick up bad habits because older staff sometimes become embittered and even downright hostile.

Most roles can be split down into a number of subroles. At varying times during the meal experience, a waiter may be expected to play a number of different parts, such as 'host', 'expert' and 'friend', and the same is true of a receptionist. What is particularly relevant from our standpoint is that receptionists should be seen as *helpful*. The key attributes you need to display are:

1 *A willingness to maintain communication*   In other words, never bring a conversation with a customer to an abrupt end if that customer wants to go on talking. If you have to turn away to deal with someone else, apologize politely and indicate that you'll be back as quickly as you can. 'Please excuse me while I just deal with this gentlemen . . .' will cover the situation (if the process takes a minute or two, you may find that your original customer has given up and gone off somewhere else). There *are* boring, long-winded guests, but it is part of your job not to reveal that you see them as such.
2 *Assigning importance to the customer's problems*   These may not always seem very important to *you*, but that isn't the point. If they are important to the guest, they *are* your business. If you can't solve them, the least you can do is to explain why and express your regret at being unable to help.
3 *Sensitivity to tension and discomfort*   You should be alert for any signs that a customer is nervous, ill at ease or genuinely uncomfortable. 'I won't keep you a moment . . .' is the least you can say to someone who has been travelling for eighteen hours and has spent the last two of them trying to fight his way through and from the airport.
4 *Being helpful with decision-making difficulties*   Never forget that no matter how familiar it is to you, the hotel is likely to be a strange and unknown environment to many of your customers. Where to go, what to see and what to do are often questions which perplex them, and suggestions are usually welcome.

This discussion does no more than scratch the surface of role theory as it applies to the receptionist's job, but it does offer a 'dramaturgical' view of what it involves and how you best prepare for it. Like an actress in a play, the would-be receptionist needs to 'learn her lines' in order to satisfy her customers' expectations. These 'lines' do not form a rigid, unchanging script because customers do vary in their expectations, but there is enough commonality in them for us to be able to detect a specific reception 'role'.

Communication

We have referred to communication a number of times, and we ought to make it clear what we mean by the term. In its broadest sense, it is the exchange of information, news, views and attitudes. The last item is one of the most important, and provides the main link with the theme of this chapter.

Nevertheless, most of our first four chapters have really been about communication, because what we have been describing are a series of procedural steps whereby information about a booking is transmitted, stored and acted upon. To begin with, the guest has to communicate his wish to stay at the hotel to front office, and front office has to communicate the availability or otherwise of rooms to the guest. Then front office has to advise the hotel's other departments of the guest's expected arrival so that they can prepare for him, and this, too, involves communication. When the guest arrives, he has to give (i.e. communicate) certain essential items of information to the receptionist as part of the registration process, and these may have to be shown (i.e. communicated) to the police. During the guest's stay he will incur various charges, and these must be communicated to front office so that they can be put on his bill. In due course this will be presented (i.e. communicated) to the guest, who may in turn ask for it to be sent (i.e. communicated) to his employers. Finally, front office must report (i.e. communicate) the results of the day's business to management.

Communication does not end there. As we shall see later on, many of front office's activities involve communication with other hotels (for example, over guests who have to be found alternative accommodation elsewhere), or with various agencies, from tour operators through to Tourist Information Centres, either because they have contacted it or because it contacts them directly in what is known as a 'direct selling' approach.

The process as a whole might be shown diagrammatically as shown below:

$$\text{Guest's firm} \rightarrow \text{Guest} \rightarrow \text{Front office} \rightarrow \begin{array}{c}\text{Other hotel}\\\text{departments}\\\text{and}\\\text{management}\end{array} \rightarrow \begin{array}{c}\text{Other}\\\text{hotels}\\\text{and}\\\text{agencies}\end{array}$$

All this means that communication is at the very heart of front office's operations. If you think about it, almost all the pieces of equipment you are likely to use in your work are in fact devices for storing, processing or communicating information. You will answer the telephone, make notes, enter data into a computer, process vouchers, make out bills and send or file letters. You will either reply to guests' questions directly or look up the answers in appropriate reference books. Just about the only items you will handle that cannot be classed as data storage records of one kind or another will be room keys and guests' valuables, and even here you will have to issue and check receipts.

There are said to be well over a hundred methods of communication within organizations. As far as hotels are concerned, they include the telephone, letters, fax, teletype, computerized displays and printouts, reports, memos, forms of one kind or another, advertisements, brochures, noticeboards and other static displays, public address systems, automated alarm systems and simple face-to-face conversations.

Most writers distinguish between 'one-way' methods, which do not anticipate a reply, and 'two-way' methods, which permit what is known as 'feedback', in other words, the exchange of information and views. Another common distinction is between 'formal' methods (usually this means those approved by management) and 'informal' (unofficial or unplanned) ones. This last distinction is important if you are analysing how a department actually works (gossip is very much part of the 'informal' system) but it is not very helpful as far as the guest–receptionist relationship is concerned, because it ought to be part of the latter's job to add little extra personal touches to the formal check-in or check-out process anyway.

No one method of communication is an ideal combination of:

1 Speed
2 Cheapness
3 Permanency
4 'Two way'-ness
5 'Quality' (i.e. the ability to convey subtle shades of meaning, feelings, attitudes etc.)

The telephone, for instance, is quick, 'two way' and reasonably inexpensive, but each caller has to make his or her own record of the conversation, and misunderstandings are not uncommon. Letters are cheap and permanent, but they are not particularly quick, and they do not encourage 'two-way' communication. Forms arrange information systematically, but they can often seem rather cold and unfriendly. One of your tasks is to choose the most appropriate method of communication for the task in hand. The fact that we often do this without conscious thought does not lessen the importance of the decision.

The communication process is actually a rather complicated one. There are at least three stages, each of which presents its own problems.

1   The person who should initiate the process must perceive the need to actually transmit the information. This does not always happen, as frequent cries of 'Oh, I forgot to tell you!' demonstrate. Hotels often introduce simple message, amendment or report forms in order to overcome this problem. Even when the need is recognized, actually arranging the material in a form suitable for transmission can be difficult. Most of us have experienced difficulties in composing important letters at one time or another, and trying to find the right form of words to console a guest who has suffered a serious loss is another example. Statistical information presents difficulties of its own for many employees: working out percentages is not everyone's strong point!
2   The information must then be transmitted. This often creates further problems, because most types of transmission equipment have their own limitations. Getting through on the telephone can be difficult (and getting past an important prospective client's secretary can be even harder). Telephone lines can be bad, or handwriting illegible. Post can be delayed, or computer links break down. There are often difficulties at your own end, too. Noise can be a problem, and guests, colleagues and managers can provide distractions. The pile up of work on your desk can create a 'log jam'.
3   Even when the message does reach the recipient, it may not be fully understood because perceptions can vary from one individual to another. This can apply to the basic information content of the message because of different interpretations. One common example is the guest who calls a hotel and asks for a room 'from the 15th to the 16th, please'. What the guest probably means is that he will be arriving on the evening of the 15th and leaving on the morning of the 16th: in other words, a one night stay. However, the receptionist filling in a manual chart or a computer reservation screen may interpret this as a *two*-night stay, since the guest has mentioned two dates (i.e. column headings on the chart). This is why many hotels ask for the stay in nights rather than a departure date. More common, and probably more serious, is the possibility that the attitudes accompanying the communication may be misinterpreted. Well-meant advice can sound patronizing. One person may see a smile as conciliatory, another may interpret that same smile as smug or superior. A lot depends upon our mood at the time: if we are tired and irritable (and guests who have travelled a long distance often are) then we are particularly liable to this kind of misinterpretation.

In theory, face-to-face conversation ought to be one of the most effective means of communication, because it is immediate and allows the maximum amount of information to 'flow' between the participants. You can hear the other person's words clearly, and you can also hear his tone of voice (without the distortion you sometimes get with the telephone) and see all his accompanying facial expressions, bodily postures and tiny, give-away gestures. This is important, because you ought to be trying to gauge your guest's state of mind. Is he hungry and impatient, or well-fed and content? Is he really seriously upset about the fact that his bedside lamp doesn't work, or just making trouble for the sake of it? You may even have to make up your mind as to whether a prospective customer is actually telling the truth about that misplaced letter of confirmation.

Because attitudes and feelings are easily communicated through what is called 'non-verbal communication' (expressions, tones of voice, posture etc.), face-to-face communication is potentially dangerous. A bored and dissatisfied receptionist may say 'Can I help you?' in such a way that the guest obtains a clear message that she doesn't really want to do anything of the sort. Studies have shown that these non-verbal clues have about five times the effect of the verbal ones. In other words, the bored receptionist is likely to give an overall impression of incivility no matter how polite her actual words might seem to be. It is not so much *what* is said, but *how* it is said that counts.

How does this link up with service quality? Well, any service process is similar to that of communication in that it affects at least two people, and is a combination of the physical and the 'cerebral' or psychological. Dore (1988) offers a model which may be helpful in understanding this process, and we have included a somewhat simplified version of it as Figure 48.

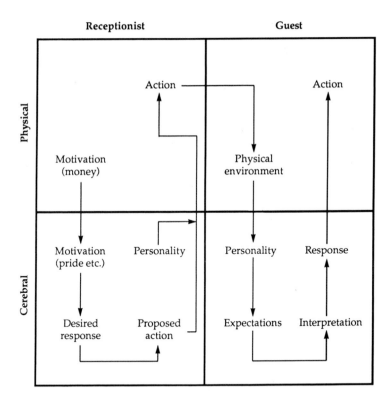

Figure 48

Let us follow this through. A receptionist greeting a newly-arrived guest is motivated by material considerations (she is paid to do so) and also by psychological ones (pride in her job and, hopefully, a liking for people in general). She wants to elicit a particular response from the guest (a feeling of satisfaction because she has made him feel genuinely welcome). In order to achieve this, she will decide upon an appropriate course of action (offering a smile and some form of greeting), and will then put this decision into effect. The actions themselves are straightforward physical ones which anyone can do, but they will be given an individual character by the receptionist's personality and physical characteristics (her accent and mannerisms, for instance).

The guest's interpretation of these actions will depend upon how they measure up to his expectations. As we have seen, these will be affected by the physical environment (since this provides a set of visual and other 'ones' upon which guests often decide what to expect from an establishment), and also by his own personality, mood and circumstances (an uncertain, defensive guest who isn't quite sure whether he really belongs in that class of establishment might feel that the smiling receptionist was being superior or even laughing at him, while a socially superior guest might feel that the same smile indicated that she was being too familiar).

The guest's interpretation of the receptionist's actions is thus a mental ('cerebral') process, and so is his response. Hopefully this will be what the receptionist intended (i.e. pleasure and satisfaction), but it may be quite the opposite (confusion, disappointment or possibly even anger). It will be expressed in some kind of physical action (a verbal protest, for instance, or a facial expression). Of course, he may try to conceal his reaction, but there is still likely to be a tangible effect, (such as a reduced tip, a failure to return or even a letter of complaint).

Dore's model is clearly akin to that needed to explain the communication process, and it makes much the same point, namely, that quality is very much a question of how certain actions are perceived by the recipient. An action (a smile, for instance, or a 'formula' greeting) is neither good nor bad in itself. It all depends upon the expectations of the person to whom the action has been addressed.

The fact that 'service' depends so much upon inter-personal contact means that staff behaviour plays a particularly important part in determining service quality. Role theory tells us much the same thing because it implies that we consciously or unconsciously act or play a particular kind of role. This 'dramaturgical' approach leads on naturally to a consideration of what are called 'social skills'. The question is: how can we actually 'project' attitudes such as sympathy, helpfulness and sensitivity? We will consider this in our Chapter 6.

Assignments

1 How far do you think guest expectations in terms of physical facilities might differ between the Tudor and Pancontinental Hotels?
2 To what extent would their expectations differ as far as the intangible aspects of 'hospitality' are concerned?
3 How can a large and busy chain hotel with a high turnover of both guests and receptionists provide 'personalized' service?
4 To what extent do you think technology can be substituted for personal service?
5 Describe the various methods by which front office might communicate with guests before, during and after their stay, indicating the advantages and disadvantages and suggesting the circumstances in which each might be used.

References

Berry, I., Zeithaml, V. and Parasuraman, A. (1985), 'A Conceptual Model of Service Quality and Its Implications for Further Research', *Journal of Marketing*, vol. 49.

Dore, C. D. (1988), 'The Interpretation of Service: An Anthropological View', *Hospitality Education and Research Journal*, vol. 12, no. 1.

Goffman, E. (1959), *The Presentation of Self in Everyday Life*, New York: Anchor Books.

Jones, P. and Lockwood, A. (1989), *The Management of Hotel Operations*, Cassell.

Kotas, R. (1975), *Market-orientation in the Hotel and Catering Industry*, Surrey University Press.

Maslow A. H. (1945), *Motivation and Personality*, New York: Harper.

Nightingale, M., 'Quality Management: Everyone's Talking About It', Paper delivered to World Hospitality Congress II.

Sasser, W. F. Olsen, M. D. and Wykoff, D. D. (1978), *The Management of Service Operations*, Boston Mass: Allyn & Bacon Inc.

6 Social skills

Introduction

Most experienced hoteliers agree that 'social skills' are vitally important to the provision of 'Service', and that they are an essential qualification for front office work. But just what are these social skills, and how can you develop them?

Being 'skilled' means having the capacity to achieve particular objectives efficiently. We all know what we mean by 'typing skills', for instance (the ability to produce acceptable quality text without taking all day over it or spoiling a dozen sheets of paper in the process), or 'cooking skills' (the ability to produce food that is both edible and appetizing). It isn't always easy to analyse just what is involved when someone exercises a skill, but the difference between a skilled and an unskilled performer is usually obvious when you compare their results.

Social skills come into play when we start dealing with other people instead of typewriter keyboards or kitchen ingredients. We still have objectives which we want to achieve (we would like the other person to do something for us, for example), but we have to employ words, expressions and gestures in order to achieve them. Social skills, in short, involve combining these elements in such a way as to modify other people's attitudes.

Most of us learn how to do this reasonably competently through the normal process of growing up and interacting with other people, but there is almost always room for improvement. Learning how to use social skills really well takes lots of practice, but the essential starting point is being able to interpret the basic elements of behaviour: in particular, those small but significant clues to people's states of mind that go under the general term 'body language'.

These states of mind can vary. You will be familiar enough with the pleasant, easy-going customer, as well as the difficult one who seems to be impossible to please no matter what you do. Understanding how and why people differ like this is a matter for the trained psychologist, but we need to have some means of recognizing what mood a customer is in, and a set of techniques for modifying this if necessary. An approach known as transactional analysis has been used quite widely for training staff in these areas, and it is worth knowing something about it.

Like any other kind of skills, social skills can only be developed through practice. Since they involve social interaction, this practice must take the form of unscripted face-to-face conversations, or 'role playing exercises'. We have provided a set of situations which require you, as receptionist, to devise appropriate responses. The important thing to remember is that it is not so much a question of what kind of solution you come up with as *how* you go about communicating it that counts.

Figure 49

Behaviour

We have used the term 'behaviour'. We must now examine this in greater detail. Let us start with a simple illustration.

Example 1

Imagine you are a guest entering a hotel for the first time. You booked your room some weeks ago and have received the normal letter of confirmation. You approach the reception desk.

The receptionist keeps her head down (Figure 49). She appears to be checking some figures. You wait for a minute or two, then cough to attract her attention. Without looking up, she says 'Just hold on a moment, can't you?' and continues with her calculations. You have plenty of time to study her closely. You see that her hair is dull and she has dandruff. Her nails are chipped, and the collar of her uniform blouse is frayed and a little dirty.

Eventually she says 'Yeah?' You tell her your name and show her your letter of confirmation. She adds a pencil tick to a list in front of her and then puts a registration form in front of you. 'Fill this in' she says, and then leans forward, arms crossed, to watch while you do it. When you have finished, she takes the form and slaps a key onto the desk. 'Room 407' she says, and goes back to her checking.

Now, what kind of impression have you formed of this hotel?'

Well, we suspect that it was a pretty poor one. It doesn't matter that you have only been in it for a couple of minutes, or that it seems to have handled your original booking efficiently enough. The receptionist's behaviour has probably been enough to put you off, and it will require an exceptionally high standard of subsequent service to make up for this initial impression.

Note that term 'behaviour'. One of the key ideas in social skills is the distinction between 'attitudes' and 'behaviour'. If you were asked to describe the receptionist's *attitude*, you would probably use terms like 'rude', 'surly', 'inhospitable', 'unwelcoming' or 'couldn't care less', and you would be right. But what gave you this impression?

The answer is the lack of attention she gave to dressing and grooming herself, the way she kept you waiting while she went on with her own routine work, her unwillingness to raise her head to look at you, and her failure to add simple phrases such 'Good day', 'Can I help you', 'Sir', 'Madam' or to use your name (which she could have seen on the letter you gave her). This is what we mean by 'behaviour', and it covers what people do, what they say, and how they present themselves.

'Behaviour' is all that we have to go on when we are meeting other people for the first time, especially when we don't know anything about them in advance. This is the usual situation when a receptionist is greeting a new guest, so it is worth looking at behaviour in more detail. It is made up of the following elements:

1   Self-presentation

This covers dress and grooming, which tell us a lot about other people even before they open their mouths. You should be able to 'read' these subtle and constantly changing statements, and you must remember that other people are equally skilled at this process and are busy 'reading' yours.

Many hotels require their staff to wear some kind of uniform because this acts as a signal, telling the guests that you are there to help them. Conventional business dress can convey much the same message, especially when you are to be seen in a position reserved for employees, such as standing behind the desk.

Notice that term 'conventional business dress'. We have no intention of trying to lay down what this consists of, because fashions and ideas about clothes are constantly changing, but there is usually a broad measure of agreement about what it comprises at any particular period (you probably conformed to it when you bought the traditional interview suit). The point is that whatever the guests' reasons for being there might be, *you* are there as an employee, and you need to 'signal' this.

Not only that: you ought to look as if you take your job seriously and are proud of your role. If you don't, the guest is likely to get a poor impression of both you and your employer. The receptionist in our example was wearing a uniform blouse, but its state suggests that she didn't think very highly of the job it stood for. Nor did she care very much about the kind of impression she was likely to make on the customers: either it didn't occur to her that they might think 'A dirty, untidy receptionist probably means dirty, untidy rooms, restaurant and kitchen', or she didn't care. Is this the kind of impression she should have been trying to give?

2   Position

Where we stand is important, not only in relation to equipment such as the desk, but also in relation to the people we are dealing with. We all have our own area of 'personal space', and any invasion of it by a stranger makes us feel uncomfortable. This personal space varies with status (note how we often talk about 'keeping our distance'), and also from culture to culture.

This concept of position can be taken further. Whenever people find themselves sitting or standing directly opposite each other with a desk or table in between, they unconsciously divide the barrier into two equal 'territories'. When our receptionist slapped the registration form in front of you and then leant forward to watch you filling it out, she was, in fact, invading your personal space. This kind of invasion makes people feel uncomfortable, even if they don't know why, and it should be avoided.

3   Posture

This covers how we stand or sit in relation to other people. Facing somebody usually indicates interest, and leaning forward shows even greater interest (unless it involves an invasion of personal space, of course).

More subtly, we can use our limbs to 'point' our bodies in the direction of the person we are interested in (study couples sitting side by side in pubs to see this mechanism in action) or we can use them as 'barriers' to shut out people we feel nervous or apprehensive about.

Our receptionist began with her body half turned away and her arm up forming a shield. When she leant forward to watch you filling in the form she was showing some interest, certainly, but even then she kept her arms folded defensively, which conveyed the impression that she wasn't very anxious to help you.

4   Gesture

This is closely linked with posture, and covers the way we send signals by moving parts of our bodies, mainly our hands, arms and shoulders. A shrug can be very irritating because it suggests that the shrugger is unconsciously trying to 'shake off' your problem. Hands are particularly important. The open palm is not only an age old sign of friendship ('Look, no weapons') but also an indication of honesty. Conversely, a lot of hand-to-face gestures like touching one's mouth or nose can indicate a degree of deceit, or at least some kind of negative feeling such as doubt, apprehension or uncertainty.

Propping one's head on a hand (as our receptionist was doing when you arrived) often indicates boredom. Is this the impression she should have been conveying?

5   Expression

The range of possible expressions is immense, but we can generally recognize friendliness when we see it. The mouth curves upwards in a smile and the eyes crinkle a little at the corners. It is unsettling to be met by a stare coupled with a blank, expressionless face, and even worse to be greeted by a sullen expression (lowered brows, a closed, downturned mouth and slightly pouting lips).

Try running through our receptionist's routine again, and then ask yourself what sort of expression you put on when you were doing so. The odds are that you automatically put on a frown, or at least found yourself deliberately adopting a blank, uncaring look.

6   Eye contact

This is of enormous importance. Looking at someone usually conveys not only interest, but also liking, and the longer and more frequently you look, the more strongly you are likely to convey these impressions (though a long, unblinking stare coupled with a grim expression can convey aggression). A dishonest person will generally avoid meeting your gaze (but then so will someone who is timid and nervous, which just shows how difficult it may be to interpret behaviour at times).

The direction in which you look is also important. The so-called 'business gaze' concentrates on the eyes and forehead in order to maintain a serious, rational atmosphere. The 'social gaze' moves between the other person's eyes and mouth, indicating a greater interest in reactions such as laughter. A receptionist needs to know which of these types of gaze to choose in respect of any particular guest, and also how to avoid the so-called 'intimate gaze', which moves between the other person's eyes and body, and signals rather more than mere social interest!

Our receptionist avoided any form of eye contact at all during the first stages of the encounter, and so conveyed a strong impression of lack of interest. Even when she did lean forward, she kept her eyes focused on the registration form, and as soon as you had finished she turned her head away, dismissing you completely.

7   Speech

Obviously, what you say is of enormous importance. Using phrases such as 'Good evening', 'Can I help you?' and 'I hope you enjoy your stay' is the clearest way of expressing your interest in your guest's welfare. Perhaps most important of all is to use the guest's name. 'Sir' or 'Madam' are all very well in their way (at least they indicate respect), but using the guest's name shows that you recognize him or her as an individual and not just an anonymous member of a group you are employed to cater for.

Obviously a good memory is a help here (being genuinely interested in the guests is even better), but there are various ways in which you can help yourself to use guest's names more. Some form of guest history record is a valuable aid, for instance, and you can always take a quick glance at the guest's registration card. 'Thank you, Mr Jones. Your room is number 305 . . .' works wonders.

Our receptionist missed two chances. You showed her your letter of confirmation, remember, but she failed to use your name, even though she must have noted it in order to check you off on her arrivals list. Then she watched you fill in the registration card, but she still didn't bother to use your name when she was handing you your key. As far as she was concerned, you were clearly just an anonymous nuisance.

8   Non-verbal speech elements

It's not just *what* you say, it's *how* you say it. You can say 'Good evening, sir' loudly or quietly, quickly or slowly, flatly or brightly. You can bring it all out together, or you can insert a pause ('Good evening . . . sir') which tends to suggest that the 'sir' was an afterthought you are not sure the guest deserves. You can lift your tone a little at the end and so turn the phrase into a question ('Good evening, sir?'), or you can lower it, as you might if you knew your guest had been waiting a minute or two and you wanted to deter any possible arguments by combining your civility with firmness.

Accent used to matter, but things have changed, and we don't think that this is true any more as long as you can be understood clearly. What really matters is your *tone*. Is it 'bright' and 'friendly', or is it 'dull' and 'sullen'? And does it sound just as bright at the end of a long and tiring shift as it did at the beginning?

How do these behavioural elements combine to form social skills? Well, studies indicate that successful practitioners use:

1   Positions and postures indicating agreement, such as leaning forward and facing their companion.
2   Gestures which indicate agreement, such as nods.
3   Frequent smiles.

4 Lots of eye contact.
5 Phrases which demonstrate an interest in the other person, concentrate on common interests, and adopt the other person's terminology and conventions.
6 Overall, a smooth, easy pattern of interaction, with few pauses or interruptions.

Social skills have an important part to play in front office work. As we saw in the previous chapter, 'service' is about meeting the guest's psychological needs and making him feel welcome, and social skills are an essential part of this process. A receptionist might use them to calm down an irritable guest, for instance, or to make a nervous one feel welcome. Social skills can be used for selling purposes, too, but we will look at this in a later chapter. For now, we will consider how they can be employed to smooth out the ordinary, everyday contacts between the guest and front office.

Let us consider another situation by way of illustration.

Example 2

It is 5.30 on Thursday evening and you are alone on the desk. You have three kinds of room, singles, twins and luxury suites. Your bookings chart indicates that your occupancy level tonight is around the seasonal norm of 60 per cent. Your arrivals list is arranged in alphabetical order and includes the following:

Langley J. Mr	303
Morris P. Mr/s	214
Naylor T. Dr	115

The door opens and you look up to see the man shown in Figure 50.

Figure 50

He strides confidently towards the desk. You smile and say 'Good evening, sir. Can I help you?', and he replies 'Yes, my name is Martin. I have a reservation for tonight.'

You check your arrivals list, but you find no such name. At this point you remember (with a sinking feeling) that your colleague Tracey (who handles a lot of advance bookings) has had personal problems and has been making a series of errors lately. You ask whether Mr Martin has a letter of confirmation. 'No, I'm sorry,' he replies, 'My secretary only made the booking a couple of days ago, and it hadn't arrived by the time I left.' What do you do now?

So what *did* you do? Well, you probably said something like this: 'I'm very sorry, Mr Martin, but there seems to have been a bit of a mix-up and I can't find your booking. There's no problem, though. What kind of room did you want, and for how long?'

This isn't bad, but it tells the guest two things which present your hotel in an unfavourable light. First, that you have mislaid his booking, which suggests a degree of inefficiency (never mind how true this may be). Second, that you are nowhere near full. He may begin to wonder why, and start to look for reasons (in which case he'll probably find a few, since no establishment is perfect). He may also begin to wonder what might have happened if you *had* been full, since you don't seem to be able to keep track of your reservations even when you're not!

How could you have avoided giving him these ideas?

Well, look at Figure 50 again and try to guess the answers to the following questions:

1   What kind of room does Mr Martin want? (We think you'll conclude that he wants a single. He seems to be alone, not accompanied, and he looks more like a single businessman than a family man who has a wife and children out in his car.)
2   How long is he likely to be staying? (We think one night. He isn't carrying much luggage, and that's how long single businessmen arriving on Thursdays usually stay, anyway.)

Now, on the basis of those guesses, try the following:

You: 'Just one moment, Mr Martin . . .' (*Glance down and have one last look for the missing booking. This gives you time to compose yourself.*) 'It was a single room, wasn't it?' (*End your sentence on a slightly rising note, making it half statement, half question.*)
Martin: (*Thinking that you are simply double checking, and impressed by your efficiency*) 'Yes.'
You: 'For one night. . . ?' (*same vocal inflexion*)
Martin: 'Yes.'
You: (*Confident now*) 'Would you just fill in this form, Mr Martin? That'll be Room 209 . . .' etc.

Now, this *could* go wrong, but the odds are that it won't. Even if it does, you are no worse off than you would have been if you had told Mr Martin right at the start that you'd lost his booking. In other words, a skilled receptionist can conceal the inevitable odd error or two by using her social skills.

Let's look at what you did in more detail and in behavioural terms.

When Mr Martin entered, you looked up at him and made a quick assessment, identifying him as a probable guest on the basis of his dress, accessories and general manner. You gave him a pleasant smile and greeted him politely, thus putting him at his ease and helping to establish a smooth pattern of interaction.

At this point it began to go wrong because you discovered that someone had mislaid his booking. However, you didn't display any outward signs of panic or confusion. You lowered your head, ostensibly to double check your records, but in reality to give yourself time to collect your thoughts. Then you took the initiative. You did this by making a couple of intelligent guesses, and then going on to choose a form of words which could be interpreted as either a question or a statement. You reinforced this ambiguity by the way you uttered them (that rising inflection, remember?). If you were right, Mr Martin wouldn't notice anything unusual, and if you were wrong, well, you had left yourself room for retreat (a quick apology and a correction). The likely result, a satisfied guest and a possible repeat booking.

Notice that there were two parts to the 'solution' in this example. The first was the 'social skills' aspect, which enabled you to combine the various elements of your behaviour into an effective pattern of interpersonal interaction. The second was what we might call 'technical' knowledge This covers your familiarity with your hotel's room and tariff structure, its current advance bookings situation and normal occupancy pattern, the habits and expectations of the single business person etc.

Most guest–reception contacts are straightforward, and their 'technical' aspects soon become second nature. Guests arrive: the process of checking them off, inviting them to complete the registration process, and assigning rooms soon becomes automatic, allowing you to concentrate on them as people. This helps you to add the important ingredients of a friendly greeting, a smile, and ideally some kind of personal touch ('Nice to see you again, Mr Johnson. How have you been keeping. . . ?).

Every now and again there will be a problem. Some of these will involve 'technical' aspects, others won't, but they will *all* require delicate and sensitive handling. The essence of most problems is that the customer wants something which for one reason or another you can't let him have. Perhaps it is someone who wants a type of room which you know happens to be fully booked, or a couple who want to vacate their room later than your housekeeping staff find convenient, or a guest who feels inclined to make more noise in his room than your other guests are prepared to accept. . . . In all these cases the question is the same: can you find a solution acceptable to both the guest and the hotel, and if not, can you manage to persuade the guest to accept an alternative with the minimum of fuss and disturbance?

Remember, all you have at your disposal are the various elements of behaviour: what you say, how you say it, and how you appear to the other person while you're saying it. It helps:

1 If you have already worked out the possible 'technical' answers as far as you are concerned (*can* you accommodate this 'chance' guest? *can* you move that one to another room?).
2 If you have also anticipated what the other person's reactions are likely to be (are they really likely to complain if they don't get their way?).

Obviously, you ought to be familiar with as many aspects of your hotel's operation as possible. However, many reception problems actually involve little or no 'technical' knowledge at all. Consider the following example.

Example 3

It is 5.45 pm and you are alone on the desk in a busy provincial hotel with a mixed clientele. There is a small queue of guests waiting to check in. At its head is a young and attractive female guest who has booked a single room as an independent traveller. Behind her are three equally young businessmen whom you are reasonably sure belong to a Sales Managers' Conference which you know is being held over the following two days. They are clearly interested in the female guest, and she is equally clearly not interested in them.

How would you handle this situation?

Now, what is your objective here? It should be to defuse a potentially awkward situation for one of your guests. Clearly, there is a risk that the young men will pester the unaccompanied female, and it would not be a good idea to let them discover either her name or (especially) her room number. They could find these out fairly easily by looking over her shoulder while she registers. Can you prevent this? Well, you might try the following:

You: (*To male guests*) 'Excuse me, gentlemen, are you waiting to register? You are? Well . . .'
(*Moving along the desk away from the female guest*) 'Perhaps you'd just like to fill in these forms here while I deal with the other guest. . . .'

This combination of words and action not only moves the three boisterous males away from the single female, but it also gives them something else to do while you are dealing with her. You are making it difficult for them to overhear her name, or her room number, or her home address, or how long she is staying. You can pass her the room key (assuming you are still using the non-computerized kind) in such a way as to conceal its number. She might not notice what you have done, of course, or say anything even if she does, but you will still feel the satisfaction that comes from having handled a difficult situation skilfully.

This is just as much a part of the receptionist's job as taking bookings, or presenting bills. In fact, many hoteliers would argue that it is a *more* important part. It requires no special knowledge of front office procedures, but it *does* require the ability to recognize potentially awkward situations, and the skill and confidence to take appropriate action.

One of the problems associated with the behavioural approach is that the elements of behaviour do not constitute a single, mutually understandable worldwide 'language'. As we all know, spoken and written languages vary considerably from one culture to another. The language of gesture varies in much the same way. There are large areas of the Middle and Far East, for instance, where giving someone something with the left hand is considered to be offensive in the extreme, and you would do well to remember this when you are handing over a registration card or a room key to a visitor from those regions.

This point has been made by writers like Michael Argyle and Desmond Morris, but personal experience is always more convincing than textbook examples, however authoritative. One of the authors of this book once worked on a small Caribbean island. The economy depended heavily on tourism (as in most of the islands), and the government was naturally anxious to know whether the tourists (mostly middle-aged North Americans) felt that they were getting good value. It therefore invited them to fill in exit questionnaires.

The results were disquieting. The tourists generally agreed that the scenery was beautiful (as it indeed was), the food good, the hotels comfortable, the sporting and other recreational facilities satisfactory, and the availability of handicrafts and other mementos adequate. However, the majority said that the service staff (in shops, bars and restaurants as well as the hotels) were 'sullen and hostile', and when asked whether they would recommend the island to their friends or come back themselves, a considerable number said 'No'.

Naturally, this worried the government, and it got together with other governments and commissioned a survey. The investigators found that while there was a small amount of genuine hostility (not surprising in view of the islands' histories), the tourists' belief that the staff were sullen and hostile was largely based on a genuine misunderstanding.

Children in the islands were brought up to behave in a particular way when in the presence of someone who might be considered a social superior. They were taught not to speak first, but to wait to be addressed. They were not supposed to look directly at a superior, or to smile (unless smiled at first), but rather to look downwards and to adopt a serious expression.

Divide into pairs and try this for yourself. One of you (the 'receptionist') should place yourself behind a desk or counter, and wait for your companion (the 'guest') to approach you. As he or she does so:

- Take a half step backwards.
- Turn your upper body a few degrees *away* from the 'guest'.
- Lower your head and direct your eyes towards the 'guest's' feet rather than his or her face.
- Adopt a serious, even solemn expression.
- Remain silent until addressed.

Now, ask your companion (who is playing the role of a North American tourist) what impression this behaviour has created, taking into consideration his or her cultural standpoint.

If you think about it, North Americans are accustomed to staff who step forward smartly, look them straight in the eye, give them a broad smile of welcome, and initiate the exchange with some such phrase as 'Good morning, can I help you?'. The behaviour *you* have just imitated is the opposite in every respect. No wonder it was perceived as demonstrating sullenness, hostility and an unwillingness to be of service! In fact, as we hope you have realized, it was simply the local way of being polite.

The government tried to solve the problem by arranging seminars and training courses for hotel receptionists and other service staff. Other islands experienced much the same problem, and one launched an intensive advertising campaign with the theme 'Every smile means a tourist dollar'. The fact that it spent scarce resources in this way indicates that it saw this kind of misunderstanding as a serious problem, and if you have read this chapter carefully you will not be surprised to see that they adopted a 'behavioural' solution by trying to get the staff concerned to act in a different way when faced with North American visitors.

This example reminds us that behaviour is only meaningful within a given situational context. Nevertheless, as far as most guests are concerned, your normal or instinctive approach is likely to be perfectly adequate.

Transactional analysis

How can you acquire these vitally important social skills? There are a number of sophisticated techniques for developing the necessary abilities, and you may well come across them at some time in your career. They include sensitivity training, interaction analysis and T groups. However, these require expert guidance and should be left to qualified professionals.

One of the best-known training techniques is transactional analysis (usually abbreviated to 'TA'). This is a theory of social action which is based on the assumption that when two or more people interact, each gains some kind of psychological benefit from the exchange. It calls such social interactions 'transactions'. These transactions include all the exchanges, conversational or otherwise, between a receptionist and a guest.

Before we go on to look at the nature of these psychological benefits, we need to understand one of the central elements of the theory, namely, that individuals can move from one state of mind to another. We all know that we and our friends can be grumpy and irritable at times, happy at others, but TA takes this rather further and distinguishes three different 'ego states'.

Ego states

These are usually shown in the form of a diagram (Figure 51).

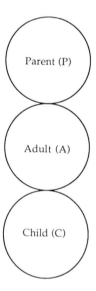

Figure 51

These terms in Figure 51 have specific meanings:

1   The parent ego state reflects the attitudes and beliefs we have acquired from our family and social upbringing. We all have these attitudes: about religion, for example, or work, or behaviour. Clearly, a receptionist who has been brought up never to answer back will react differently to an awkward customer than one who has been taught to stand up for herself whenever she is attacked. The parent state can be subdivided into 'nurturing' and 'critical' parents. A nurturing parent is driven to look after people, to minister to their wants and to soothe them when they are upset. A critical parent, on the other hand, is always finding fault. A nurturing parent might react to a late arrival who has neglected to make an advance booking with something like 'Oh dear, I really *am* sorry . . .', whereas a critical parent would say 'Well, sir, you really should have made a reservation. . . .'
2   The adult state represents the rational, logical, realistic approach which we ought to adopt when we are confronted by new problems. It has nothing to do with actual age: indeed,

many people actually become less adult as they get older and their attitudes become increasingly out of date. The adult ego state is the one which is capable of exploring alternatives, calculating the balance of advantages, and arriving at a logical decision. It is not affected by either prejudice or sentiment. It doesn't waste time trying to establish where the blame should lie, or commiserating with the victim, but gets down to the business of seeing what can be done about the situation. An adult receptionist faced with our walk-in would say something like 'I'm sorry sir, we are fully booked at the moment. Would you like me to call another hotel and see whether they've got a room?'

3 The child ego state represents the basic 'I', the part that underlies all the acquired social attitudes (the parent) and the limitations imposed by other people and things (the adult). People in a child state behave, quite literally, as they would if they were children. They can be selfish and unreasonable ('I want it *now!*'), but they can also be spontaneously affectionate. The child state can be subdivided into the 'natural child' (the spontaneous, impulsive character we have just described), the 'adapted child' (the one who has learned some manners but who may consequently be repressing his or her natural emotions and be harbouring resentment as a result), and what is called 'the little professor' (the imaginative, creative part of our personalities). The most effective form of problem solving comes when we combine our little professor with our adult. This allows us to bring all our creativity to bear on real-life problems and to recognize when a solution is practicable.

How can you recognize these ego states? There are various combinations of words and expressions which act as indicators as shown in Figure 52.

	Parent	*Adult*	*Child*
Words:	'You should' 'You must' 'Oh dear!' 'That's terrible!'	'What?' 'Why?' 'I see' 'Well, let's see what we can do'	'I need' 'I feel' 'I don't care' 'I don't know'
Expressions:	Frowning Concerned	Attentive Straightforward	Pouting Delighted

Figure 52

Note how 'behavioural' these indicators are. TA teaches that it is very much a question of what people actually say and how they say it which matters. It tries to teach you how to 'read' behavioural clues in order to detect underlying states of mind.

Complimentary and crossed transactions

Transactions can be 'complementary' or 'crossed'. A complementary transaction occurs when both sides of the transaction are in harmony. A guest might initiate a conversation in adult mode, for instance, and find that the receptionist responds in kind (Figure 53).

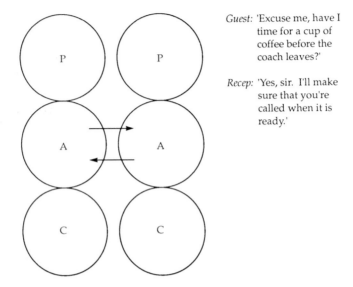

Guest: 'Excuse me, have I time for a cup of coffee before the coach leaves?'

Recep: 'Yes, sir. I'll make sure that you're called when it is ready.'

Figure 53

Alternatively, a complementary transaction might be between two different, but linked, ego states. Such a conversation might take place between the guest's child and the receptionist's nurturing parent (Figure 54).

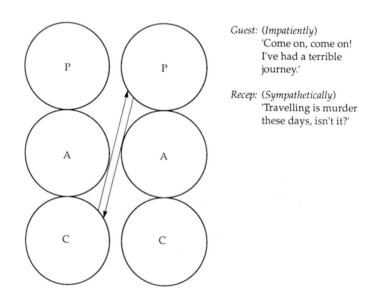

Guest: (*Impatiently*) 'Come on, come on! I've had a terrible journey.'

Recep: (*Sympathetically*) 'Travelling is murder these days, isn't it?'

Figure 54

A crossed transaction takes place when the response is not appropriate. An adult query might be met from an angry parent's point of view (Figure 55).

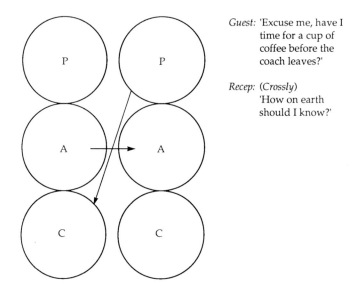

Guest: 'Excuse me, have I time for a cup of coffee before the coach leaves?'

Recep: (Crossly) 'How on earth should I know?'

Figure 55

Alternatively, a childlike opening remark might be met by a critical adult response (Figure 56).

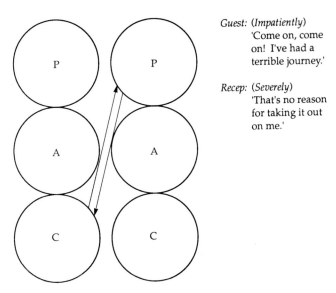

Guest: (Impatiently) 'Come on, come on! I've had a terrible journey.'

Recep: (Severely) 'That's no reason for taking it out on me.'

Figure 56

Crossed transactions are not constructive. They lead to rebuffs or recriminations, at the end of which the guest is no further forward. The aim of everyone in a service situation ought to be:

1 To cancel any negative or non-constructive adult or child feelings on the part of the guest, and then:

2   To move the transaction as smoothly as possible to an adult level.

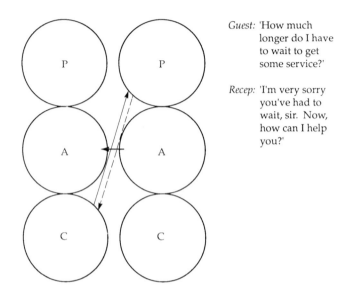

Guest: 'How much longer do I have to wait to get some service?'

Recep: 'I'm very sorry you've had to wait, sir. Now, how can I help you?'

Figure 57

In Figure 57 the receptionist has begun as a nurturing parent, sympathizing with the guest's obvious annoyance, and then quickly moved into a progressive adult mode by asking the guest what precisely he wants. The guest may continue to display annoyance about the hotel's slowness, of course, in which case more sympathy and apologies may be called for, but eventually he will have to tell you what his problem is, and the conversation can finish on an adult basis.

Strokes and trading stamps

Transactional analysis describes the psychological benefits we derive from interchanges with other people as 'strokes'. A stroke is any form of recognition, such as a look, a smile, a greeting or even something more tangible, such as a tip. The use of a guest's name is a good example of positive stroke.

One interesting aspect of strokes is that we seem to try to avoid any form of 'stroke deficit'. In other words, we keep a kind of mental tally and try to give as many as we receive. If someone smiles at us, we usually feel obliged to smile back. If we usually exchange daily strokes with someone ('Good morning', 'Good morning') and then don't see them for a week or so, we feel obliged to make up the deficit by having a much longer conversation ('Hello, haven't seen you for a while . . . Been anywhere interesting. . . ? Oh, did you enjoy it. . . ? Well, see you tomorrow. . . .') This has implications as far as selling is concerned, because a customer finds it more difficult to say 'No' if he has been the recipient of a series of positive strokes.

Strokes can be negative as well as positive. Again, we keep a kind of mental score card and try to give as good as we have got. If someone shouts at us, we tend to shout back, and if we are not in a position to do this then we try to get our revenge in some other way (by deliberately putting them in one of the least pleasant rooms, for instance).

People tend to 'collect' strokes, and to reward themselves when they have acquired enough of them. TA calls this process 'cashing in your stamps' (by analogy with the kind of trading stamp which entitles you to free gifts if you collect enough of them). We feel justified in celebrating if we receive an important positive stroke such as a promotion, just as we are liable to blow up and lose our tempers if we receive too many negative strokes.

Some people seem to make a point of collecting negative strokes ('dirty stamps') so that they can have a really good row or sulk when they have assembled enough of them. TA's explanation of this process is that such people have been conditioned during their childhood to *expect* such negative strokes, to such a point that they are not really comfortable unless they are receiving them.

This brings up the question of the 'the OK corral'. Some fortunate individuals seem to grow up with positive attitudes towards both themselves and everyone around them, while others acquire much more negative outlooks. The 'OK corral' can be expressed as shown in Figure 58.

I'm not OK You're not OK	I'm OK You're not OK
I'm not OK You're OK	I'm OK You're OK

Figure 58

The attitudes summarized on the left-hand side of Figure 58 are clearly much more pessimistic than those on the right. Those who share the 'I'm not OK: You're not OK' are likely to be thoroughly difficult guests, unable to enjoy themselves and viewing all your efforts to cheer them up with suspicion. Those in the 'I'm not OK: You're OK' quadrant will also tend to be gloomy, though they won't regard this as your fault. Even people with the 'I'm OK: You're not OK' outlook can make difficult guests, because if anything goes wrong it will always be your fault and not theirs'.

Games

The idea that people 'collect' different kinds of strokes according to their basic outlook on life is expanded into the notion of games. A game is a transaction in which one person ('player') manoeuvres the other into providing the desired kind of stroke as a payoff. These payoffs need not be pleasant: indeed, there are many games in which the payoff is a negative stroke.

The idea of games is fundamental to TA and was first developed in response to the observation that a great many people do appear to play curiously negative 'life games'. There are individuals who seem determined to get themselves fired from every job they hold, for instance, or who seem to stir up trouble wherever they go.

It is important to realize that a games player is trying to *manoeuvre* you, often quite

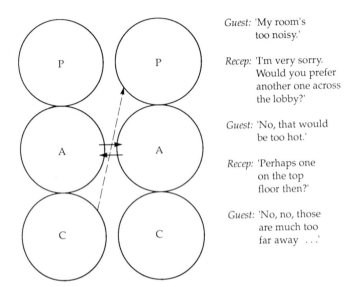

Guest: 'My room's too noisy.'

Recep: 'I'm very sorry. Would you prefer another one across the lobby?'

Guest: 'No, that would be too hot.'

Recep: 'Perhaps one on the top floor then?'

Guest: 'No, no, those are much too far away . . .'

Figure 59

unconsciously, into providing a particular response. This means that the transaction is being conducted on two levels, one the apparent, surface one, the other the hidden or psychological one. Take the situation in Figure 59.

Here it is becoming increasingly clear that the guest is going to find fault with every suggestion the receptionist makes, and that what appeared to be a rational, adult discussion is in fact nothing of the sort.

There are a great many games. Some of the more common ones are:

1   'Yes, but . . .'   This may be what is being played in the example above. The guest may appear to be acting as an adult but is actually behaving like a spoiled child, hoping to get the receptionist to behave like a nurturing parent. Eventually the receptionist will run out of alternatives and the guest will have 'proved' to his own satisfaction that the hotel doesn't have anything suitable.

2   'Uproar'   Alternatively, the guest in the example may be being difficult in the hope that the receptionist will finally lose patience and say something critical, even rude. In this case the guest would be playing a child in the hope of provoking the receptionist's critical parent. The guest would then be able to 'switch' ego states and become critical himself, making a scene and demanding to see the manager.

3   'Kick me' or 'Why does this always happen to me?'   Some individuals seem to derive an obscure sort of satisfaction from proving themselves to be so useless that the people they are dealing with eventually lose patience with them. Staff may play this game: if one of your colleagues is making mistake after mistake without any serious attempt to cover them up then this is a serious possibility. The player's payoff is a feeling of perverse pride arising from the fact that his misfortunes are greater than anyone else's.

The significance of games is that they help to explain why some of your customers seem to behave unreasonably. Although a conversation may appear to be couched at a normal adult–

adult level, it may in fact be being conducted according to a concealed 'script' of which the receptionist is not aware. Fortunately, most people don't take the games they play too seriously, but look out if you find yourself having to deal with an obsessive third degree player of a nasty game like 'Now I've got you, you son of a bitch!', because the player's payoff comes when he catches you out in a mistake!

Role playing

We have already said that one of the best ways of developing any skill is practice. This applies to social skills just as much as to riding a bicycle. Situations do recur again and again, and a lot of the confidence displayed by the experienced receptionist comes from having dealt successfully with very similar ones in the past.

If you are already in a job, then you should be getting this practice as a matter of course. We recommend that you pay careful attention to the way your more experienced colleagues handle the situations, and then try to follow their example. Don't be too uncritical, though: not every experienced receptionist handles every problem in the best possible way, and your aim ought to be to do even better.

If you haven't yet entered full-time employment, you can still develop your social skills by means of role play exercises. In fact, we have already asked you to do a bit of this earlier in this chapter. Role playing gives you the opportunity to practise your social skills in a face-to-face situation.

Try the role play exercise at the end of this chapter. It is designed to help prepare you for the kinds of situations which may crop up from time to time, and to help you practise the necessary social skills. You can rehearse it over and over again because what you should be concentrating on is improving your own performance each time, and not on the 'technical' aspect of the problems.

The exercise works best if you observe the following guidelines:

1   There should be two or more 'players'. One should take the role of the receptionist and the other (or others) should play the guest (or guests). The guest's opening sentences are 'scripted', but it is up to the receptionist to produce appropriate responses. We haven't 'scripted' the guests' parts any further than their opening lines because what they say subsequently depends very much on what sort of answer the receptionist produces.
2   Obviously, the guests should try to play their parts as realistically as possible. It is particularly important that they should recognize when to give way. Most of the conversations should only continue for three or four exchanges, after which you should stop and review how they went.
3   The exercise should be 'unrehearsed'. In other words, the receptionist and the guest shouldn't get together beforehand to work out how the rest of the conversation should go. Effective social skills involve reacting to other people's initiatives, and you need to practise this aspect.
4   On the other hand, the receptionist *should* read through the problem first and try to work out any 'technical' implications (sometimes there aren't any: it is just a matter of applying common sense). This is because the receptionist should be concentrating on the Social Skills aspects. It's not so much knowing *what* to do that's important here, it's knowing *how* to do it.

Room	Last night	Tonight	Tomorrow	Day after	etc.
1 T	← ——————— Foster —————— →			← Mason ——	
2 S	← Smith →		← Price ——		
3 TB	← Jones —————— →		← Bloggs ——		
4 D	← Thomas —————— →		← Parry ——		
5 D	← Johnson →	← Lovell ————————— →		← King ——	
6 TB	← Timms →		← Baxter ——		
7 TB	← Frazer —————— →				
8 S			← Meads →		
9 D		← ———— Harris ———— →			
10 TB	← Marks →	← Gomez ——			

Room rates:
Singles £20
Doubles and twins £30
TBs (twins with bath) £40

Figure 60

5   The exercise should be conducted in front of an audience (e.g. the rest of the group). This is because you are trying to develop a kind of 'performing' skill, and while solitary rehearsals are all right if you are simply learning your lines, they are no substitute for the real thing. Once the exchanges have come to a natural end, you can throw the discussion open to the rest of the group. As observers rather than performers, they will have seen more than either the 'receptionist' or the 'guest', and they can often offer valuable feedback and suggestions.

6   It is even better if you can act out the roles in front of a videocamera and then play the tape back. We often have no idea of how we appear to others until we have seen ourselves in action in this way.

7   It helps, too, if you have a few 'props' such as a desk, a key rack, a couple of telephones, and some bills or letters of confirmation which have been pre-prepared along the lines indicated in the dialogues. They aren't strictly necessary, but they do help to set the right 'pace' for the dialogues. After all pauses constitute quite a large part of most conversations, and what you do during them is an important aspect of 'body language'.

8   Following on from the above, it helps if you look the part. Take the trouble to put on that interview suit, and see what a difference it makes to your whole carriage and bearing. That's partly what you are supposed to be practising, isn't it?

9   Finally, take it seriously. Clowning around and playing it for laughs may seem fun at the time but it is really rather shortsighted. This is a very important aspect of the receptionist's skills, and it should be treated as such.

A final point. In one or two cases the problems may involve you in determining your hotel's policy. In reality, you would probably be able to consult a senior manager, but for the purposes of this exercise *you* are the senior manager as well as the person on the spot!

Assignment: Reception role play problems (or 'Just another day on the desk . . .')

The following problems should be tackled in conjunction with the bookings chart and arrivals list shown in Figures 60 and 61 though it is not absolutely necessary to update these as you go along. The 'Receptionist' should respond appropriately in all cases.

Arrivals list (tonight)

Name	Stay	Room	Remarks
Lovell Mr/s	2N	5D	Regulars
Harris Mr/s	2N	9D	Arriving late
Gomez Sr/Sra	4N	10TB	From Brazil

Figure 61

Problem 1: Time 7.30 am

Guest: 'Marks, Room 10. Can I have my bill, please?' (*Pause*) 'What's this? £40 for the room? But when our travel agents made the booking for me they were told your twins with bath were £30! Look: here's the confirmation they sent me'
Shows receptionist the travel agent's letter to Mr and Mrs Marks, which does indeed say 'Twin Room with Bath £30'. The receptionist has no record of any special rate being agreed, but knows that the head receptionist (unfortunately not available) has authority to do this.

Problem 2: Time 7.45 am

Guest: 'My name's Timms, Room 6. My bill please,' (*Pause*) 'What's this? £3.00 for a phone call? I only made one local call. It was after 6 pm and I only spoke for a couple of minutes. . . .'
The receptionist was not on shift at the time but is aware that calls are

monitored automatically, that the equipment is modern and accurate, and that the hotel's policy is to charge for calls at 250 per cent of cost.

Problem 3   Time 9.15 am

Guest: 'Good morning. I'm Mr (or Mrs) Johnson from Room 5. We were going to leave this morning, but I'm afraid we've had to take our car in for repairs and it won't be ready until tomorrow at the earliest. Is it all right if we stay another night?'

Problem 4:   Time 9.30 am

A member of the housekeeping staff has discovered undeniable evidence of the overnight use of dangerous drugs in Room 4D. This has been reported to the general manager, who has instructed the receptionist to insist that the Thomas's should leave immediately. Mr (or Mrs) Thomas happens to pass the desk. . . .

Problem 5:   Time 1.45 pm

The receptionist discovers that Mr (or Mrs) Smith in Room 2 has not checked out, then sees him (or her) leaving the restaurant and asks why.

Guest: 'Oh, I thought I mentioned when I arrived that I wouldn't be leaving until late afternoon. . . .'
There is nothing in the records to confirm this statement. The hotel's standard terms state that rooms should be vacated by 12.00 noon and that the full room rate is due in respect of any day or part of a day that the room is occupied.

Problem 6:   Time 2.45 pm

Guest: (*On telephone*) 'Hello, my name's Parry. We're booked in for tomorrow. I've just checked your letter of confirmation and I see you've given us a double room. I wonder if you could change that to a twin, please?'

Problem 7:   Time 3.15 pm

Guest: 'Foster, Room 1. We were booked to stay another two nights, but we've just had a phone call to say that our house has been burgled and we ought to return as quickly as possible. Do you mind if we check out immediately?'

Problem 8: Time 3.30 pm

Guest: (*On telephone*) 'Hello, my name's Marks. I checked out this morning. I've just realized I left my watch in the room. It's a very expensive gold one and it was on the bedside table beside the lamp . . .'

On checking with the housekeeper the receptionist will be told that no such watch has been handed in.

Problem 9: Time 4.00 pm

Guest: (*On telephone*) 'Hello, my name's Mr (or Mrs) Franklin. I'm due to meet my mother (or father) at the airport near you the day after tomorrow. Can I have two single rooms please?'

Note: Whoever is playing Franklin should quote a parent of the opposite sex.

Problem 10: Time 4.30 pm

Guest: 'Good evening. I'm Mr (or Mrs) Frazer from Room 7. Last evening I asked for a faulty switch to be repaired. You sent your maintenance man up to my room to do it. It took about ten minutes and I was in the bathroom for some of the time. Well, I've just discovered that there's a ten pound note missing from my wallet. . . .'

The receptionist knows that the maintenance man has been with the hotel for several years and has an unblemished record to date.

Problem 11: Time 6.15 pm

Guest: (*Approaches desk*) 'Hello. I wonder if you could spare a moment? I'm Mr (or Mrs) Lovell from Number 5. We've just arrived. I'm afraid that although we booked a plain double room, my wife (or husband) hasn't been very well, and we really should have asked for a room with a private bathroom. Would it be possible to change to one, please?'

Problem 12:   *Time 6.25 pm*

Guest: (*Who has just been shown to room.*) 'Hello, it's me again, Mr (or Mrs) Lovell. That room you've just given us hasn't been serviced. The bed's not been made and the bathroom's filthy!'

The receptionist is aware that there are no housekeeping staff on duty and that the only other person available is the assistant manager.

Problem 13:   *Time 6.30 pm*

Guest: (*Approaches desk and speaks slowly, with a strong foreign accent.*) 'Er, good evening. My name Gomez. I 'ave reservation.'

Problem 14:   *Time 6.45 pm*

A male and a female approach the desk. They appear sober, respectable and well-behaved.

Male (or Female):   'Hello. My girl (boy) friend and I were travelling to London, but we've been held up. Can you let us have a twin or a double room for the night, please?'

Problem 15:   *Time 7.00 pm*

Guest: (*Approaches desk*) 'Good evening. My name's Carter and my wife (or husband) and I have a reservation. Here's your letter of confirmation.' (*Shows receptionist letter, which confirms Carter's statement.*) 'One double room arriving tonight and staying for two nights. . . .'

Problem 16:   *Time 10.45 pm*

Guest: 'Good evening. Our name is Harris. We reserved a double room some weeks ago and told you we'd be arriving late.'

The receptionist notices that they are accompanied by a small dog. The hotel's policy is 'No Dogs', and this is clearly stated on all brochures and confirmation letters.

Problem 17:   Time 11.45 pm

A guest approaches the desk. He (or she) appears respectably dressed but carries no luggage.

Guest: 'Good evening. My name's Skipper. I'd like a room for the night. I've just arrived from Paris but I'm afraid my luggage hasn't! You know what airlines are like, ha ha!'

The receptionist checks the black list and discovers that a guest answering to a similar description has disappeared from several hotels recently without paying the bill.

Problem 18:   Time 00.15 am

Guest: 'Excuse me. I'm Mr (or Mrs) Frazer from Room 7. I'm sorry to bother you, but our room's over the bar, and there seems to be some sort of party going on. There's a lot of noise coming from it, and we can't sleep.'

Room 7 is in fact over the bar. The party is being thrown by the Jones' from Room 3, who are regular and generous guests, and is scheduled to go on until 3.30. The other rooms are all quieter.

Problem 19:   Time 03.45 am

Mr and Mrs Jones have retired to their room, where they are singing, dancing and generally behaving in a noisy and boisterous fashion. (Note: 'Mr and Mrs Jones' should respond negatively to the receptionist's initial approaches. They might indulge in a certain amount of invective and even resort to threats of violence.)

Problem 20:   Time 04.00 am

During the process of calming down the Jones's, the receptionist notices that they have smashed the bedside tea making machine. This particular machine cost £35 when it was purchased two years ago.

7 Sales

Introduction

Most of the expenses involved in letting accommodation are fixed. This means that once sales have passed the break-even point, any additional receipts are virtually pure profit from the department's point of view. The implication is that effort put into generating additional room revenue is worth more in terms of profit than equivalent effort put into selling liquor or food, where there are important variable costs such as food costs to consider. Of course, better value for money in terms of food and drink can generate extra accommodation income, but the fact remains that in many hotels the bars and restaurants often do little more than break even and it is the rooms which generate the profits.

This means that we ought to devote a lot of attention to raising room revenue. This is usually seen as a marketing problem. However, there *are* measures which front office staff can take to increase revenue, and they form the subject of this chapter.

The basic point to grasp is that there are two ways of increasing revenue. One is to bring in more customers, the second is to persuade each customer to pay more.

To demonstrate this, imagine a hotel with 100 beds, an average guest rate of £50, and an average annual occupancy of 70 per cent. The average nightly accommodation revenue will be:

$$70/100 \times 100 \times £50 = £3,500$$

Now, let us assume that we can somehow add another 7 per cent to the occupancy rate. The figures now become:

$$77/100 \times 100 \times £50 = £3,850$$

Alternatively, let us assume that we can somehow persuade each guest to pay £5 more. The figures then become:

$$70/100 \times 100 \times £55 = £3,850$$

This example may be somewhat contrived, but it does underline the point that there are two ways of increasing revenue. Of course, combining them gives even better results. If we can increase both occupancies and average spends in these proportions, the figures then become:

$$77/100 \times 100 \times £55 = £4235!$$

So let us see what front office staff can accomplish in these areas.

Increasing occupancies

Although front office has little to do with the main means by which guests are attracted to a hotel (advertising and direct sales, for instance) this does not mean that receptionists have no scope at all for increasing occupancies.

'Juggling' bookings

If the hotel uses a conventional chart, skilled receptionists can show ingenuity in plotting the bookings in order to fit the maximum number in. We have already looked at this earlier, but to remind you, consider Figure 62.

Room	1st	2nd	3rd	4th	5th	6th	7th
101 (T)	← Chalmers →			←	Howard		→
102 (T)	←	Webb	→		← Turner		→
103 (T)	←	Clifford		→	←	Fleming	→

Figure 62

Now suppose you receive a request from Mr and Mrs Morrison, who want a Twin room for the nights of the 3rd and 4th. An inexperienced receptionist may well say 'Sorry: we don't have a twin for both nights.' Someone with more experience would quietly switch the Chalmers with the Webbs, leaving Room 102 free for two nights for the Morrisons.

You can also help to fill a hotel by 'doubling up', or persuading unrelated singles to occupy twins. It used to be quite a common practice in the old days (indeed, guests were often expected to share the same bed!) but is now much less frequent. However, it makes sense to try it if you have too few singles and too many twins. Groups such as conference delegates are worth approaching because they may know each other already and are likely to have something in common. Some form of inducement such as complimentary drinks or a price reduction is well worth considering.

'Splitting down' is another practice which could help if you have too few twins and too many singles. You will often find that pairs of friends travelling on their own account will choose a twin room in order to reduce costs. If you offer them the option of taking two singles at no extra charge, they may well jump at it. You don't get any extra money directly, but you do free one of the scarcer twins.

Handling enquiries

Most shop assistants ask 'would you like anything else?' as a matter of course. Few receptionists do. This is a mistake, because a lot of calls come from agents of various types who have to make multiple bookings. It saves them time and money if they can reserve several with one call, and although their other clients may have expressed preferences for other hotels, your question may just tip the scales and lead to them all being placed with you.

In the same way, never respond to a request for a single room on the 15th with 'I'm very sorry, we're full'. Haven't you got anything else you could offer? Your order of priority ought to be:

1   *A different type of room*   Don't you have a twin you might offer at an appropriately reduced rate?
2   *A different date*   Obviously you won't persuade the majority of prospective customers to change their dates of stay, but it is surprising how flexible some guests can be, and if you only win 10 per cent of the time you will still be well ahead.
3   *A companion hotel*   If you are located in a large city, you may well have one or more 'sister' hotels nearby. The relationship is often one of mutual competition, but it makes sense to see whether one of them can take your overflow.
4   *Another hotel*   If you can't fit your caller into one of your own group's hotels, then try someone else's. This helps your image with the customer (who might well try you again first next time) and also makes it more likely that you'll get the other hotel's surplus when they are in an 'overflow' situation.

Repeat business

Another very important way in which front office staff can help to increase occupancies is to try to boost repeat business. Obviously, the guest must have been satisfied with the hotel during his current stay, otherwise you stand little chance of his coming back. This means:

1   That front office should have dealt with him efficiently from pre-arrival through to post-departure. This means no errors over room reservations, no mistakes over the charges, no failures to pass on messages and so on. We must not give the guest any reason not to want to come back.
2   That front office should have dealt with him politely and pleasantly. It is not enough to make sure that he has no complaints: we must try to make him *want* to come back.

If all has gone well, the moment of departure is a good time to try some forward selling. Many hotels ignore this opportunity, but there are good reasons for trying to capitalize on it. One of the main problems hotels face in terms of marketing is that they are seldom able to engage in face-to-face selling, since bookings are usually arranged in advance, over the telephone and often through agents of one type or another. Never forget that *a guest in the hotel is a potential future customer*. Somebody who has come to your area once may very well do so twice, and if your hotel suited him then, it ought to do so again.

There is another and more subtle point. A hotel is a kind of home. It may seem a little intimidating at first, but most guests soon get over that and come to regard it as a familiar, even friendly place. Departure is often a somewhat comfortless time: the guest has to set off into the cold, unfriendly world once more, and it is at this moment that he is likely to be particularly receptive to the suggestion that you would like to see him back sometime. You can ask 'I hope you enjoyed your stay?', and if you get an affirmative answer, go on to 'Are you going to be coming back this way again? Can we make a provisional booking?' Even if only a few guests are able to give you a definite answer there and then, you have planted the idea in the others' minds, and it may well develop into a firm booking eventually.

The same point applies to the use of 'follow-up' techniques. Commercial firms often pay considerable sums of money for address lists which might include a high proportion of potential customers. Your registration cards represent precisely such a list. These are people who have already had reason to come to your area, have chosen your hotel, and have (presumably) been happy with their choice. We shall return to this point when we look at marketing.

'No shows' and overbooking

The most difficult and controversial issue in connection with increasing occupancies is the way you respond to the problem created by 'no shows'. These are people who make bookings and then fail to honour them. We can include early departures and late cancellations in this category because the effects are the same. A guest who books for two nights and then leaves after one is just as much of a loss to the hotel as somebody who books for one and then never turns up at all. However, early check-outs are not quite so serious from the hotel's point of view because they do give longer notice (you tend to find out in mid-morning rather than the late evening), allowing you more chance to relet. The effects of 'no shows' as a whole can be demonstrated in the following example:

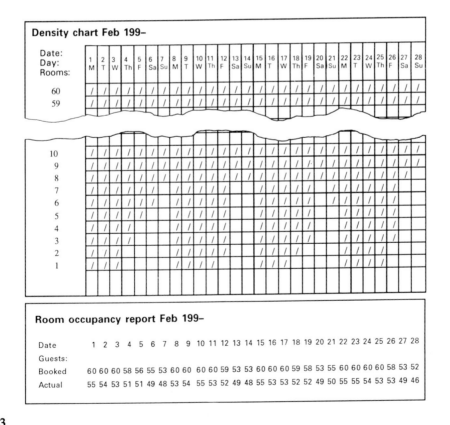

Figure 63

You are presented with the (simplified) density chart for a four-week period, together with the accompanying (equally simplified) occupancy report (shown in Figure 63). The average room rate is £40 per night.

What is your room revenue for the period, and how might you increase it?

Well, the percentage of arrivals to bookings averages about 90 per cent. In other words, the no-show rate is 10 per cent, which means that you are regularly losing five or six guests every night. The effect on room revenue is easy enough to calculate. The total of actual room nights was 1454, which yielded £58,160 over the period. However, if everyone who had booked had turned up, you would have had 1615 room nights yielding £64,600, a difference of £6,440.

This is a substantial sum to lose (especially for a relatively small hotel), and as a front office manager you should not be happy about it. This is why the question goes on to ask how you might increase the revenue.

What can a hotel do to offset the impact of no shows? There are several alternative approaches, namely:

1 Reduce the number of no shows.
2 Impose financial penalties on no shows.
3 Find alternative last-minute bookings.
4 Overbook in order to offset the impact of no shows.

Let us consider each of these in turn.

1 *Cutting the number of no shows*

The first point to make is obvious but often overlooked. Front office staff ought to check guests' stays and 'chase' any unconfirmed bookings using letters, telephone or whatever other medium is appropriate. This is particularly important as far as groups are concerned, but it really applies to anyone.

Second, the hotel should make sure that it has a clause in the standard booking contract specifying that rooms are only held until a specified time unless otherwise agreed. Most hotels do this, and the time is usually somewhere between 6 pm and 7 pm. This doesn't necessarily reduce the overall number of no shows, but it does allow the hotel to identify them in time to take some remedial action, and thus reduce their impact.

2 *Imposing financial penalties*

In principle, a hotel can sue a no-show guest for breach of contract if it has not been able to relet the room (after making a reasonable effort to do so, of course). This is often difficult because guests come from far away, and unproductive because the amounts are relatively small. Nevertheless, it is still worth sending a letter requesting compensation: even a few favourable responses will more than cover the postage costs, and it does tend to discourage future repetitions of the offence.

Collecting non-arrival charges is facilitated by the practice of taking a credit card number on booking. You are then able to charge them to the cardholder. He can dispute the charge, of course, but the onus is on him to prove that it isn't legitimate.

A hotel can always ask for a non-returnable deposit. This is much more satisfactory, not because it covers the hotel's losses in the event of a no show (it is usually only a proportion of the final bill) but because it makes the potential no show think twice about booking at all.

Another very similar practice is to include a provision entitling you to a cancellation fee as part of the booking contract, though there is no guarantee that you will actually get it.

As we have said, some no shows take the form of early check-outs. Since the guest is repudiating (i.e. breaking) his contract, you can demand payment for the unused night in the same way as if he had failed to arrive at all, though you must also be prepared to refund that payment if you are subsequently able to relet. All this tends to deter early check-outs, and they are not so much of a problem as non-arrivals.

3   Finding last minute bookings

No shows tend to increase along with demand. The reason is that many guests know that last-minute bookings can be difficult to make at peak periods, so they tend to reserve accommodation on the off-chance that they will want to use it. This means that you should be able to relet at such periods providing that you can 'tap into' the demand.

One way of doing this is to have a waiting list. You will probably find that you will continue to receive enquiries after you have filled your bookings chart. All you need to say is 'We're very sorry, we don't have any vacancies for that date at the moment, but if you will leave your telephone number we'll get back to you if we can.' You may not be able to do this, and even if you can the guest may well have found a room somewhere else, but your action in calling back shows him that you are both efficient and courteous, which may cause him to contact you first in the future. In any case, you should be able to fill two or three rooms from a wait list of twenty or so names.

Another method is to contact one of the organizations which receive a lot of last-minute enquiries. They include the airlines and commercial hotel booking agencies, together with the local Tourist Information Office. One of the latter's roles is to put would-be guests in touch with local hotels, and it is likely to be receiving enquiries up until closing time (indeed, with modern computerized displays, it can still direct customers to you even after that).

4   Overbooking

Overbooking means deliberately accepting more bookings than you have room for. If you get it right, you *should* end up with just about the right number of guests, and your room revenue for that night will be close to the optimum. However, this is a controversial issue, because it raises the question of whether the practice is legal.

The civil law position is quite clear: a guest who fails to take up accommodation he has reserved is guilty of breach of contract, and a hotel which fails to supply the accommodation reserved is also guilty of breach of contract. We have already discussed your obligations in that respect. However, it is worth repeating that you have an obligation to minimize your losses. A prudent hotelier who *expected* a certain number of no shows might well argue that overbooking was simply a way of doing this.

Criminal law is another matter. The problem is that telling a guest that he is booked when you are actually following a policy of overbooking may constitute a false trade description, and thus an offence under Section 14 of the Trades Descriptions Act. It can be argued that if you tell sixty-six customers that you are reserving rooms for them when in fact you only have sixty rooms, then you must be telling someone a lie. On the other hand, if you are reasonably sure that in the event only sixty of those customers will actually turn up, then you are making the statement in good faith. The one is a false statement, the other a 'fallible forecast'.

Unfortunately, this issue has not been resolved. The leading case is *British Airways Board* v.

Taylor (1975). In this case an airline 'bumped' a passenger, admitting that it had been overbooking and had got it wrong. The question of whether this was a criminal offence was taken all the way up to the House of Lords, but then had to be dismissed on technical grounds unconnected with the central issue. However, their Lordships did find that the justices were entitled to find as a fact that the airline's letter of confirmation *was* false within Section 14 of the Act. The general issue remains undecided. Unless or until it is clarified (possibly by someone else fighting a case through the Lords), we can't be sure. Our best guess is that double booking a specific room on a conventional chart almost certainly *isn't* legal, whereas overbooking using a density chart probably *is* (because you are not claiming to reserve a specific room). However, you need to be careful about overbooking limits. If you overbook to an extent which more or less guarantees that someone will be left without a room each night, then you may well be infringing Section 14, and you should keep this in mind while reading the following paragraphs.

Having done our best to clear up the legal position, let us consider the question of judicious overbooking using Figure 63. Clearly, you can't overbook the Fridays, Saturdays and Sundays since you are not fully booked for those nights anyway. However, you *can* do it for the Monday to Wednesday period, since you have almost certainly been turning bookings away (a 100 per cent booking rate usually reflects a much higher level of enquiries and actual requests).

We will take Monday the 1st as a basis for our calculations. As our density chart shows, we actually took sixty bookings for that night. This almost certainly meant that we had to turn away a number of later requests. Suppose we had accepted enough of those to compensate for the expected no shows? Let us compare what actually occurred with what *might* have happened:

Actual		*Possible*	
Bookings	60	10 per cent overbooked	66
No shows	5	No shows (10 per cent of 66)	7*
Arrivals	55	Arrivals (90 per cent of 66)	59*
Revenue (55 × £40)	£2,200	Revenue (59 × £40)	£2,360
Revenue gain: £160			

* We have rounded off these figures to whole numbers: you can't have 6.6 people failing to arrive!

Note that there is a built-in safety margin here, since the expected number of no shows increases with the number of bookings taken and not the number of rooms. In this example, if you overbook by six, the number of no shows is more likely to be seven.

The revenue gain is clearly to our advantage, and the case for overbooking is simply that it should bring actual receipts closer to the optimum room revenue (in this example £2,400). However, most receptionists contemplating overbooking for the first time worry about what happens if they *don't* get it right and too many people turn up. Let us consider this, using the same example.

The actual no-show rate varies between 8 per cent and 12 per cent. If you overbook by 10 per cent (i.e. accept sixty-six bookings) and the worst happens (i.e. only 8 per cent fail to turn up), you should be faced with sixty-one arrivals (the figure is actually 60.7, but we've rounded that upwards for the reasons already explained). So what happens now?

Well, it is quite likely that you will be able to 'stretch' your accommodation in some way or other. There may well be a suite which you can convert in a hurry, or a staff room you can take over, or some other expedient. This is how many hotels record occupancy percentages of over 100 per cent on occasion. However, let us look on the black side and assume that you *can't* accommodate the extra guest. What do you do now?

The usual answer is to find a room for him somewhere else. This is called 'booking out', or 'walking'. It may mean some frantic last-minute telephoning, but an experienced receptionist should have seen the crisis coming and made arrangements in plenty of time. Many hotels have reciprocal arrangements to cover exactly this kind of situation. Obviously, you will try to find a room in an equivalent class hotel. If the alternative is much poorer than your own establishment, the guest is likely to feel aggrieved, and if it is much better, you will have to pay the difference in price.

This raises the important issue of just what you are liable for. Failure to provide the room you said you were going to provide is breach of contract, and you are liable to compensate the guest for any losses incurred as a result. These would cover any additional travelling expenses, or any increase in the price of the alternative room, but it doesn't generally include compensation for disturbance or annoyance since these are very difficult to assess in financial terms.

With these points in mind, let us look at our problem again. We can accommodate sixty, but we actually have sixty-one arrivals. What are we going to do with the extra one? Fairly obviously, we are going to take him on one side, apologize profusely, tell him that we have arranged suitable accommodation elsewhere, offer to call and pay for a taxi to take him there, and offer him a complimentary drink or so to help him pass the time while he is waiting for it.

Now, how much will all this cost? On balance, we are likely to lose a little as far as the accommodation is concerned, because sometimes we will have to book the guest out into a more expensive room, which means we have to pay the difference, whereas if the cost of the alternative is the same as ours we don't lose anything, and if it is cheaper we can't claim the difference back *from* the guest (because we are not supposed to profit from breaking our contracts). However, we will only find ourselves paying out in a minority of cases, and even then the differentials are likely to be fairly small. We might perhaps allow an average of £5 per guest for these payments.

What about the taxis and other expenses? The full retail rates might well be fairly expensive, but then it isn't the guest who is paying but the hotel, and if it hasn't already negotiated a contract on favourable terms with the taxi firm then it shouldn't be in business! In the same way, the drinks it offers are complimentary ones, and all that the hotel loses is their basic cost. Again, being generous, we might allow about £5 per guest, making £10 in all.

The calculations now look like this:

10 per cent overbooked	66
No shows (8 per cent of 66)	5 (rounded off)
Arrivals	61
Roomed (@ £40 per guest)	60 yielding £2,400
Booked out (@ £10 per guest)	1 costing £10
Net receipts	£2,390

You will notice that this is £30 more than we achieved in our last example. In other words, overbooking pays, and overbooking close to the margin can pay even more, because booking out doesn't cost as much as you think.

This kind of problem responds well to the use of a spreadsheet. Let us demonstrate this with the same figures as we have used above (i.e., sixty beds at £40 each, a no-show rate varying from 8 per cent to 12 per cent, and a book-out cost of £10 per head) – see Figure 64.

A	B	C	D	E	F	G	H	I
O'Bkg (%)	Number booked	Arrivals @ 8% no show	Arrivals @ 10% no show	Arrivals @ 12% no show	Rev. @ 8% no show (£)	Rev. @ 10% no show (£)	Average @ 12% no show (£)	rev. (£)
8	65	60	59	57	2,400	2,360	2,280	2,347
9	65	60	59	57	2,400	2,360	2,280	2,347
10	66	61	59	58	2,390	2,360	2,320	2,357
11	67	62	60	59	2,380	2,400	2,360	2,380
12	67	62	60	59	2,380	2,400	2,360	2,380
13	68	63	61	60	2,370	2,390	2,400	2,387
14	68	63	61	60	2,370	2,390	2,400	2,387
15	69	63	62	61	2,370	2,380	2,390	2,380
16	70	64	63	62	2,360	2,370	2,380	2,370
17	70	64	63	62	2,360	2,370	2,380	2,370
18	71	65	64	62	2,350	2,360	2,380	2,363
19	71	65	64	62	2,350	2,360	2,380	2,363
20	72	66	65	63	2,340	2,350	2,370	2,353
21	73	67	66	64	2,330	2,340	2,360	2.343
22	73	67	66	64	2,330	2,340	2,360	2,343
23	74	68	67	65	2,320	2,330	2,350	2,333
24	74	68	67	65	2,320	2,330	2,350	2,333
25	75	69	68	66	2,310	2,320	2,340	2,323

Note: The formula used are as follows (the actual format may vary slightly from one spreadsheet to another):

B (No. booked): $60 + (60/100 \times A)$
C (Arrivals @ 8% no show): $B - (B/100 \times 8)$ (rounded off to whole number)
D (Arrivals @ 10% no show): $B - (B/100 \times 10)$ (rounded off to whole number)
E (Arrivals @ 12% no show): $B - (B/100 \times 12)$ (rounded off to whole number)
F (Revenue @ 8% no show):   IF C (=60, THEN C×40: IF C‹60, THEN 2400 − ((C−60)×10)
G (Revenue @ 10% no show):   IF D (=60, THEN D×40: IF D‹60, THEN 2400 − ((D−60)×10)
H (Revenue @ 12% no show):   IF E (=60, THEN E×40: IF E‹60, THEN 2400 − ((E−60)×10)
I (Average Revenue): $(F+G+H)/3$

Figure 64

As you would expect, average revenue falls as the overbooking percentage rises (because you are having to book more guests out). Interestingly enough, however, it is at its peak when you overbook by 13–14 per cent, which is a higher rate than one would expect. Of course, this rate is true *only* for this particular set of figures. However, the 'optimum' overbooking rate is generally higher than you would think, and the demonstration does show the value of using spreadsheets as a guide to management action, though you *must* remember that consistent overbooking to a point which guarantees that some guests will have to be 'walked' may constitute a Trades Descriptions Act offence.

A final point is that overbooking is not just a question of figures. It has an inter-personal aspect, too, because you are dealing with *people*. What usually happens is that you begin to be aware that there is a problem looming when you find your stock of unallocated rooms dwindling more rapidly than the outstanding names on your arrivals list. Eventually you realize that you are going to have to 'walk' one or two of the remainder. Three questions now present themselves. Which ones do you 'walk', what do you tell them, and who should do the telling?

The criteria for deciding who to 'walk' will vary from hotel to hotel. The fairest method would seem to be 'first come, first served' but this means that you may have to do it to favoured regulars or customers linked to important clients. Avoiding this can involve you in some difficult decisions, especially if there are only a couple of rooms left.

The question of what to tell those you are booking out is even more difficult, especially since they may arrive before those to whom you have given preference. It certainly doesn't do your customer relations much good to tell a guest that he is going to be unlucky because you have overbooked and got it wrong! There are tales of hotels which have maintained an 'Excuse of the Day' book in order to avoid repeating the well worn 'I'm sorry, we've had an accident with the central heating and your room is uninhabitable' story. We will have to leave this to your own personal sense of ethics and (if appropriate) your imagination.

Who should do the telling? This is an unpleasant task, and one which is often shirked. Any receptionist *ought* to be able to handle it, but if you look at it from the customer's point of view you will realize that it is properly the responsibility of the reception manager or someone of equivalent status. After all, the hotel is really letting the customer down, and it ought to show that it is treating the matter seriously.

Increasing average room rates

The second possible line of approach is to get the guest to spend more. Since we are only concerned with room revenue here, we will not consider the way in which front office can help to promote the hotel's other services and facilities, though this is also an important part of the job. We will also ignore the most obvious way of increasing the average spend, namely, raising the tariff rates, since that is a marketing decision, and in this chapter we are only looking at what front office staff can do. You may feel that this doesn't leave very much, but you would be wrong. What you can do is *sell*.

Selling accommodation is much like selling any other product. There are a number of simple techniques which are taught on sales courses, and which you should keep in mind. They are (in no particular order):

1 *Sell hospitality* This involves using the appropriate body language, including smiles. Nobody ever sold much by looking gloomy. You have to make your customers like you, and the simplest way to do that is to show that you like them. It also includes lots of eye contact. This shows that you are interested in the other person and concerned for their welfare, which is exactly the impression you want to convey. Nobody ever sold much by looking disinterested and unconcerned, either. Remember, too, that your body language

can 'signal' whether you are telling the truth or not. Open hands and a clear, steady gaze spell 'trust' in most cultures, whereas a sideways look and a nervous movement of the hand towards the mouth suggest duplicity.

2 *Use the prospective guest's name, and keep on using it*   People respond well enough to 'Sir' or 'Madam', but these are still a little impersonal. Addressing somebody by their name (e.g. 'Mr Johnson') still shows respect, but adds a touch of personal recognition as well. Whatever you do, *don't* refer to them by their room number (e.g. 'Number 447')!

3 *Sell value*   The main problem you face is that rooms are generally booked 'sight unseen': in other words, at a distance and some considerable time before the accommodation is actually used. In these circumstances it is difficult to convince the would-be guest of the superior advantages of the higher-priced rooms. It is much easier if he can see them side by side with the cheaper ones and compare their facilities. Outside hotels, a lot of selling is done in this way: you go into a store to buy something with a low price tag, then find yourself walking out with something much more expensive because the salesperson has taken the opportunity to show you a better quality product (sometimes very cheap items are deliberately advertised to bring customers in and give the sales staff the chance to push the more expensive items: this is called 'switch selling'). 'Showing' rooms is difficult but not impossible. In a small hotel you can actually take a guest up to the rooms and literally show them the different facilities: you will often find that they will agree to take a more expensive room once they have seen that it really *is* better. In a larger hotel this is more difficult, but you can still do a lot. Some hotels use photographs, while others rely on the receptionist's descriptive powers. Try to learn all about the facilities, and endeavour to find something extra to say about the more expensive types of room. Don't just say 'We have some singles at £45. . . .' Try 'We have some very comfortable singles at £45: they all have baths and toilets en suite and excellent views of the lake. . . .' You may not have a lake nearby, of course, but you can always find *something* good to say about the facilities on offer. Make a point of finding this out before you have to deal with any enquiries.

4 *Use the 'sandwich'*   No, this isn't something sent up by room service, but a term used to describe the salesperson's technique of putting an unwelcome bit of news in between two 'nice' ones. In most cases the unwelcome news is the price. The 'nice' bits can be almost anything which makes the would-be guest feel better or gives him some justification for spending that amount of money. For instance 'Singles, sir? Yes (smile), we *do* have a number of singles available. The larger ones are priced at £45, but they all have baths and toilets en suite and they also have excellent views of the lake. . . .' This approach starts with two or three positive touches (the 'Sir', the smile, the welcome news that you *do* have some singles). It then goes on to the (presumably) unwelcome news that the rooms cost £45, but follows that up immediately with a number of reasons why.

5 *Sell high*   You might well have two classes of single, a cheaper one at £30 and a better one at £45. If someone rings up to ask the price, don't do as so many receptionists do and say 'We have some at £30 and some others at £45. . . .' That way you are really telling the guest that he can enjoy all the public facilities of your hotel for £30. It is very difficult to persuade a customer to move upwards once you have indicated your lowest price, whereas it is fairly easy for you to come down. Launch into your spiel about the advantages of the dearer rooms. If your caller says something like 'Well, I don't know . . .' in a doubtful tone, you can always go on to add something like 'Of course, we also have some slightly smaller rooms at £30 each. They don't have baths or toilets en suite, but they do have a shower cubicle and they're very comfortable. . . .'

6 *Assume that the prospective guest wants to stay at your hotel*   It is possible to convert an enquiry

into a booking by subtly 'nudging' a caller so that he moves from an uncommitted standpoint to one where he finds himself confirming a booking, almost without realizing that the decision has been taken. Consider the following dialogue:

Recep: 'Smoothline Hotel, Tracy speaking. How can I help you?'
Caller: 'Would you have a single room for two nights, arriving next Tuesday?'
Recep: 'Just a moment, please: I'll check. What name is it, please?'
Caller: 'Mr Johnson.'
Recep: 'Thank you, Mr Johnson. I won't be a moment.' (*Pause*) 'Hello, Mr Johnson, yes, we *do* have room available. The rate is £45 and the room has a bath and toilet and an excellent view of the lake. . . . Would that be acceptable?'
Caller: 'Er, yes.'
Recep: 'What time would you be arriving, Mr Johnson?'
Caller: 'Er, about half past six I should think. Maybe a little later if I get held up on the motorway.'
Recep: 'No problem, Mr Johnson. I'll put it down as a possible late arrival. Could you give me a telephone number, just in case?'
Caller: 'Well, my . . . my work number is.' (*Gives number.*)
Recep: 'Thank you, Mr Johnson. And your address?'
Caller: 'Er . . .' (*Gives address.*)
Recep: (*Briskly*) 'Thank you very much, Mr Johnson. That's a provisional single booking for Tuesday next, possibly arriving a little late. Can you confirm that for us before then?'
Caller: 'Well, yes, I suppose so.'
Recep: 'Fine, Mr Johnson. We'll look forward to seeing you, then.'

Hopefully this shows how someone who is initially only making an enquiry can be 'nudged' gently but firmly into confirming a booking. The receptionist starts with a relatively neutral question ('What name is it, please'), then moves on from that (using the caller's name as often as possible) to describe the room (note the use of the 'sandwich' and how she 'sells high': if the caller sounds doubtful about the price she can quickly go on to mention the cheaper singles). These are followed by more loaded questions ('Would that be acceptable?' and 'What time would you be arriving?'), carefully using the conditional tense at this point. As the caller commits himself by revealing more and more information, the receptionist moves in to clinch the sale, briefly summarizing the details of the contract and making it clear that she *expects* the caller to go through with it.

There are other approaches which can be used to increase the average spend. When business is slow and rooms plentiful you could try suggesting to a couple who want a twin that they might prefer two singles instead. You would have to pick your customers very carefully: this isn't likely to appeal to a pair of obvious honeymooners, but it *might* to a more elderly couple who normally occupy separate rooms at home. Two singles at reduced rates should still net you a bit more than one twin, and it would be value for money as far as the guests were concerned.

This last sentence is important. You are not trying to 'con' anyone out of money. You are trying to draw their attention to the superior facilities on offer, and to convince them that these are worth the extra money. If you genuinely *believe* this, then you will sound convincing, and conviction is vitally important in selling. In the end, the foundations of successful selling are simple:

- *Know* your product.
- *Believe* in your product.

An example

In 1974 the well-known American hotel writer and consultant C. DeWitt Coffman wrote an article in the *Cornell Quarterly* describing how he went about improving sales revenue in hotels. Coffman said that 'In almost any hotel it is possible to get the average daily room rate increased over what it was in the month just passed – without raising the posted rates.'

This sentence needs careful analysis. The reference to the *average* rate means that Coffman was not concerned so much with increasing the occupancy percentages as with actually persuading each guest to pay more. And this was to be done without raising the tariffs (i.e. the 'posted rates').

How Coffman went about this provides an object lesson in terms of (a) accommodation selling and (b) management approach. The latter, as you should be aware, involves planning, organizing, motivating and controlling. Let us see how Coffman's approach illustrated each of these functions.

1 *Planning*   Coffman's first step was to establish realistic targets. He did this by taking the average occupancy percentage and then multiplying this by the maximum listed rates, assuming the best possible set of circumstances (e.g. all the 'dearest' rooms being sold first). This established the *maximum* possible letting revenue. He then did the same calculation using the worst possible set of assumptions (i.e. all the cheapest rooms being sold first). This established the theoretical *minimum* letting revenue. He then compared these figures with what the hotel was actually achieving. In theory, this should have fallen in between the maximum and minimum figures. In practice, it generally didn't, because of discounts and various other concessions. Coffman cited a 200 room motel with an average occupancy of 70 per cent, where the maximum revenue should have been around $1,250,000 and the minimum $1,000,000: the *actual* revenue was $900,000. Finally, Coffman established a target increase. In the example quoted, this was about $100,000, which is slightly over 10 per cent. Remember that this was to be achieved within a month or two, and without any increases in tariffs.

2 *Organizing*   Coffman began with a process which he called 'guest testing'. He or his assistants would pretend to be would-be guests and make a number of calls, using letters, telephone calls and personal visits and spreading these over the hotel's working week to cover as many of the staff as possible. Some of the calls would purport to be from important executives, others from special groups such as honeymooners or nervous little old ladies. The receptionists' performances were analysed under the following headings:

- 'Appearance' (including voice)
- Courtesy
- Promptness
- Sales efficiency

Obviously, the 'bookings' would not come to anything, but this would not matter since they would be written off as no shows. Having obtained a full picture of the hotel's current practices, Coffman would then visit the hotel and address a meeting of all the front office staff. There he would describe his 'guest testing' programme and outline his findings. This would involve criticizing some of the things the receptionists had been doing, but Coffman would never identify any individuals. Instead, he would take the opportunity to launch a training programme to set things right. The programme included a training manual which covered many of the points we have already looked at, such as persuading doubles to occupy separate singles during slower periods, persuading singles to 'double up' in peak periods (perhaps not so easy in todays' climate of opinion), using the 'sandwich' when quoting rates, and discouraging the indiscriminate offering of special rates. However, the main technique he advocated went further. It involved some of the points we have looked at, but was based primarily on the idea of actually getting the guest into the lobby *before* the contract was finalized. As you should be aware, face-to-face selling is by far the most effective method and this becomes impossible if the contract is concluded at a distance. The technique was tailored to suit the typical American situation where a lot of enquiries come in via courtesy phones at stations, airports and similar places. Such enquiries normally involve 'same day' bookings, and Coffman's receptionists were trained to adopt a three-part strategy.

(a) On receipt of such a call, they simply confirmed that there were rooms available and invited the traveller to come direct to the hotel, where they assured him he would be made very comfortable. On arrival, he was then allocated one of the higher-priced rooms without any discussion about rates.

(b) If the would-be guest asked about rates (either over the phone or after arrival), Coffman's instructions were to 'sell high': in other words, to quote the highest feasible rate and if possible to avoid quoting any other.

(c) If the would-be guest tried to negotiate a lower rate, Coffman's instructions were to avoid confirming this in advance. The manual contained a number of standard phraseologies, and the one suggested for this situation was 'we can't guarantee that rate, but we'll do our best to give it to you, or one close to it.' If the guest then turned up at the hotel, the receptionist was supposed to follow rule (a) and move him up at least one rate.

Obviously, these recommendations could not be followed in all cases, but their overall effect was that a significant number of guests would be likely to end up in somewhat more expensive rooms than they would have selected if allowed to choose for themselves.

3 *Motivating* Coffman recognized that many receptionists would be reluctant to practise this kind of 'hard selling' without some kind of incentive. He accepted that it was difficult to assess individual contributions to increased room rates targets, and suggested that the healthiest scheme was a central pool, with something like 10 per cent of any increase being divided among the room clerks, sales manager and night manager's sections in proportions to be agreed by the staff themselves.

4 *Controlling* Coffman knew perfectly well that staff would not be able to put these ideas into practice all at once, so the final part of the process was a series of follow up 'guest tests', with refresher classes as necessary and a set of 'reminder' cards and posters displayed over a period of time.

Obviously, this approach would not be suitable for all types of hotel, nor for all market segments. We have quoted it here because it is one of the best examples available of 'hard selling' taken to its logical conclusion, and because it does give us some idea of the limits of the possible. Remember that Coffman was a successful hotel consultant, and that he had actually put these ideas into practice. Remember, too, Coffman's contention that average room revenue could be increased by something like 10 per cent without increasing either occupancies *or* room rates.

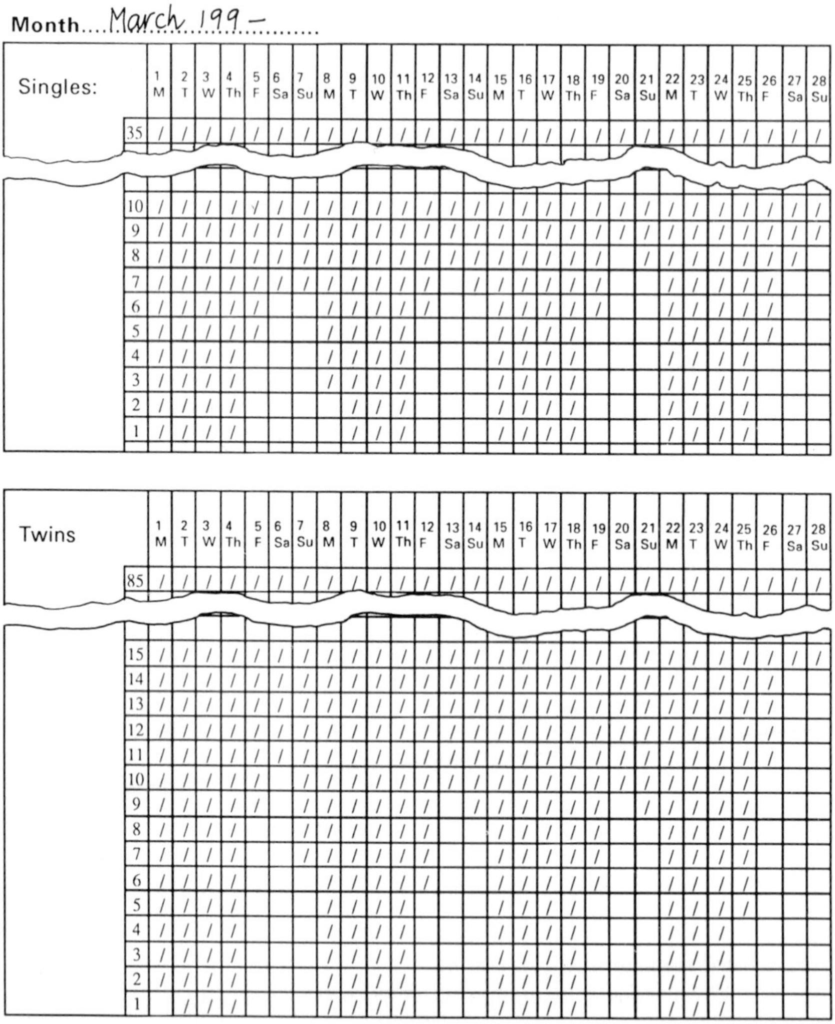

Month....March 199 —........

Figure 65 — reservations/occupancy chart

Singles:

Top row total: 35

Rows (10 down to 1): density chart of bookings for days 1–28 (M T W Th F Sa Su repeating).

Twins

Top row total: 85

Rows (15 down to 1): density chart of bookings for days 1–28 (M T W Th F Sa Su repeating).

Occupancy report:

	1	2	3	4	5	6	7	8	9	10	11	12	13	14	15	16	17	18	19	20	21	22	23	24	25	26	27	28
	M	T	W	Th	F	Sa	Su	M	T	W	Th	F	Sa	Su	M	T	W	Th	F	Sa	Su	M	T	W	Th	F	Sa	Su
Singles	32	33	33	32	27	26	30	32	33	32	27	26	30	31	33	31	27	23	26	32	33	31	31	28	24	25		
Twins	78	76	76	78	69	66	69	74	72	79	78	70	68	71	82	79	76	77	72	67	65	77	78	76	74	66	61	62

Figure 65

Assignments

1   A hotel has thirty-five singles and eighty-five twins. The singles are priced at £38 each and the twins at £68. The preceding four-week period yielded the figures shown in Figure 65 and you expect the booking pattern for the next period to be very similar. Calculate the optimum overbooking rate on the assumption that the average cost of booking out is £12 per person.

2   The hotel is the same as in Assignment 1. Although one of the standard booking conditions is that the room will only be held after 6.30 pm if prior notice of late arrival is received, this provision is seldom enforced. On Day 2 of the following period (a Tuesday) you have taken thirty-eight single bookings. Of these, thirty-three have checked in and registered by 7.30 pm and you are left with the following outstanding names on your Arrivals List:

Name	Stay	Confirmed	Comments
Armstrong G Mr	1 Night	Yes	Regular. Usually arrives by car by 6.00 pm or earlier. No explanation for delay.
Jones Ls Mr	3 Nights	Yes	Not known. Three-month old booking reconfirmed last week, but no note about late arrival.
Tibbs S Miss	1 Night	Yes	Booked through travel agent: known to be elderly, disabled and likely to arrive late.
Schmidt J Herr	2 Nights	Yes	German, booked through regular account customer (a large local company). No note re late arrival, but flights known to be delayed.
Palfrey S Mr	1 Night	No	Booked two weeks ago, request for confirmation ignored. Claims to know your company's chairman. No note of late arrival.

You have an arrangement with a nearby hotel, and you have already confirmed that they can take two or three extra guests. You also have one 'chance' customer in the lobby, a Mr Atkins, who wants to stay for three nights. He is respectably dressed, carries appropriate luggage and appears able and willing to pay. What should you do? (*Note*: There is no reason why you shouldn't run this like the role playing exercises in the previous chapter. Appoint one person as receptionist, and another as front office manager. Let them confer. Then allocate the 'customer' roles to other members of the group, and let them enter one by one in random order.)

3   You are a receptionist at the Takem Inn, operating on Coffman's principles. You have three classes of singles available, respectively £75, £60 and £45 each. You are required to respond to the following callers, all of whom are using your courtesy phone at the local airport and who need accommodation for tonight. There is little spare accommodation elsewhere:

Caller A: Should be timorous, reluctant to make a fuss and rather nervous about the prospect of not being able to obtain accommodation at all.

Caller B: This caller will try to establish the room price, but should be fairly easy going and not too hard to influence. It may help to think of him as being able to charge the cost against expenses.

Caller C: A competitive and aggressive character keenly interested in limiting his expenses.

(*Note*: This should be conducted on a role play basis in conformity with the suggestions outlined earlier. The roles should be switched around and the 'calls' taken in random order.)

4 Discuss front office's role in increasing the hotel's *overall* sales (i.e. food and beverage and other receipts as well as room revenue).

5 Outline a possible incentive scheme for front office staff which might be introduced by either the Tudor or Pancontinental Hotel.

8 Marketing aspects

Introduction

We have seen that front office can do more than is sometimes thought in terms of selling accommodation. However, the real task of bringing the customers in is properly the concern of the marketing department. Much of the work of this department lies outside the scope of this book, for a number of reasons. First, it is concerned with the hotel as a whole, including banqueting and other facilities as well as rooms. Second, it is often concerned with a whole group of hotels, and third, marketing itself is a much broader concept than mere 'selling'.

According to the British Institute of Marketing, 'Marketing is the management process responsible for identifying, anticipating and satisfying customer requirements profitably.' We might quibble at the last word, since non-profit making organizations ought to be doing these things too, but the definition shows that marketing covers a number of activities which do not form part of the day-to-day work of the front office department, such as consumer orientation (buyer behaviour and social changes within the environment), market research (assessing consumers' needs and competitors' activities), competition analysis (finding out what the opposition is offering and how it compares with your 'package'), product analysis (your package's strengths and weaknesses), pricing, promotion (including advertising and selling) and marketing control.

Nevertheless, these activities *do* impinge on the work of the front office manager and staff, and everyone ought to be aware of the importance of what is called a 'marketing orientation'. As we have already pointed out, room revenue is vital to a hotel. Accommodation staff *must* rid themselves of the old-fashioned attitude that they are only there to handle bookings, and that how the would-be guest comes to hear of the hotel in the first place, or what he thinks of it as a result of his stay, is none of their business.

Hotel marketing as a whole is too large a subject to compress into one chapter, and we recommend that you read one of the many excellent texts on this subject. We do not propose to deal with the intricacies of market research, for instance, nor with advertising or public relations. However, there are certain 'borderline' topics which do properly form part of the business of front office staff (and are sometimes not fully covered by the straightforward marketing texts), and we propose to devote the remainder of this chapter to these.

Reaching the customer: advertising

Hotels as a whole face a peculiar problem in terms of reaching their markets. Apart from the giant corporations involved in the mass-consumption markets (soap powders, confectionery etc.), most commercial organizations fall into one of two classes in this connection:

1   Their market is local, and thus easily reached through media such as local newspapers, TV, cinema advertisements and the like. Most restaurants fall into this category.
2   Their market is dispersed over the country as a whole, but is linked together by a common enthusiasm so that it can be reached via 'special interest' journals. There are any number of these magazines available, catering for interests as diverse as boat-owning, computing, dog breeding and walking.

Hotel groups are not usually large enough to be able to afford mass-media advertising. This means that they must be more selective. However, the hotel's market is, by definition, not a local one. There are always some guests who live nearby (they may be moving house, for instance, or reluctant to drive home after a celebration), and a certain number of bookings which result from local recommendations (neighbouring businesses will often arrange accommodation for visitors with nearby hotels), but the greater part of a hotel's business comes from people who live some distance away and who have few ties with the locality (if they had, they might well be invited to stay in private houses). Moreover, guests do not usually come from one particular region alone. There are of course exceptions to this (North Wales has traditionally drawn many of its visitors from the North West, just as North East England has attracted a large number from Central Scotland), but in most cases visitors come from a variety of regions and even countries. This makes localized advertising difficult.

Nor is the hotel's market a specialized one. There are business people, true, but they are seldom restricted to only one sector of industry, and there are also lawyers, teachers, engineers, painters and little old ladies visiting their nieces or nephews at college. All these people have little in common except a need to stay in a particular locality for one or more nights. In other words, the market is very heterogeneous, and this makes it difficult to reach it via any of the 'special interest' periodicals we have mentioned.

All this creates considerable problems, and hotels commonly use third parties as intermediaries as a result. This makes sense since hotels are often situated a long way from their customers, and it is a good idea to get some local agency to do the selling for them. This costs money in the form of commissions, of course, but then so does advertising.

Reaching the customer: intermediate agencies

Let us consider the various means by which hotels and their customers can be brought together (Figure 66).

One of the points to consider in connection with Figure 66 is whether the intermediary is an 'agent' in law or a principal. If a travel agent books accommodation on behalf of a customer, your contract is with the customer, not with the agency, and since an agent cannot be liable for the actions of his principal, you cannot claim damages from him if the customer does not turn up. On the other hand, tour operators normally book accommodation on their own account directly with the hotel. If they are then unable to persuade enough people to come on the tour, that is their loss. The question of whether someone is acting as an agent or a principal can be a difficult one, but it is clearly important.

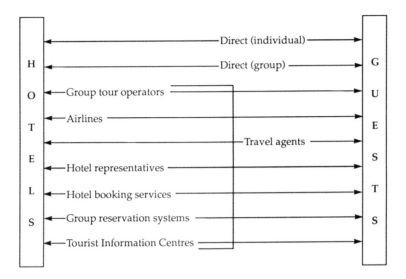

Figure 66

Direct individual sales

This first mechanism is the most obvious one. The would-be guest somehow obtains information about the hotels in his chosen destination, chooses one, and then contacts it by letter, telephone or some other mechanism. The process is a basically simple one, and the only parties involved are the hotel and the customer.

Of course, the customer has to find out about the hotel first. This involves some kind of advertising or promotion. We have already invited you to come to your own conclusions about this, but you should be aware that typical methods include mentions in guide books, local accommodation brochures, or directories such as the AA or RAC handbooks. Since one of the themes we shall be emphasizing in this section is that hotels have to *pay* to reach their customers, we might point out that such 'mentions' are seldom free. There is usually a charge of some kind, even if it comes in the form of a subscription to whatever local agency might be promoting and distributing the brochure.

One of the main problems with direct contact is that the customer is usually located a considerable distance from the hotel. This means that he has to place a long-distance telephone call in order to make an advance booking, and might have to repeat this several times in order to obtain a room at a particularly busy period. This costs money and (what is often worse) often takes a good deal of time. Most of the intermediaries shown in Figure 66 exist in order to save the customer this kind of trouble.

However, not all travellers bother, or are able, to arrange accommodation in advance, and a hotel can always appeal directly to these. Roadside advertisements are examples of this approach, especially when combined with displays saying 'Vacancies' or 'No Vacancies'. Motels in particular often rely largely on these, for obvious reasons. Advertisements in or near local railway stations can serve much the same purpose. One of the best illustrations of this approach is the row of courtesy phones to be found in American airports: leased by local hotel companies they put the passenger through directly to the hotel's front desk. Hotels have actually located their own front desks and receptionists at some airports (Hong Kong, for instance). All these are examples of the hotel trying to lessen the 'distance' between the would-be guest and its sales desk.

Direct group sales

Many 'direct' bookings are actually made on behalf of groups of one sort or another. Some of these are relatively small, such as sports clubs outings, overnight functions etc., but others can be very large, such as major conferences. These are sometimes arranged by specialist agencies, but quite often the organizer prefers to deal with the hotel directly.

We shall look more closely at conferences later. At the moment, we are only concerned to note that such groups are such an important source of business that they are an exception to the usual rule that it is not worth the hotel's while to try to contact the customer directly for some face-to-face selling. A conference organizer might bring in several hundred visitors, with all their ancillary expenditure.

As members of the group doing the booking, conference organizers are not usually entitled to any kind of commission. However, they *are* influential, and they do quite often relieve the hotel of a certain number of administrative chores, so that some kind of personal incentive is both called for and justifiable. The size of the group itself can be reflected in the price reduction offered to members, whereas the conference organizer can be rewarded (or compensated) by a complimentary room.

Travel agents

These are a familiar feature of every high street. There are two main types of travel agent in existence:

1   *Retail agents*   These are the common and familiar high street agents who sell direct to the public. Their business is to arrange holidays for their customers, including coach and rail trips, cruises, flights and (this is the bit which concerns us) hotel accommodation. Some are actually retail outlets for large tour operators, but most are small, independently-owned businesses.
2   *Company agents*   Some city centre agencies specialize in business house travel. However, organizations such as the major multinational companies are so big that it is worth their while to have their own travel agency to handle all their business. Sometimes they buy one outright, sometimes they simply invite a small agency to specialize in their business. Either way, the agency is likely to handle a lot of valuable bookings. It receives commission in the usual way, though some of its profits are likely to be passed on to its parent company or major client.

Travel agents can, and do, deal directly with hotels. However, much of their work lies in selling 'packages' for other specialist firms, so a large part of their business has been channelled through these. This situation may well change as a result of developments in booking systems described later.

Travel agents make their money from commissions received on the sale of ticket and bookings. Since tickets are fixed in price the mechanism is fairly simple. The agency simply carries a stock of blank tickets and simply remits the money, less the commission, to the carrier when it sells one. Hotel accommodation is more awkward because the cost of the final bill is unknown (there may be 'extras' like drinks and laundry, for instance). In some cases the agency simply arranges the booking and then invoices the hotel for its commission in due course. This has been known to lead to delays and even non-payments. Since there is generally a time lag, the records are difficult to check and may not show that the booking was an agency one anyway, and of course, the guest may not have turned up. It also leads to problems in terms of currency exchange, since the amounts are often relatively small and are sometimes exceeded by the clearing charges (though Utell International, one of the big international booking agencies, will cash such cheques in their country of origin and pay you the equivalent).

In other cases, the travel agent may get the customer to pay a deposit, which it then forwards to the hotel after deducting its commission. This is more satisfactory, except that the smaller agencies have been known to have cash flow problems and sometimes the customer arrives before the deposit. Credit facilities should only be extended to travel agents if they have been approved by IATA and are members of their own national association.

Finally, the agency may charge the customer the whole of the accommodation cost in advance and issue him with a voucher in exchange. He presents this to the hotel, which then credits him with the amount. The hotel then presents the voucher to the travel agent concerned and receives payment less commission in return. Agency vouchers are very convenient for the agencies (which get their payment in advance) and for the customers, but they need to be inspected with some care since there is no standardization. Some agencies issue impressive looking 'passports' which actually do not commit them to paying anything at all.

Group tour operators

These include the familiar names whose brochures you will find in a retail travel agent. Many of the larger ones have their own retail outlets, which offer the usual high street travel agency services as well. In all, they sell an enormous number of holiday 'packages' and book a comparable amount of space at hotels.

This category also includes a vast number of smaller operators of various sorts. Some undertake 'speciality' work, arranging battlefield or birdwatching tours, safaris, ski trips and the like. Others specialize in arranging conferences. One of the fastest-growing sectors is that of incentive travel, usually arranged by a company for its clients or its successful sales staff and agents. This is a specialized field, and it has attracted its own full-time incentive travel companies which provide a range of consultancy and administrative services for firms wishing to arrange such trips.

Group tour operators do not receive commission because they are not introducing clients but rather booking the space themselves. They make their money from the difference between the cost of the separate elements of the 'package' (transport, food, accommodation, entertainment etc.) and the price they are able to charge for it. Clearly, the more cheaply such an operator can obtain hotel accommodation the better from his point of view, so negotiations with them are keen, especially since the volume of business they control gives them enormous leverage.

Foreign tour operators often delegate local arrangement to specialist companies called 'ground handlers', who make transportation, tour and other arrangements on behalf of their principals. This means that while your basic contract is with the tour operator, detailed arrangements may be in the hands of someone else. Since the ground handler is usually local, this is helpful rather than otherwise.

We shall look at the operational problems associated with dealing with groups later.

Airlines

The major airlines are in a special position, since they are very large and commercially very powerful. The nature of their operations means that they are constantly having to send their flight crews to 'overnight' in hotels all over the world, and this in itself means that they create a considerable amount of business.

In addition, they deal with an enormous number of travellers. Most of these book their flights initially through travel agents, but there are still many who do so directly with the airlines. In either case, such travellers often find it convenient to arrange other services such as car hire and hotel accommodation at their destinations as part of the booking process. This puts the airlines in much the same position as the nineteenth-century railway companies, who also used to make hotel bookings for their passengers, and who even found it profitable to own and operate their own hotels.

Moreover, the airlines frequently have to make arrangements for travellers who may miss their onward connections through no fault of their own. Arranging overnight accommodation for a planeload of passengers held up by fog or some other operational problem is a common task for airline staff, and can be a useful source of business for hotels in the vicinity of major airports.

All this means that airlines are often able to insist on 'free sale' arrangements, whereby you allocate a block of rooms for them to sell, but they incur no penalty if they remain unsold.

One of the important points to note about the airlines is that they have developed superb bookings systems, which are increasingly being linked with the hotel industry's own group reservation systems. For a decade or more British travel agents have been able to confirm seat availability and make bookings on virtually any airline flight, even though each airline has its own computerized central bookings system. This has been made possible by means of a sophisticated central switching and translation service known as 'Travicom', which eliminates the need for each travel agency to have lots of different terminals. The system is shown diagrammatically in Figure 67.

Figure 67

Clearly, this offers a model for the hotel industry. As we shall see, the major hotel groups all have their own sophisticated central reservations systems, but as yet there is no equivalent to Travicom which would allow a travel agent direct access to each or any so that he could make bookings directly in the same way as he can now book flights. In the United States the situation is somewhat different. There the various airlines have their own 'single access' reservation systems. However, these are much more closely linked to the main hotel (and car hire) reservations systems so that the travel agents are able to book accommodation as well as seats on a 'real time' basis. Various developments are now underway in Europe to link airline and hotel reservation systems, and these are likely to have a profound effect on the way in which bookings are carried out.

Hotel representatives

Hotel representatives were originally an American institution, developed because the United States is a large country with widely dispersed centres of population and a lot of business travel. Hotel representatives base themselves in one such area (some now have worldwide representation) and act as sales and reservation agents on behalf of a number of non-competing hotels from other regions or countries. Local travel agents are able to make bookings for their clients quickly and cheaply, rather than incurring the expense involved in long-distance telephone calls. Representatives will also distribute your brochures and other promotional material locally. They are usually paid an annual fee plus commission on all the reservations they make.

Hotel booking agencies

Some areas are short of hotels and it is particularly difficult to find accommodation in them at busy times of the year. This is fine for the local hotels, but not much fun for those trying to make bookings there. This has led to the development of specialized hotel booking agencies.

Some of these offer this service to individuals. You can often find their outlets in important travel centres such as major railway stations. They are a particularly useful source for 'last-minute' bookings. As with most intermediaries, they make their money by charging commission on the bookings they arrange. This is frequently levied in a somewhat roundabout fashion. The client pays the agency a booking fee (typically about 12.5 per cent of the first night's accommodation charge) and receives a receipt. He then presents this to the hotel and has an equivalent amount deducted from his bill. This provides a quick, simple and foolproof mechanism for paying the agency.

Other hotel reservation agencies deal mainly with travel agents and offer a national, continental or even worldwide service. Smaller, participating hotels without elaborate computer facilities continue to use telex links between themselves and the agency, but the latter recognize that travel agents accustomed to interactive computerized airline booking do not want to continue booking hotel accommodation by telex or telephone, and have been investing in linking their own computers to the larger group reservation systems. Additional links with the airlines' own reservation systems are likely. Such agencies earn their living from commissions in the usual way, though there is usually also a 'systems' charge to cover the installation of any specialized equipment.

Group reservations systems

These are designed to help customers to book accommodation at any of the hotels within a group, usually with one local telephone call. They offer a useful service to the kind of travel agent which specializes in large business accounts and which may have to make a number of bookings at different locations at the same time. However, the facility can also be useful to the individual tourist, who is able to make a booking at a distant hotel with one local call. Another incidental advantage is that they make it easier for the group to monitor overall booking trends.

Although we have used the term 'group' reservation systems, independent hotels can offer the same facility by joining what is known as a reservations consortium. At its simplest, this means that each participating hotel undertakes to recommend its partners, which it guarantees will be of equivalent standard. A rather more elaborate version of this system actually sets up a central reservations system which operates on the same lines as those run by the larger chains.

Group reservation systems began in the United States, where there has always been a considerable amount of long distance business travel. Hilton and Sheraton developed systems based on teletype connections. British groups also developed their own systems during the late 1960s. There was even an attempt to create a national system in 1969 under the auspices of the HCIEDC (Hotel, Catering and Institutional Economic Development Council). However, many of the larger groups refused to join this because they feared that the business it brought them would be 'substitutional, not additional' (in other words, people who would normally have booked with them directly would now go through the new system). This doomed the HCIEDC scheme, which operated at a loss for three years and was wound up in 1972.

This underlines the basic problem with the earlier schemes, namely, that they were expensive to operate. They usually required a central reservations office *in addition* to the hotel's own back offices, and that cost money. Typically, a customer would ring the central office and enquire about room availability at a particular hotel. In some cases the central office would have to ring the hotel and then ring the customer back: in others the system was streamlined so that the central office had 'free sale' rights unless or until these were withdrawn by the hotel. In either case, the central office would have to let the hotel have details of the bookings as quickly as possible. This meant that each booking had to be handled twice, once by the central office and once by the hotel. Moreover, the communication costs were transferred from the customer (who only made a local call) to the hotel group (which still had to transmit the information from the central office to the hotels).

It is difficult to be precise about the actual level of costs. One major group made its central reservations office a separate subsidiary which they charged the group hotels 15 per cent of the accommodation cost for all bookings made through it. Other groups did not reveal their central reservation unit's costs, but there are indications that these were usually around 10–12 per cent of the value of the bookings handled. Even if they did not create separate subsidiaries, good accounting practice would have led them to charge their participating units in proportion to the amount of use they made of the service.

As a result, individual hotels tended to use central reservations agencies (both group and independent) when they needed to boost their occupancies (in other words, they 'bought' bookings), but tended to opt out when they thought they could fill up without their help. This was of course precisely when the customers needed the service most! As a result, the groups handled only about 10 per cent of their bookings through their central reservations systems.

They were mainly used by travel agents, and there were some indications that the systems were not actively promoted once usage had reached a certain level.

This situation began to change following the introduction of computers. As early as the 1960s, Holiday Inns introduced a computerized system whereby all their hotels were linked to one central computer, allowing would-be guests to book at any member of the chain through their local Holiday Inn. This was based on a large central mainframe computer, which effectively replaced the central reservation office and was probably equally expensive. Nowadays, much smaller computers located in individual hotels can communicate directly with one another, eliminating the need for a separate central office or facility and thus reducing the cost. The two alternative approaches are shown diagrammatically in Figure 68.

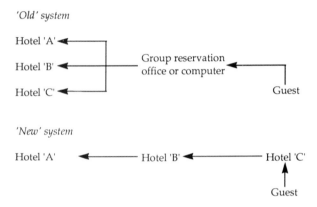

Figure 68

Under the new system, the guest can call the group hotel nearest to his home (Hotel 'C' in this case) and make a booking at any hotel within the group. The various hotel computers are linked by leased cables, and the receptionist can call up either her own booking chart *or* the charts for Hotels 'A', 'B' etc., and make a booking directly into one of the latter.

The advantages are obvious. The costs are very much reduced because the bookings are now only handled *once*. In theory, there should be little or no extra work for the receptionist (it is possible that those in 'outlying' hotels might find themselves handling more enquiries for popular ones in central locations, but the overall effect will be to distribute the national workload more evenly). The cost of the necessary computer hardware and software can be discounted, because the computers themselves would have been introduced in any case and the cost of the extra programming required to support the interchange of information is relatively insignificant. This leaves communication as the only cost penalty still being incurred (the customer is only making a local call and the charge for transmitting the details from Hotel 'C' to Hotel 'A' falls on the group), but this is acceptable because the service to the customer is greatly improved. It is not surprising that groups which have introduced this type of system claim that usage has increased dramatically (a rise from 10 per cent to something like 50 per cent has been mentioned).

At the time of writing, British hotels have not yet gone as far as some other organizations in making their systems accessible to travel agents and other intermediaries. As we have seen, travel agents have had access to airline central computers for some time, and the advantages of being able to make bookings directly have become clear. More recently, hotel bookings agencies and the major tour operators have done much the same thing, and the hotel industry has begun to follow their lead. This would allow travel agents to book comprehensive 'tailormade' packages combining both transport and accommodation. As we have indicated previously, this trend is likely to continue.

Tourist Information Centres

The idea behind the Tourist Information Centre is quite different to that of the group reservation system. The latter aims to help customers to book at group or consortium hotels anywhere in the country (or sometimes the world). A Tourist Information Centre aims (among other things) to help customers to book accommodation at any hotel within its own local area. It resembles the hotel booking service except that it is not a commercial enterprise but a local government service.

The Tourist Information Centre also differs from most of the other intermediaries in terms of the type of customer it deals with. Group reservation systems tend to be set up by the big international hotel chains and used by agencies specializing in business travel services. Tourist Information Centre booking services tend to be used by private individuals interested in much cheaper accommodation, often of the bed and breakfast type.

Information services for tourists are very much a European institution. Holland introduced them as long ago as the 1890s, and now has close to 500 'VVVs' (the Dutch term) at village, district and provincial level, all coordinated by a national advisory body which has standardized reservation procedures. Most other European countries have similar systems. Some are operated by local authorities, some by regional governments.

The basis for their financing differs in detail, but typically some 60 per cent of their funds comes from the local or regional government, 20 per cent from registration fees paid by listed hotels and other establishments (restaurants, camp and caravan sites and the like), and 20 per cent from profits on the services provided for tourists (the sale of maps, guides, profits on sightseeing tours etc.).

The Tourist Information Centres' main role is to provide information about local tourist facilities in general, including details of shops and restaurants, historic buildings and other sights, current and forthcoming events like festivals and other celebrations. They stock maps and directories, and sell or arrange tickets for attractions such as the 'Son et Lumiere' displays to be found throughout France during the summer. They often arrange trips and employ their own tour guides. They also provide details of local hotels and boarding houses, and the great majority will undertake to arrange accommodation booking.

Although such accommodation booking is only one of their activities, it is the one which concerns us here. In principle, every establishment within the municipality is registered with the Tourist Information Centre and classified according to location, type, facilities and price (you should remember that most European countries have compulsory registration, classification and grading of hotels, and frequently a degree of price control as well). A clerk approached by a tourist seeking accommodation can then ask 'Which part of town do you want to stay in, and how much do you want to pay?', select an appropriate hotel on the basis of the responses, ring it up and make a booking on behalf of the tourist.

This has sometimes seemed to present a problem to those unfamiliar with the system, such as visitors from America, where the system is much less widely developed. The argument is sometimes advanced that an employee in a state or subscriber-based system cannot be impartial in recommending individual hotels. In practice, European agencies have been doing so for nearly a century now, and there have been very few accusations of bias.

The establishment of a system of Tourist Information Centres was a major priority for the English, Scottish and Welsh Tourist Boards when they were set up in 1969. England now has over 400 TICs, divided into three levels:

- Local: Covering the immediate vicinity only.
- Regional: Covering the Regional Tourist Board area.
- National: Covering the region and also providing a basic service covering the whole country.

In common with most European systems, the Tourist Information Centres are basically financed and staffed by the local authorities, but the English, Scottish and Welsh Tourist Boards provide signs, publicity material, displays, equipment, badges and uniforms, undertake training and provide some financial assistance.

For many years it was not obligatory for all British Tourist Information Centres to offer an accommodation booking service, but this became compulsory in 1988. These tourist accommodation services have typically been operated by maintaining lists of registered establishments (sometimes on sheets, sometimes on card indexes) and then either telephoning proprietors or asking them to telephone the centre with details of vacancies. The systems have varied considerably in terms of elaboration because of the differing size and resources of the Tourist Information Centres. The most sophisticated was probably the budget accommodation service operated by the London Tourist Board: this dealt with hundreds of clients daily over the summer high season and used a 'queueing' system whereby the customer was given a number and asked to wait while the staff rang round until they found him accommodation.

One of the problems with Tourist Information Centres has been that since they are staffed by local authority employees working under nationally agreed terms and conditions of service, they have often tended to be a little inflexible in terms of opening hours. This does not matter too much as far as much of their business is concerned, but it does create problems for the benighted traveller desperately searching for accommodation at 10 o'clock at night. The usual answer to this problem has been some form of window display giving the names, locations and phone numbers of local hotels. Over the past few years these have been computerized to some extent: typically, a VDU placed inside the window displays a 'menu' of information available: the customer can select the items he wants by pressing various buttons placed on the outside of the window. Although technically ingenious, these displays are still static rather than dynamic: in other words, they do not display current room availability.

All these were local services. There was also the national 'Book A Bed Ahead' Service, which was introduced in 1973 and operated mainly by the larger Tourist Information Centres. This guaranteed to find the traveller accommodation at any other location covered by the scheme up to twenty-four hours ahead. It was thus only an advance booking system in a very limited sense of the term. The mechanics were similar to those of the local service: the Tourist Information Centre telephoned its counterpart at the desired destination, which rang round its own local hotels until it found a suitable vacancy and then rang back. Since this generally involved two long-distance telephone calls, the customer was required to pay a fee for the service. The system as a whole is shown diagrammatically in Figure 69.

In principle, this arrangement could be developed into a national computerized reservations system, with each participating hotel being linked to its local TIC, and each TIC being able to access each other computer. However, this would require a very considerable

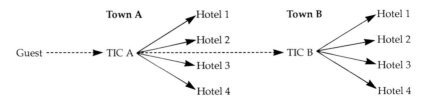

Figure 69

investment in terms of computer hardware and software. The Tourist Information Centres themselves could be equipped with similar computers all operating the same standard program, but the participating hotels come in all shapes and sizes, and many are likely to remain non-computerized in the foreseeable future, so that full realization of the ideal remains very distant.

Some preliminary steps have certainly been taken. During the early 1980s the English Tourist Board pioneered a viewdata system called 'Reservision'. More recently the Welsh Tourist Board has established three computerized central reservations services in its offices at Colwyn Bay (covering North Wales), Machynlleth (Mid Wales) and Swansea (South Wales). As with the hotels' own group reservation systems, some two-thirds of the usage has been by travel agents.

In addition, there is now at least one commercial service which links the individual hotel to its local Tourist Information Centre. The hotel's particulars (location, rooms, prices and special features) are stored on a microcomputer in the Tourist Information Centre. When a customer walks into the Tourist Information Centre, he is asked for his preferences in terms of location, price etc. The clerk enters these into the computer, which then displays a list of appropriate hotels. The hotels themselves rent terminals which they use to record details of current vacancies (these can be changed daily, hourly or even minute by minute if necessary). These terminals can be 'interrogated' by staff at the Tourist Information Centre via the ordinary telephone to determine current vacancies. When the customer selects a hotel, the Tourist Information Centre clerk checks its current room availability on the computer, then rings the hotel and makes the booking in the usual way. When the hotel accepts this, the Tourist Information Centre computer prints out a confirmation letter or slip, together with a receipt for any deposit which might have been requested.

Tourist Information Centres might seem to be an exception to the usual rule that intermediaries have to be paid in some way or other. However, this is not the case. As we have seen, they are financed out of central and local taxes. In addition, establishments have to pay to be listed (which entitles them to a 'Crown' classification in Britain) and sometimes have to pay an additional fee to become members of the accommodation bookings service. After some initial reluctance, the Boards now pay travel agents commission for bookings, which forms part of their operating expenses. In effect, the local hotels are paying such commission jointly through the agency.

The future

As we have indicated, booking systems are going through a series of major changes. The result is likely to be much more flexibility, with travel agents being able to tap into a great many more interactive hotel and Tourist Information reservation systems to make bookings directly on behalf of their clients.

There is a further possibility which needs consideration. The traditional direct booking has remained unaffected by all this technology, but this will not necessarily be the case in the future. 'Armchair shopping' is likely to become perfectly feasible, and the principle can easily be extended to accommodation booking. There is no technical reason why a householder should not be able to call up the hotel database covering his proposed destination (in other words, browse through a kind of vast electronic brochure), select whichever hotel he prefers because of its location, price and facilities, check its room availability, make a booking and even pay a deposit, all without having to leave the comfort of his home. Indeed, with fax-type facilities becoming more and more widespread, it is likely that he will be able to receive an immediate confirmation slip as well.

This prospect has aroused opposition from some travel agents, who see their own role as high street retailers being threatened. However, the number of hotels remains immense, and if the example of the airlines is anything to go by, rates are likely to become more rather than less complicated. Customers will still want help with these and advice regarding destinations in general. In the same way, the convenience of the specialized services offered by tour operators, hotel booking agencies and the like should continue to ensure their survival.

Moreover, people will still make last-minute travel decisions, and travellers will still be benighted by unforeseen events such as fog and strikes. In other words, there will always be a role for that oldest and most direct of all booking methods: the last minute walk in.

Selling to intermediaries

We have seen that intermediary booking agencies such as airlines, group tour operators and conference booking agencies are able to deliver large numbers of guests. It is thus well worth investing time and effort in trying to 'sell' the hotel to them. This is not usually part of the job of the ordinary receptionist but hotel sales departments are increasing in importance and you may find yourself involved in that side of operations one day. Moreover, front office managers sometimes have to do it. You should thus have some idea of what is involved.

The activity can be looked at under two headings:

1 Direct sales
2 Negotiating

Direct sales

The difference between direct sales and the kind of selling you do on reception (which we looked at in our last chapter) is that instead of waiting for the customers to come to you, here *you* go to them.

The first step, therefore, is to decide who are to be your sales targets. You have to analyse your sources of business, both actual and potential, so that you can increase the former and penetrate the latter. This comes under the heading of market research, which we do not propose to discuss at any length because it is dealt with fully in a number of excellent marketing textbooks.

The one point we would stress is that such research doesn't stop with the construction of the hotel or the preparation of the annual marketing plan. It should be a day-to-day activity. Does the local paper contain a report of a forthcoming event? It doesn't matter what this is: it can be a one-off centenary, an annual festival or a dog show; the question should be, is there any business in this? And just who would be able to deliver it? The organizers, perhaps, the local travel agents, or the local Tourist Information Centre? Again, the weather forecasts are worth watching. If fog is expected, the airline schedules might well be disrupted, and they and the tour operators may be in the market for beds. National or international transport strikes can have the same effect.

The targets for direct sales include travel agents, tour operators, exhibitors, short course organizers and conference organizers. And don't forget the local businesses, who often make a whole series of bookings for their visitors throughout the year. How do hotels go about selling to these individuals?

First, they find out who is the decision maker. Sometimes these are professionals who are easily identified, but quite often businesses delegate course or conference organization to somebody relatively junior. Organizing committees present yet another kind of problem since it is very often difficult to know precisely who carries the main 'clout'. A great deal of effort sometimes goes into the lobbying of delegates to the major national and international associations. This is a job for professionals and is outside the scope of this book, but the essential principles remain the same: discover who really makes the decision and concentrate your efforts on *him*.

Next, they choose the most appropriate method of approach. There are a number of these, and, like many other things, they are best used in combination. Let us look at them.

Direct mail

Direct mail is the term used for the kind of circular letter outlining some opportunity or other which we often find in our morning mail. It is superior to advertising in that it can be addressed to a specific group of people and can outline a particular selling point in considerable detail. Take as an example a hotel introducing a complicated new weekend break tariff. It would be wasteful to advertise this nationally since the message would have to be simplified to the point where those interested would need to be told to write in for further details: besides which, it would inevitably reach a whole lot of people who wouldn't be interested no matter how persuasive it was. By contrast, a direct mail shot could be aimed precisely at the travel agents, who would then have details of the new offer in front of them.

The problem with direct mail is that people often take one look at the envelope and then throw the contents away unread. This is partly because circulars are often perceived as being impersonal. You can get round this to some extent by using the mail merge facilities on your computer to produce personalized letters, but this still doesn't get over the other basic problem, which is that your letter is also perceived to be irrelevant. This is because there is no guarantee that it will arrive just at the time the recipient is about to make a decision. People don't throw away direct mail which is relevant to their immediate problem. Timing is thus crucial to successful direct mail selling.

This brings us back to market research. One of the key things you need to know is *when* these key decisions are made. Conferences are often arranged eighteen months or more in advance, for instance, so there's no point in sending out direct mail soliciting bookings for next week.

Moreover, experience suggests that there's not much point in sending out just *one* mail shot either. Direct mail makes its point by repetition, so if you are targeting a particular group of people you should send out three or more 'shots', starting well in advance of their decision date, repeating your basic message but emphasizing something slightly different each time.

Letters

Unlike the circular, a letter is addressed specifically to one particular reader. It is a good deal more flattering to the recipient because he usually has a pretty good idea of how much it actually costs to draft and type such a letter. You can emphasize this by adding some kind of personal touch like 'It was nice to meet you at the Conference last month. . . .' This has become even more important lately, since technical developments are making the better quality 'personalized' circular letter increasingly difficult to distinguish from the real thing.

In the old days, letters tended to be fairly formal, with a lot of phrases like 'We beg to assure you' and 'I enclose herewith'. The modern trend has been towards simpler, more colloquial sentences, but one thing hasn't changed, and that is that the letter should look and feel impressive. Good quality paper, an impressive heading, wide margins and clear type all convey one clear message to the recipient, and that is *quality*. Spelling and grammar need attention, too. It is no use having an impressive letterhead and expensive paper if the letter itself says something like 'We got sum luvly rooms . . .'

Letters should be simple, direct and above all, orientated towards the recipient. He's not interested in your facilities: he's interested in satisfying *his* requirements, and the only reason he is reading your letter is that he thinks you might be able to help him. He knows, too, that he is going to have to pay something for this service, so don't try to hide the price. Wrap it up by all means (remember 'the sandwich'?), but let him know it fairly early on so that you have space to tell him all the nice things he is going to get for it.

Finally, personalize your signature. You're not just 'A. Clerk', you should be 'Angela Clerk', or 'Alan Clerk' or whatever your full name happens to be. In spite of all your efforts, a letter is still a relatively cold and formal means of communication. This suits some situations, but it isn't ideal for selling. Other things being equal, a customer will buy from the friendliest salesperson available. You can demonstrate that friendliness by inviting your prospective client to use your first name from the start. That doesn't mean that you should use his, of course. A touch of deference at the start doesn't do any harm.

Telephone selling

The first big advantage of telephone selling over letters is speed. It takes time to draft and type a letter, time for the Post Office to deliver it, and often time for the recipient to get around to reading it. Most business people will drop what they're doing in order to answer the telephone. That gives you your opportunity.

The second great advantage is personalization. A letter is just a piece of paper and it is easy to throw in the wastepaper bin because the writer isn't there to see it happening. A telephone caller is a *person*, and there's no way to cut a call off brusquely without giving offence. Some business people don't mind doing this, but most will try to be reasonably civil. Again, much depends upon timing. You stand a far better chance of being listened to attentively if you have got the timing right and you can show that what you are offering will solve one of your listener's immediate problems.

Telephone selling is difficult, and like all difficult things, it needs both preparation and practice. Let's consider how you should prepare.

1   Make sure you know exactly who you want to talk to, and get through to him yourself instead of getting your own secretary (if you have one) to do so. After all, you are making an unsolicited call and you don't want to waste your target's time by making him wait for you to come on the line. For the same reason, try to avoid interrupting him if he is involved in an important meeting. Make an ally of his secretary first: one of her jobs is to protect her boss from timewasters, and she will be inclined to favour a caller who understands her importance.

2   *Plan* what you are going to say. What questions do you want to ask and what information do you want to convey? List your main points (on one sheet of paper) and work through them briskly but thoroughly. Have a pencil handy and tick them off as you deal with them: after all, your prospective client may ask questions of his own or volunteer information in the 'wrong' order as far as your list is concerned, and you have to be flexible.

3   Relax. This is easier said than done, but there *are* relaxation techniques and you should find some that work for you. Try to sound easy and natural, and don't push *too* hard.

4   Use short, simple sentences and try to stress the key words ever so slightly. What key words, you ask? Well, your listener's name, for instance, your own first name (that friendly touch, remember?), your own establishment (stress the word 'hotel' rather than its name at this point because you want to get him thinking about accommodation (he probably has lots of other problems too), and take every opportunity to say 'you'. For instance: 'Good morning, Mr *Client*. My name's *Angela* Clerk and I'm calling from the Smoothline *Hotel*. Am I right in thinking that *you* hold an annual sales conference in July? Good. Well, I realize that *you* will have made arrangements for this year, but I'd like to tell *you* what we can offer for *your* future conferences.' Notice how this tries to bring the client into the conversation as quickly as possible, even if it's no more than a non-committal 'Yes' at this stage.

5   Follow up. This is where the letter comes into its own. Telephone calls have one serious disadvantage, and that is that they leave no permanent record. However, you *have* made a personal contact, and you can capitalize on this with a personalized letter. The letter also allows you to spell out what you have to offer, and to include whatever brochures or tariffs the contact requires.

Personal calls

The personal call is potentially the most effective means of all, because you are dealing with your target on a face-to-face basis and can interpret and respond to every nuance of expression (remember the importance of being able to 'read' body language?). Moreover, you can take all the information you need, select and emphasize exactly those features the discussion calls for, and then leave your brochures or price lists for the client to consider at leisure.

Everything we have said about telephone selling applies to personal calls. You have to identify who you want to talk to and then get in to see him, so you will need the cooperation of his secretary just as you did when you were telephoning.

You should *plan* what you want to say and try to say it as smoothly and persuasively as possible. There's a problem here in that it isn't as easy to refer to a checklist as you can with telephone sales, though if the visit is a follow up to a phone call during which the prospective client has raised certain points, it *is* permissible to refer to your notes. After all, this shows that you are taking him seriously.

You should also try to structure the discussion so that it focuses on your client's specific problems and interests. If you are trying to sell your hotel to someone organizing some kind of senior citizens' get together, the fact that you have childminding facilities is likely to be irrelevant at best and positively off-putting at worst.

Finally, you should follow up with a letter, just as you did with the phone call.

Salespeople making personal calls should be fully equipped with all the information they need. Some kind of glossy presentation folder with colour photographs of the accommodation, floor plans, sample menus, wine lists and copies of letters from satisfied and prestigious clients is ideal.

All this assumes that you are calling on the client. It is of course much better to persuade the client to call on *you* if you can. This not only allows him to see what you have to offer, but also capitalizes on one of the hotel's biggest advantages, namely, that it can offer hospitality at cost. Of course, any reasonably intelligent client knows this, so any entertainment offered has to be of the very highest standard. The slightest slip up will lead the client to think 'If that can happen when they're really putting themselves out to impress me, what would it be like when it's just another function?'

Negotiating

The other great difference between selling to intermediaries and the usual reception sales activity is that the former usually involves negotiations. Of course, some individual customers may try to bargain over the price, but negotiating is a much 'larger' activity, implying approximately equal status between the participants and often involving complicated tradeoffs between different elements of an extensive 'package' of services.

A typical example of a negotiating situation arises when you are approached by a tour operator. He wants inclusive accommodation at a reduced price over your peak period: you want him to guarantee to take as many rooms as possible during the months when you are only half full. There is a lot of room for discussion here: the type of rooms offered, the cost and range of choice of the meals supplied, the ratio of peak to off-period period rooms, the price to be paid for the package as a whole and even the number of complimentary rooms to be conceded will all enter into the equation.

Negotiation is the process by which two parties seek to resolve their differences and reach agreement. It implies that they both have an interest in reaching such an agreement. However, it also implies that they have different interests. When you start the negotiating process, you will have some idea of your most favourable position (i.e. the best possible outcome as far as you are concerned). You will also have some idea of your limit (i.e. the least favourable outcome you are prepared to accept). Your opponent will also have similar positions. Hopefully, they will overlap, leaving an area in the middle which is called the Bargaining arena:

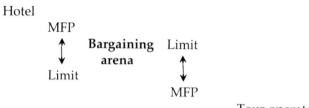

Tour operator

If there is no overlap, then you are not going to be able to reach agreement unless one side or the other revises their limit.

The process of negotiating is so important that you should study it in much greater depth if you find yourself involved in it seriously. In outline, however, you should go through the following steps:

1 *Prepare* Try to predict your opponent's limit (don't bother to pre-guess his most favourable point because he will probably start with that anyway!). Establish your own objectives and make sure that you have all your own facts and arguments ready.
2 *Argue* You won't be able to persuade your opponent unless you produce reasonable arguments, so use the very best you can. Don't make the mistake of thinking that argument means repeating your own point of view in increasingly louder tones. It doesn't. It means *listening* to what your opponent says, and then producing counter arguments to show him where he is wrong. This is best done in quiet and reasonable tones because shouting will merely get him angry too. You can call on our old friend body language here. Remember that leaning forward shows interest and that 'open' hands and arms indicate sincerity and a willingness to consider your opponent's points, whereas leaning back with your arms and legs crossed demonstrates a closed mind. You may find it useful to use the latter position as a tactical ploy occasionally, but on the whole you will do better with the first.
3 *Bargain* Negotiation implies movement. Your MFP and his limit are unlikely to coincide, so be prepared to concede some points. Don't do so at once ('sell high', remember?) but don't be too obstinate either. Try to link these to corresponding concessions on his part ('Look, if you agree to take up more rooms in October, then we'll agree to reduce the price by £10 per head. . . .') Notice the *if you . . . then we . . .* structure of this sentence, which follows the classic 'cost/benefit' selling sequence. In other words, don't give anything away free. Concede your least damaging points first, but try to keep one up your sleeve as a 'sweetener' that you can throw into make the final agreement more acceptable to your opponent.
4 *Close* If you think you are close to agreement, then try to summarize what has been achieved so far, detailing the concessions made by *both* sides and adding in effect 'We've both moved a long way and it would be a pity not to agree now when we're so close. Don't you agree?' If your opponent says 'Yes' then you are practically home and dry. This is the moment for your 'sweetener'. If he says 'Yes, but . . .' and brings out one last objection, then you can pin him down with something like this 'Are you saying that if we move a bit more on that point you would agree?' The idea here is to get him to commit himself to one last reservation: deal with that and he will find it difficult to stall any longer.
5 *Summarize* Never rely on an oral agreement. Get the points down in writing. Send your opponent a letter detailing these as quickly as possible. Make sure that the wording shows that these points were *agreed* and are not open to further discussion.

Assignments

1 Collect five different examples of hotel advertising (note: by this we mean examples of the hotel being advertised to the public at large, and not just specimens of what we might call 'internal' promotions such as leaflets drawing guests' attention to special events in the restaurant). Annotate your examples (which could be cuttings, photographs etc.) with the answers to the following questions:

   - Where did the advertisement appear?
   - What was the target market?
   - What were the key points of the advert (e.g. 'image', price etc.)?
   - Were they (a) Informative, (b) Persuasive or (c) Some other category?
   - What was the approximate cost of the advertisement?

2 Choose either the Tudor or the Pancontinental Hotel and prepare a direct mail shot to attract new short, weekend break business.

3 You are front office manager for either the Tudor or the Pancontinental. You have learned that the management of Marberry plc, a large local manufacturing business, is planning a training course for its sales executives to introduce them to a new portable computer system which it proposes to introduce. Draft a letter to the sales manager of Marberry with a view to securing this business.

4 Prepare and make a sales call to the Marberry sales manager. (Note: this is a role playing exercise. One member of the group should take the role of the target's secretary and another that of the target.) The exercise can be repeated with the following variations:

   (a) Target receptive to proposal.
   (b) Target busy with important meeting but likely to be receptive when finally contacted.
   (c) Target has already signed contract with another hotel.

5 Compare the roles of group reservation systems and Tourist Information Centres in bringing prospective guests together with suitable hotels.

'Well, Mr Blenkinsop, if the computer says your bill comes to £2,045,734.65, that's what it comes to.'

Part Three

Management Aspects

9 Tariffs

Introduction

So far, we have said little about how a hotel goes about deciding how much to charge for its services. This is clearly something which affects its marketing policy and is likely to play an important role in the negotiating process we outlined at the end of the last chapter.

Tariff construction is not something that is likely to concern the average receptionist very closely. However, it *is* a matter for the front office manager, and you ought to have some understanding of the principles.

There are two fundamental methods of approaching the problem of accommodation pricing:

1 *Cost-based pricing* In these systems, the tariff is designed to cover the basic costs of operation at a given level of service, plus a given rate of return.
2 *Market-based pricing* These systems start from an idea of what the customer is prepared to pay and use this as a starting point. The hotel then tries to tailor its costs so that it achieves a reasonable rate of return on that basis.

Of course, no hotel can determine its costs without having some idea of what the customer wants by way of service, so even cost-based pricing contains an important market element. However, the distinction outlined above does reflect two different approaches to the problem.

They may be linked with two other approaches to the problem. There is evidence that the hotel industry is divided into 'price makers' and 'price takers'. The former (usually the larger market leaders) use sophisticated costing and market research techniques to determine the optimum price levels for their hotels. The latter (usually the smaller hotel operators) then compare their establishments with those of the price makers, and adjust their prices accordingly.

The former will generally use a cost-based approach (though modified, as we have said, by marketing considerations), while the latter will adopt what is effectively market-based pricing. In other words, they will compare their services and facilities with what their larger neighbours are offering, and then say 'If the Superbe is charging £50 per night for a modern room with a good view and every possible facility, we can't ask more than £35 for our less attractive ones. . . .'

Let us look at these different approaches.

Cost-based pricing

The 1:1,000 *rule*

This is the simplest of the cost-based systems. It is very much a 'rule of thumb' approach. It simply states that you should charge approximately £1 per night for every £1,000 of room cost. In other words, if the room cost £25,000 to build, your room rate should be about £25 per night. The rule works in other currencies, too. If you built an American hotel with a room cost of $50,000, your room rate should be around $50 per night, and if your calculations were in Japanese Yen, about 50.

The rule was devised quite a long time ago, when rates of interest, tax levels and expectations about appropriate rates of return were very different. It is affected by what you expect to make from the restaurant and bar, too, and how much your other commitments are likely to be. However, it does reflect the fundamental importance of fixed costs in determining a hotel's profitability, which in turn reflects the importance of site values. If you tried to build a hotel in a major metropolitan city centre, you would have to pay a high price for the land. This would be reflected in the room cost, which might well exceed £150,000. As the 1:1,000 rule indicates, you would then have to charge around £150 per night to have any chance of recovering your investment. This helps to explain current London room rates.

'Room cost', incidentally, includes the cost of the public areas as well, which are averaged out over the rooms as a whole. Essentially the calculation is:

$$\frac{\text{Cost of land} + \text{building} + \text{fixtures and fittings}}{\text{Number of rooms}} = \text{room cost}$$

The old 1:1,000 rule ignored inflation, but it is obvious that this must have an effect. Many of the hotels built at the turn of the twentieth century had room costs measured in a few hundred pounds rather than tens of thousands. It would be ludicrous for such hotels to be charging 50p per night today, and of course they don't. What the operators *should* be doing is revaluing their major fixed assets (land, buildings etc.) every few years or so, and then calculating new room rates on that basis. In practice, many pursue a more conservative approach, so that their land and buildings remain undervalued in balance sheet terms. In applying the rule, therefore, it is better to take the *current* cost of building an *equivalent* room rather than the (possibly misleading) historical cost.

With this reservation, the 1:1,000 rule still offers a rough and ready guide to hotel prices. It is not at all precise, but if you know (say) that a group with a number of hotels totalling 1000 rooms has just been bought for £40,000,000, then you can assume with some confidence that the average room rate will be closer to £40 per night than £20 or £80.

The Hubbart formula

The Hubbart formula is a method of establishing an average room rate for a new hotel. It is based on a calculation of total costs plus the desired rate of return. This figure is then divided by the total number of anticipated room nights in order to produce an average room rate. The basic calculation may be summed up as:

$$\frac{\text{Operating costs} + \text{required return} - \text{income ex other departments}}{\text{Expected no. of room nights}} = \text{average room rate}$$

It is rather more complicated than this in practice, but there is still nothing particularly difficult about it. The steps are as follows:

1 Calculate the total amount invested in the hotel (this will include both share capital and any long-term loans such as debentures).
2 Decide on the required annual rate of return on this investment (again, discriminating between dividends and loan interest, and allowing for the effects of any tax deducted before the profits are distributed).
3 Estimate the overhead expenses (interest, administration, heating and lighting, repairs etc.) for the next year.
4 Combine 2 and 3 to find the required gross operating income (in other words, the amount you need to make to cover your expenses *and* keep your investors satisfied).
5 Estimate the probable profits from all other sources other than rooms (i.e. restaurants, bars, health clubs, concessionary shops etc.).
6 Deduct 5 from 4 to find out how much profit you need to make from room lettings.
7 Estimate the accommodation department's expenses for the next year (front office and housekeeping wages, laundry etc.).
8 Add 6 and 7 to find out how much you need to make from the rooms.
9 Estimate the number of room nights you are likely to achieve per annum (this may be established by taking regional tourist board averages for comparable hotels).
10 Divide 8 by 9 to find out the average room rate you should charge.

Let us take a practical example.

Mike Allott has bought a plot of land near a motorway intersection in order to build a motel on it. His architect calculates that he can fit twenty rooms on to this site, plus appropriate car parking and access routes, a restaurant, a small swimming pool and the necessary stores and offices.

He estimates that the land and buildings will cost him £500,000, the fixtures and fittings another £100,000, and that he will need another £10,000 for initial working capital. He proposes to borrow £50,000 by means of 12% debentures and to raise the remainder of the capital required by issuing shares at a premium.

Mike decides that he wants a return of 18 per cent on his investment, though he recognizes that about a third of this will be taken in tax. He estimates the operating costs and goes on to calculate the required average room rate as follows:

Total investment:		
Fixed assets	600,000	
Working capital	10,000	610,000
Total capital employed:		=====
Share capital	500,000	
Share premium account	60,000	
12% debentures	50,000	610,000

Required net profit before tax:		
Required return less tax	67,200	
Tax at 30%	28,800	96,000
Operating costs:		
12% debenture interest	6,000	
Operating expenses	27,900	
Property expenses	25,600	59,500
Required gross profit:		155,500
Profits from other depts:		
Food	15,000	
Bar	34,000	49,000
Required profit from rooms		106,500
Estimated rooms expenses		45,000
Required room income		151,500
Estimated room nights p.a.		
(20 rooms at 70 per cent occupancy)		5,110
Required average room rate		30

You will notice that this average room rate bears out the 1:1,000 rule. The room cost was about £30,000 (total cost £600,000 divided by 20), and the rule predicts that the average room rate should be around £30. It will not necessarily be exactly that (you could get a different result by altering the food profit figure, for instance), but we have used fairly 'standard' ratios in preparing Mike's forecasts for him, and even if we changed some of these we would still expect the result to be somewhere in a range of £25 to £35 per night. This suggests that the 1:1,000 rule still has some validity.

Differential room rates

One of the problems of both the 1:1,000 rule and the Hubbart formula is that they only produce *average* room rates. These are satisfactory as long as the hotel is operating with only one type of room, but they do not allow for the fact that the price often has to vary according to the type of room (e.g. single, twin etc.), its facilities (size, furnishings, accessories, location, noise etc.), and the number of people occupying it.

Since these considerations affect most hotels, the calculation of an average room rate is usually only the first step in the process of tariff creation. In most cases, such a rate needs to be broken up in order to offer differentials between different room types. Let us consider this problem with the aid of another example.

Let's assume that we have taken over an old and somewhat run-down hotel, refurbished it, and now have to work out a new tariff. By using the Hubbart formula we discover that the average room rate ought to be £35 per night. The hotel has the following rooms:

20 singles   (washbasins and showers)
30 doubles   (washbasins and showers)
10 de luxe doubles   (bathrooms en suite)

Our problem is to work out appropriate rates. Our initial choice has to be between a 'per room' and a 'per guest' rate. In this situation we would probably choose the former, since the rooms vary in terms of size and amenities. Most couples would regard two singles as offering rather more than one double, and so worth paying something extra for. In the same way, a single person occupying a double room would have considerably more space at his disposal, which is also worth something extra. A simple 'per guest' rate would ignore these considerations and lead to some guests feeling disadvantaged while others felt that they had got a bargain.

However, we can't begin to work out suitable rates without having some idea of the probable occupancy figures. Our Hubbart formula calculations assumed an average room occupancy percentage of 65 per cent, but this is likely to vary according to the type of room. Let us assume that our estimates are as shown in Table 6.

Table 6

Type		*Rms*	*Occ%*
S	(single, single occupancy)	20	68.0
D(s)	(double, single occupancy)		20.0
D(d)	(double, double occupancy)	30	60.0
LD(s)	(Luxe D, single occupancy)		9.0
LD(d)	(Luxe D, double occupancy)	10	48.0
Total		60	
Average			65.0

As you can see, we have had to allow for the fact that the double rooms can be let to singles as well as couples (they might even sleep more if we added cots or 'Z' beds, but we will ignore that complication for the moment).

We have also had to allow for the fact that we have a different number of rooms of each type. A 10 per cent change in the doubles occupancies would have more effect on the overall rate than a 20 per cent change in the de luxe doubles occupancy, simply because there are three times as many of the former.

In order to arrive at a suitable rate per night for each type of room, we have to decide on appropriate 'weightings'. In other words, if a single room cost (say) 1, how much more would

Table 7

Type	*Rms*	*Occ%*	*AOcRms*	*Wght*
S	20	68.0	13.6	1.0
D(s) }		20.0	6.0	1.4
D(d) }	30	60.0	18.0	1.8
LD(s) }		9.0	0.9	1.8
LD(d) }	10	48.0	4.8	2.4
Total	60			
Averages		65.0	43.3	

we expect to pay for a double? These weightings are very much a matter of judgement, and your final decisions may not be the same as ours. However, most people seem to agree that a single person occupying a double should pay more than the standard single rate (after all, he has more space) but not the full double rate, and that a double should normally cost rather less than twice the single rate (it doesn't cost twice as much to service, for one thing), so our proposals, shown in Table 7 are within the normally agreed limits.

Now, we know that our original target revenue per night must have been £1,365 (£35 average rate × 60 rooms × 65 per cent occupancy rate). Our problem is to split the average rate up in a way which will reflect the varying number of rooms, the different occupancy rates *and* the differential weightings, so that the actual revenue will come to the required £1,365 per night. A possible way to do it is shown in Table 8.

Table 8

Type	Rms	Occ%	AOcRms	Wght	AOxW	B/E£pn	R. Rate	Rnd'd	T. Rev
	(1)	(2)	(3)	(4)	(5)	(6)	(7)	(8)	(9)
S	20	68.0	13.6	1.0	13.6	275.0	20.2	20.00	272.0
D(s) }	30	20.0	6.0	1.4	8.4	169.8	28.3	28.00	168.0
D(d) }	30	60.0	18.0	1.8	32.4	655.2	36.4	36.50	657.0
LD(s) }	10	9.0	0.9	1.8	1.6	32.5	36.1	36.50	32.8
LD(d) }	10	48.0	4.8	2.4	11.5	232.5	48.4	48.50	232.8
Totals:	60					1365.0			1362.7
Averages:		65.0	43.3		67.5				

The meaning of the various columns in Table 8 is as follows:

1 The number of rooms of each type. There are two kinds of occupancy to consider as far as the doubles and de luxe doubles are concerned, but the total number of rooms remains the same at sixty.
2 Room occupancy percentages (as before).
3 Average number of rooms occupied per night. The calculation is:

$$(1) \times \frac{(2)}{100} = (3)$$

In the case of the doubles and de luxe doubles, the combined total of occupied rooms cannot exceed the total number of rooms of that type (i.e. thirty and ten respectively).

4 Weights as previously agreed.
5 Average occupancies times weights, or (3) × (4). This produces a combined weighting which reflects both the 'value' of the room *and* the expected occupancies.
6 This divides the required nightly revenue of £1,365 in the proportions shown by Column (5). In other words, the singles figure is calculated as follows:

$$1365 \times \frac{13.6}{67.5} = 275$$

and so on. The point of this is to calculate how much each type of room needs to contribute to the nightly target given its expected occupancy and its 'weight'.

7   This column establishes how much each individual occupied *room* needs to contribute to the target. We find this by dividing the total target figure for the room type (this is what we calculated in Column 6) by the number of occupied rooms (Column 3). The singles figure, for example, is calculated as follows:

$$\frac{275.0}{13.6} = 22.2$$

You will notice that the room rates we obtain still bear the same relationship to each other as the original weightings. The de luxe doubles, for instance, are still 2.4 times as expensive as the singles.

8   This simply rounds off the figures in Column (7) to commercially acceptable sums. Your answers here might not be exactly the same as ours, but that doesn't matter very much.

9   Final revenue total per night. This is necessary to check that your rates do actually achieve something close to the target figure. One result of the rounding off process in Column (8) is that our final revenue total doesn't come out exactly to £1,365, but this doesn't matter as long as it is reasonably close. After all, most of the original figures were only estimates anyway.

All this can be done without any great difficulty on a spreadsheet. It may take an hour to set up, but once this has been done you can file it and use it again. For instance, if your target revenue figure changed you could easily recalculate your rates, or revise them on the basis of different weightings if they turned out to be wrong.

Seasonal rates

Another of the problems that an average rate doesn't deal with is that of seasonality. Almost all hotels experience some fluctuations in occupancy levels at different times of the year, and these are particularly marked in the case of resort hotels. The case for varying the rates between different seasons is that setting a low rate during the off season helps to attract business, while setting a higher rate during the busy season maximizes profit.

Some specialized kinds of operation (hire boats, for instance, or holiday camps) can have a whole range of different rates, with the main holiday periods attracting the highest ones, but hotels generally have fewer. The most common approach is to have a high season rate and a low season one. In Europe the high season is in the summer, but in tropical holiday areas where tourists go to escape the northern winter (like the Caribbean) it is the winter.

We face the same problem with seasonal rates as we did with different room types, and we can use the same approach. Indeed, we can even combine the two. Let us extend our last example to see how.

You will remember that we had estimated average annual occupancies for each type of room. In practice, these would vary from week to week, being relatively low in the winter (possibly with an increase around Christmas), and higher in summer.

Let us assume that there are two reasonably clearly marked seasons, a low and a high. Let us also assume for the sake of convenience that each of these lasts six months (October to March, say, and April to September). The occupancies for the different types of room might then break down as shown in Table 9.

Table 9

	Rooms	Low%	High%	Av. Oc%
S	20	63.0	73.0	68.0
D(s) }	30	18.0	22.0	20.0
D(d) }	30	50.0	70.0	60.0
LD(s) }	10	6.0	12.0	9.0
LD(d) }	10	30.0	66.0	48.0
Total:	60			
Averages:		56.5	73.4	65.0

As before, the averages take account of the fact that there are differing numbers of each type of room.

You will notice that the seasonal differences are greater for some types of rooms than for others. In the case of the de luxe doubles, for instance, the summer occupancies are twice as high as the winter ones, whereas the increase in the singles occupancies is nowhere near as great. This may well lead you to think about raising the differential in the case of the former by more than for the latter. However, to keep things simple, let us assume that you decide that the winter rates should be three-quarters of the summer ones (or, to put it another way, the summer rates should be a third higher than the winter ones).

The problem is how to divide up our set of average room rates so that they reflect this difference while still achieving the target revenue figure of £1,365. Fortunately, we can use the

Table 10

	Rooms	Occ%	Av'ge Occ.%	Av'ge Oc. Rms	Room W'ght	Seasnl W'ght	AvOc xW't	B/E £pn	Room rate	Rnd'd rate	Total r'vue
Low:	(1)	(2)	(3)	(4)	(5)	(6)	(7)	(8)	(9)	(10)	(11)
S	20	63.0		12.6	1.0	3.0	37.8	106.4	16.9	17.0	214.2
D(s)	30	18.0		5.4	1.4	3.0	22.7	63.8	23.6	23.5	126.9
D(d)	30	50.0		15.0	1.8	3.0	81.0	228.0	30.4	30.5	457.5
LD(s)	10	6.0		0.6	1.8	3.0	3.2	9.1	30.4	30.5	18.3
LD(d)	"	30.0		3.0	2.4	3.0	21.6	60.8	40.5	40.5	121.5
High:											
S	20	73.0	68.0	14.6	1.0	4.0	58.4	164.4	22.5	22.5	328.5
D(s)	30	22.0	20.0	6.6	1.4	4.0	37.0	104.0	31.5	31.5	207.9
D(d)	30	70.0	60.0	21.0	1.8	4.0	151.2	425.6	40.5	40.5	850.5
LD(s)	10	12.0	9.0	1.2	1.8	4.0	8.6	24.3	40.5	40.5	48.6
LD(d)	10	66.0	48.0	6.6	2.4	4.0	63.4	178.4	54.0	54.0	356.4
Totals:	60		65.0 (Av.)				484.9	1364.9			2730.3
											(Av.) 1365.2

same 'weighting' technique that we have already outlined above. Even more fortunately, we can combine the two sets of calculations, as shown in Table 10.

This looks fairly formidable, but it is in fact only an extension of the technique we used earlier. What we have done is to combine the two kinds of weighting, so that the final figure reflects both the relative 'value' of the rooms *and* the seasonality factor.

The columns are calculated as follows:

1   Actual number of rooms, as before. Once again, note that the double and de luxe double figures have to reflect two types of occupancy, but that the total of available rooms remains sixty.
2   Occupancy percentages, this time divided into low and high.
3   Annual average occupancy percentages for each type of room. There is only one figure for each type of occupancy because there can only be one annual average! It is only incorporated as a check on the accuracy of the seasonal figures, and we won't be using it in the subsequent calculations. The calculation in this particular case is quite simple, but it would be slightly different if you had seasons of different lengths. This is easy to demonstrate:

(a)   6 month high season
      6 month low season

$$\frac{(63 \times 6) + (73 \times 6)}{12} = 68$$

(b)   4 month high season
      8 month low season

$$\frac{(4 \times 73) + (8 \times 63)}{12} = 66$$

4   Average number of rooms occupied per night for each type of occupancy. The calculation is:

$$\frac{(1) \times (2)}{100} = (4)$$

5   Weights as previously agreed.
6   Seasonal weightings. As already noted, we decided that the high season rates should be a third higher than the low season ones. This is achieved by giving the former a weighting of 4 and the latter a weighting of 3.
7   Average occupancies times *both* weights, or (4) × (5) × (6). This produces a combined weighting which reflects the probable occupancy, the 'value' of the room, *and* the seasonal weighting.
8   This divides the required nightly revenue of £1,365 in the proportions shown by Column (7). The low season singles figure is calculated as follows:

$$£1,365 \times \frac{37.8}{484.9} = 106.4$$

and so on. This works out how much each type of room should be contributing to the nightly target.

9   This shows how much each individual occupied *room* needs to contribute. We find this as before by dividing the total contribution for the type (Column 8) by the actual number of occupied rooms (Column 4). The low season singles figure, for example, is calculated as follows:

$$\frac{106.4}{12.6} = 16.9$$

You will notice that the resulting room rates within each of the two seasons still bear the same relationship to each other as the original weightings (the de luxe doubles, for instance, are still 2.4 times as expensive as the singles). Moreover, the low season rates are almost exactly 75 per cent of the high season ones, which is what we wanted.

10 Again, we have rounded off the rates in Column (9) to produce commercially acceptable figures. This is a question of judgement, and your decisions may not be the same as ours, though in this particular case the answers are fairly obvious.

11 This column simply confirms that the various rates will actually produce the required average annual nightly revenue target figure. The calculation is actual occupied rooms (Column 4) times the rounded off room rate (Column 10). The only point to note is that the final total (£2,730.3) has to be divided by two, since each separate rate only applies for a six month period (i.e. *half* the year). This produces our Hubbart formula starting point of £1,365 per night, which is an average of both the low and high seasons. As we said before, if you had seasons of unequal length, this calculation would have to be modified. The simplest way to handle this in practice would be to work from an *annual* target rather than a nightly one. This would involve multiplying each *nightly* room rate by the actual number of nights during which that particular rate would apply. The total would then become the annual target revenue figure rather than the nightly average. This is probably more accurate, but it means we have to handle rather large figures in each spreadsheet 'cell', which is why we have not used it here.

Weekday/weekend rates

Another related problem appears when we need to split our average rates between the weekdays (usually Monday to Thursday) and weekends (Friday to Sunday). As a general rule, weekend occupancies are lower than the weekday ones. This is because relatively few offices are open on Saturdays or Sundays, and most business travellers prefer to return home for the weekends. Touring and resort traffic may not be affected to the same extent, but there is often a drop in this kind of business too.

Hotels may differentiate between weekdays and weekends for the same reason as they use seasonal rates. Differential rates maximize revenue when demand is high, and encourage occupancy when it is low.

The problem as far as rate setting is concerned is the same as before, and the technique we have already described *could* be extended if necessary. You would have to decide how much more the weekend rate should be as compared with the weekday one, and then introduce an appropriate weighting. You might decide, for instance, on one in the proportion of 2:3 (in other words, with the weekend rate only two-thirds of the weekday one). You would then have a table with *four* separate blocks of rates (low/weekend, low/weekday, high/weekend and high/weekday). This would be rather complicated, especially since you would have to allow for the fact that the total number of weekend nights is different from the total of weekday ones (there are 156 weekend nights and 208 weekday nights, plus one which might be either).

In practice, few hotels would use differential weekend rates calculated in this way, since they complicate the tariff structure and make billing more difficult. However, there *is* a case for differential weekend rates where the weekday and weekend business are self-contained and mutually exclusive. Hotels have commonly had lots of guests from Monday to Thursday, and relatively few over the weekends (this is sometimes known as 'four-sevenths occupancy'). Some years ago the more enterprising decided to do something about it, and began to promote 'weekend packages' in association with the major transport undertakings or tour operators. The method they used to price these weekend packages was different to the ones we have described so far, and we shall discuss it in the next section.

Marginal or contribution pricing

Traditional cost-based pricing tries to make sure that revenue covers the total costs plus the target profit. Marginal pricing is aimed at ensuring that the price charged for any individual service covers the variable cost of providing that service plus a contribution to the establishment's fixed costs.

Marginal pricing is particularly suited to what have been described as 'secondary pricing decisions' (Sizer, J. (1975) *An Insight into Management Accounting*, Penguin Books), which means any supplementary business such as special weekend packages, occasional conferences and the like. One example might be the 'four-seventh' type of hotel, where the main market is the Monday to Thursday business traveller. The hotel still has to remain open over the weekend, however, and thus incurs extra costs. Some of these can be reduced (the number of staff on duty can be cut, for instance), but overheads such as depreciation, insurance and local taxes remain unaffected. If the establishment can create new weekend business, these overheads can be 'spread' over a larger number of customers.

It is usually not possible to attract such weekend business at the normal weekday prices, which means that there will have to be considerable reductions. The aim of marginal pricing is to make sure that these low weekend prices still cover the variable costs, together with a contribution towards the fixed costs. The actual size of this contribution is often secondary: the basic idea is to fix the selling price so that it is attractive enough to bring in *some* additional business and thus make *some* contribution.

Let us consider a simple example. As you know, variable costs usually form a very small proportion of the cost of letting an additional hotel room. They involve little more than the laundry charges and a few disposables (such as soap), plus whatever guest amenities you provide. Strictly speaking, direct labour is only a semi-variable (you don't normally take on an extra receptionist to deal with one extra guest, though you may have to in order to deal with twenty), though it is usually included as well. Even with labour included, the variable costs do not usually amount to much more than 25 per cent.

Let us assume that these variable (direct) costs are actually 25 per cent, and that our normal (i.e. weekday) rack is £40. Our figures would then look something like this:

	£
Normal room rate	40
Les variable costs:	10
Normal contribution	30

If we can obtain more than £10 for our room at the weekends, then we are getting a contribution towards the fixed (overhead) costs. If we charged £15, for instance, we would be getting £5 contribution. It may not sound much, but it is a great deal better than nothing at all. The 'floor price' (i.e. the minimum we could charge) would be £10, the 'ceiling price' (i.e. the maximum) usually not more than £40 (the normal rate). This gives us a 'price latitude' or range of possible prices of £30, which provides a lot of scope to develop a flexible pricing strategy, and even to explore totally new markets.

Marginal pricing can be used to advantage in the following situations:

1   Where facilities are otherwise likely to remain empty.
2   In any situation where there are rapid and marked fluctuations in demand, making the uniform rack rate inappropriate (in these circumstances marginal pricing will at least tell you the lowest price you should charge).
3   Where you are quoting a price on a 'one off' basis, especially in a competitive situation.

The areas where marginal pricing is most likely to be useful are thus weekend breaks, off-season holidays, conferences and special events. Hotels have also been known to respond to last-minute enquiries by reducing their prices (airlines follow the same reasoning with regard to unsold seats), which amounts to the same thing.

Generally, marginal pricing should only be used as a supporting technique, since it does not offer any guarantee that all the fixed costs will be covered. It should, therefore, be combined with some other form of 'cost-plus' pricing. One approach might be to rely on the staple business (in our case, the Monday to Thursday guests) to cover the basic costs (all the fixed costs plus the variable ones incurred by that business), and use the weekend business to provide the extra 'jam'. However, this depends on the 'sales mix' (the relative proportions of the two market segments) and the extent to which it is possible to develop a profitable weekend business.

There are, of course, problems associated with marginal pricing, notably the difficulty of establishing just what the variable costs actually are (especially in small businesses), the risk that frequent price changes may affect customer goodwill and thus repeat business, and the difficulty of deciding just what price level will maximize demand. These last two considerations lead us on to a consideration of market pricing.

Market-based pricing

Price taking or 'price followership'

As we have already indicated, many smaller hotels simply 'follow' the prices established by their larger competitors. This may be the only strategy open to numbers two and three in a small resort town, for instance. The rates are usually set at 5–10 per cent or so below those of the price leader, and are changed whenever the leader's rates alter.

Strictly speaking, this is competitor-based pricing, but since the 'price maker' is usually basing his prices on a sophisticated analysis of what the market will bear, it is also a form of market-based pricing too. It can also be seen as a mechanism for updating the 1:1,000 rule: the price makers have tended to be the larger modern hotels, and price followership has worked to keep rates in the older establishments in line with current construction costs.

The problem with price taking is that it does not take any account of the follower's capital structure, profit targets or operating costs. If the 'price maker' is much more efficient (through better room design, reducing heating costs, for instance) this puts the 'price taker' in the difficult position of having to cover relatively higher overheads with relatively lower revenue.

'Top-down' pricing

This approach is often used by companies proposing to enter a new market. It starts with an analysis of that market aimed at identifying a 'gap' which is currently unfilled. We might look at an old-fashioned resort town, for instance, and find that while there are one or two well-established traditional hotels and a lot of smaller private hotels and boarding houses, there is no medium-sized modern hotel with a conference centre and rates which fit somewhere in between the two levels available.

Once this market opportunity has been identified, the procedure is very similar to that used in the Hubbart formula. The main difference is that we now start 'at the top' by establishing how many rooms we think we can let per annum at the given rate, and then working downwards through the cost figures to see whether these will result in an acceptable rate of return.

If our calculations do not result in an acceptable return, then the cost figures must be re-examined. It may be that reductions can be made in the cost per room, or staffing ratios can be reduced, or a greater contribution obtained from the restaurant.

It might be argued that 'top-down' pricing is still cost based because ultimately it is still the costs which decide whether we can achieve an acceptable rate of return. The advantage of the approach, however, is that it puts the emphasis firmly on what the customer wants, and stimulates innovative thinking about the various cost elements, rather than taking these as fixed.

Many traditional aspects of hotel services have been modified as a result. One example is the labour-intensive, early morning tea tray, replaced by teamakers in all but the most expensive hotels without any serious objection on the part of the customers. Another and more radical example is the Japanese 'cubicle' hotel, introduced after research had shown that Japanese customers wanted much cheaper city centre overnight accommodation and would not mind sleeping in self-contained insulated cylinders with communal washing facilities just so long as they cost only 25 per cent of the usual room rate. Here the sequence of thinking began with the question 'How can we provide accommodation at a quarter of the usual city centre room rate?', and came up with the answer 'Pack four times as many guests into the same space'.

Rate cutting

Most approaches to pricing assume that demand will increase if prices are lowered. However, rate cutting can be a risky expedient, because the increases in occupancy needed to offset the drop in revenue are surprisingly high, as Table 11 demonstrates.

Some of these increases are clearly unobtainable, even though a hotel can sometimes achieve more than 100 per cent by bringing additional beds and rooms into play.

What is perhaps more important is that a unilateral cut may begin a round of competitive

Table 11   Occupancies required to offset rate cuts

		Cut of 5%	Cut of 10%	Cut of 15%	Cut of 20%
Current Occ %	50 *Required:*	53	56	59	62
	55	58	61	65	69
	60	63	67	71	75
	65	68	72	76	81
	70	74	78	82	87
	75	79	83	88	94
	80	84	89	94	100
	85	89	94	100	106
	90	95	100	106	112
	95	100	106	112	119

rate cutting which would end up in everyone making losses and the weaker hotels (possibly yours, especially since you were the one who felt the need to start it in the first place) going to the wall. This is why the industry as a whole frowns on what is sometimes called 'discounting'.

Prestige product pricing

It is not always true that demand will increase if prices are lowered. We have already suggested that raising the price may well make the hotel more exclusive and thus change the nature of the product (marketing people explain this in terms of 'product differentiation'). Whatever the explanation, the fact remains that hotels can sometimes *increase* occupancies by *raising* their prices, in apparent defiance of the laws of economics.

It is said that when the first modern hotels were built in Central London after the Second World War their initial occupancies were disappointing, and it was only after they increased their rates so that they were in line with the older, higher-cost establishments that occupancies picked up.

This strategy will only work where the market is not particularly price conscious, and is thus only open to establishments in a position to cater for the more exclusive kind of clientele. It may well work for a luxury cruise ship, for instance, but not for the cheap weekend market. Nevertheless, it underlines the fact that pricing is very much a *psychological* activity. The point about the modern Central London hotels was that although their initial rates were actually based on lower costs, these were perceived (rightly or wrongly) as reflecting lower *quality*.

In the same way, prices are often modified to convey particular messages. £39.50 sounds much lower than £40 than it really is, and £105 can 'signal' prestige and quality much more clearly than £95. This is why we added a 'rounding' column to our earlier tables.

Inclusive/non-inclusive rates

So far, we have not considered the question of whether to include meals in our rates. There are four main kinds of tariff available:

1   *Fully inclusive (room plus all main meals)*   This is the European 'En Pension' rate, frequently known as 'American Plan' because nineteenth century US hotels often catered for long-stay full-board residents.
2   *Semi-inclusive (i.e. room plus breakfast and* one *main meal, usually the evening one)*   This is often called 'Modified American Plan' or 'MAP'. It is aimed at the guest who may be staying for a few nights and is likely to be out and about during the day, though it also suits the overnight traveller who arrives in time for the evening meal and departs after breakfast.
3   *Bed and Breakfast ('B&B')*   This is self-explanatory.
4   *Non-inclusive rate (i.e. a separate charge for each item such as room, meals, drinks, extras etc.)*   This is often known as 'European Plan' because it was characteristic of the large European hotels Americans stayed at on their travels.

No rate can ever be fully inclusive, because guests vary so much in their requirements. Some drink a lot, others don't. Even if you include wine with the meal, they may ask for an expensive premium vintage instead, or round it off with liqueurs and cigars. Some guests will make considerable use of the telephone while others won't, some will require laundry services, or newspapers, or flowers. All these are extras which will have to be charged for separately. 'Inclusive' is thus a relative term.

The question is, what kind of approach to adopt? This depends upon two factors:

1   Guest characteristics

The tariff type has to be related to the guests' own requirements. The main factors affecting these are as follows:

(a)   *Length of stay and meal requirements*   There is a broad relationship between these two factors. Most overnight stays will want an evening meal, whereas week-long stays may not want to be tied down to a single restaurant (this is why large modern hotels often offer a range of 'meal experiences'). Long-term stays tend to regard the hotel as 'home', and only eat out occasionally. The class of customer and pattern of stay also come into this. A Spa hotel is likely to have a number of relatively immobile long-term residents who will require three meals a day and certain regular services such as laundry, whereas an airport hotel can't even be sure that its guests will be staying for a full night or that they will have time for breakfast.
(b)   *Alternative eating facilities*   Guests at a country hotel miles from any other restaurant are more or less forced to eat there. On the other hand, a city hotel located in the centre of the restaurant district has little chance of 'holding' its guests for more than one night of their stay (one imaginative solution is to provide vouchers which the guests can use at a variety of local restaurants).
(c)   *Spending power*   An inclusive tariff implies a table d'hôte menu with a restricted range of

dishes, all costing more or less the same to produce (it would be difficult for a hotel offering a full à la carte menu to levy a standard meal charge because some guests might choose caviar and others an omelette). Since standardized menus offer the advantages of economies of scale, they usually mean lower prices, and thus appeal to customers with relatively low purchasing power. Since inclusive rates are also known in advance, they help such customers to budget for their stays. By contrast, more upmarket customers are accustomed to a wider range of choice and are prepared to pay for this.

(d) *Homogeneity*   Inclusive rates are more acceptable if all the guests have similar tastes. This is characteristic of much specialized holiday accommodation (holiday camps, for instance), group tour business and conventions. A related consideration is the extent to which requirements are likely to vary from night to night. A business traveller may eat a plain, solitary meal one night, then entertain a group of clients lavishly the next, which makes an inclusive tariff more awkward to operate.

2   Hotel characteristics

Some hotels will find it easier to operate inclusive tariffs than others. The main considerations are:

(a) *Grade*   A five star hotel will have a higher staff:guest ratio than a cheaper one. Although most of these extra staff should be involved in direct guest service, the hotel ought to find it easier to produce itemized bills. Nowadays, this factor is increasingly linked with computerization.

(b) *Size*   This does not necessarily mean that there are more staff to guests, but it does mean that the cost of equipment such as expensive computers and point of sale terminals can be spread over a larger number of customers. Moreover, the larger the hotel, the more sophisticated its costing system needs to be, and this also tends to lead to itemized bills.

(c) *Length of stay*   The longer this is, the greater the relative burden of itemizing every separate charge. If a guest incurs four charges a day (room, breakfast, lunch, dinner) and stays for seven days, then the bill will be twenty-eight items long (not counting extras). This could be reduced to only one by using an inclusive weekly rate, whereas seven separate one-night stays still mean seven separate bills. The administrative advantage of an inclusive rate is stronger in the former case.

(d) *Marketing considerations*   An inclusive rate helps to 'fix' guests as far as the restaurant is concerned. They are often uncertain as to whether credit will be allowed for meals not taken, and think that as they are paying for them they might as well eat them. This is probably most important in smaller hotels (where the unexpected absence of a relatively small number of guests might seriously upset restaurant calculations) and those working on very narrow margins. One interesting variation on this theme is the increasing use of 'meal allowances'. Many hotels offering inclusive rates allow guests to choose either the standard table d'hôte menu *or* to set off the cost against an à la carte meal. This often encourages guests to take advantage of the latter's wider choice because they feel they are getting a substantial allowance towards the cost, and thus helps to increase restaurant sales figures.

Turning a room rate into an inclusive rate is easy enough in principle because all you have to do is add the meal prices to the room rate. Of course, you have to remember that double occupancy means *two* people, and thus two sets of meal charges, which is why most inclusive rates are 'per person'.

The process is not so easy in practice because you have to decide what should be included in the meals (coffee? wine?), and how much you should charge for them. You also have to decide on whether to make an allowance if the guest does not consume one or more of the meals, how much to allow, and how to check that the meal was not eaten. Breakfasts used to be a particular problem: receptionists in hotels operating bed and breakfast rates were sometimes faced with early check-outs who claimed that they had not had time for breakfast, and had little option but to take the guest's word for it and make an appropriate deduction there and then. One of the advantages of electronic point of sale billing is that it reduces this kind of uncertainty.

Assignments

1 Compare the tariffs likely to be found in the Tudor Hotel with those of the Pancontinental. Which is the more likely to include inclusive elements?

2 Paragon Hotels are considering building a 150 room hotel in a city centre location. The estimated building costs are £5,000,000, the fitting out costs £2,000,000, and the working capital required £500,000. The project will be financed by borrowing £6,000,000 at 15 per cent per annum and providing the remainder from internal sources. Paragon's policy is not to undertake any new investment unless the overall return is 15 per cent net of tax (currently 30 per cent on net profits). The annual operating expenses are estimated to be £2,500,000, the food and beverage contribution to be £400,000, and the room servicing costs to be £300,000. The hotel will be open all year round and the average occupancy is expected to be 75 per cent. Calculate the average room rate using the Hubbart formula.

3 Paragon Hotels have just acquired the Queen's Hotel, which has the following characteristics:

Rooms: 15 singles with shower
15 singles with bath
20 doubles/twins with shower
20 doubles/twins with bath
5 luxury doubles/twins

Expected clientele:
30% business (year round, mainly S, stay 1/2 nights)
20% transit (year round, mixed S/D, stay 1 night)
20% touring (seasonal, mainly D, stay 1 night)
20% resort-based (seasonal mainly D, stay 4/7 nights)
10% group (seasonal, mixed S/D, stay 2/3 nights)

Studies suggest that average monthly occupancy percentages will be as follows:

	Jan	Feb	Mar	Apr	May	Jun	Jul	Aug	Sep	Oct	Nov	Dec
S	65	65	65	67	69	73	77	82	80	76	67	66
SB	48	49	52	65	75	84	88	93	90	73	52	45
D/T	75	78	82	83	84	88	93	95	94	74	56	62
D/TB	28	32	35	46	54	59	78	89	93	56	30	42
LD/T	25	31	34	45	51	57	70	88	85	47	32	48

These figures can be assumed to be consistent over the probable price range. Friday–Sunday occupancies are likely to average 60 per cent of Monday–Thursday ones.

Table d'hote meal charges (exclusive of liquor) are expected to be as follows:

Breakfast   £3.00
Lunch   6.00
Dinner   9.00

Room revenue is required to cover operating expenses plus overheads together amounting to £400,000, plus a profit of 20 per cent (ignore tax).

Design a suitable tariff and demonstrate that this will meet the prescribed accommodation revenue target on the basis of the information given.

4   You have a thirty bedroom hotel with a low weekend occupancy. A neighbouring hotel is operating weekend packages (i.e. full board for two days) successfully at £40 per person over a six month (i.e. twenty-six week period). You would like to enter this market. You estimate that the costs to be taken into consideration are as follows:

(a)   Food £8 per person per day.
(b)   Laundry and other direct guest costs £6 per day.
(c)   Additional part time staff: thirty hours at £2.00 per hour.
(d)   Fixed Cost Allocation £5,000.
(e)   Advertising and promotion £5,000.

Propose a suitable package rate and demonstrate the average occupancy level at which this will: (a) Break even; (b) Yield a net profit of £2,000 over the period.

5   It is said that some hotels can actually increase demand for their services by raising their prices. How far is this true of hotels as a whole, and what is the explanation?

10 Yield management, groups etc.

Introduction

So far, we have paid relatively little attention to the problems created by the need to cater for different types of market segment. In reality, a large hotel may accommodate a mixture of independent business travellers, holidaying families, group tour members, conference delegates and airline cabin crew on stopovers, to name but a few.

Moreover, guests in identical adjoining rooms may be paying markedly different rates, even though they are enjoying the same services and facilities (a situation very similar to that which applies in the airline business, where fare structures have become increasingly complicated and passengers seated side by side may have paid very different amounts for their tickets). Some of these guests will be charging their bills to company accounts, others will be paying for themselves. Some will be arriving and departing in large groups, others as separate individuals. We need to look at the implications of these differences.

There are two main questions:

1 *What type of business should the hotel accept?* Nowadays, more and more are negotiating preferential rates with favoured customers. At the same time, differences between market segments with respect to the length of time between booking and arrival have also become more marked. Relatively low-price group bookings are often arranged months or even years in advance, whereas many high-price single bookings are only made a few days before arrival. There is thus a risk that a hotel may find itself having to turn away lucrative business because it has already committed itself to a less profitable type. The effect of this development is that hotels are having to pay much more attention to their 'sales mix', in other words, the proportion of bookings of different types taken. This has always been a consideration when taking group business, but the proliferation of different rates has made it much more important nowadays. At the same time, the development of computers has made the process of calculating the optimum sales mix much more effective. The result has been a great expansion of interest in what is called 'yield management'. We shall be looking at this in the first part of this chapter.

2 *What are the operational implications of group business?* So far, we have been considering guests mainly as individuals. We have made various references to the modifications in procedures needed in the case of groups, but it is useful to bring these together and look at their implications as a whole. At the same time, we can consider the implications of one or two other types of booking, including the special case of timeshare reservations. These together form the second part of this chapter.

Yield management

Differential rates

Our discussion of tariffs left out one factor which has come to be of increasing importance in recent years. Hotels have always charged different rates for different nights of the week, just as they have always varied their rates according to the season. Until recently, however, they have generally charged most guests the same rate for a given room on any given night. That is no longer the case.

We have already seen that travel agents can earn discount on any booking made through them, and we have described the mechanism by which this is paid. The larger credit card companies can negotiate similar discounts. The customer still pays the full rack rate, of course, but this is immaterial as far as the hotel is concerned.

Many large associations are offered the same kind of concession. It is quite common for their members to be eligible for discounts in this way. Their purchasing power as individuals may not be very significant, but collectively they represent an important source of business. This applies to trade associations, professional bodies, unions etc. In these cases the individual guests *do* benefit from the discount.

Companies also negotiate special rates. Many hotels offer a special 'corporate rate' almost as a matter of course, but important companies responsible for providing a significant amount of business can hold out for much better terms than these. A large local firm may account for some 20–25 per cent of a medium-sized hotel's business, for example, and its bargaining power is considerable. The same applies to the bigger travel agencies, tour operators or airlines.

The actual level of rates available are likely to vary considerably, and are usually confidential. However, one informed assessment indicates that they cover the range shown in Table 12.

Table 12

Rack rate (%)	
100	Single private and 'chance' bookings
90 } 80	Travel agents, groups eligible for discounts and regular guests' corporate rates
70 } 60	Special corporate rates for larger multiple travel agencies and major companies
50 } 40	Very large national or international companies

Source: Hodgson A. (1987), *The Travel and Tourism Industry*, Pergamon, 7 p. 117

Booking horizons

Holiday guests generally make their bookings much further ahead than business travellers. This is mainly because holidays are planned in advance, whereas many business trips are often decided upon at short notice.

This is particularly true of group tour business, where the organizers often book large blocks of rooms long before they actually sell them to their customers (in other words, the rooms are booked even before the holidaymakers get around to planning their vacations). A 'time horizon' of two years or more is common with large block bookings in busy centres. This is also true of conference bookings, which share many of the characteristics of package tourism.

On the other hand, leisure bookings are generally much more price sensitive than business bookings. There are several reasons for this:

1 In most cases leisure bookings are paid for by individuals rather than firms.
2 Holiday travel is less dependent upon location than business travel. If one resort turns out to be too expensive, the holidaymaker can usually go to another, whereas business travellers generally have to go to one specific destination.
3 The longer leisure booking time horizon allows 'bargain hunting'.

Very competitive bargaining over rates is characteristic of group tour operators and large scale conference organizers. On the other hand, there is a good deal of evidence to indicate that business travellers are not as price sensitive as leisure travellers.

What this means is that a hotel which 'fills up' with leisure bookings well in advance runs the risk of having to turn away higher value business customers close to the date of arrival. This situation is made worse by the fact that this business will almost certainly go to its competitors, who will thus earn more money than the original hotel.

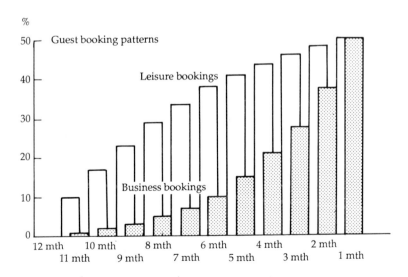

Figure 70 *Leisure and business bookings*

The differences between leisure and business booking patterns are shown graphically in Figure 70. For the sake of simplicity, we have assumed that each accounts for 50 per cent of the hotel's bookings, and that there is no unsatisfied demand. These figures should not be regarded as typical. They will vary considerably in practice, but the general relationship remains broadly true. In our example, over half of the 'leisure' bookings (i.e. 25 per cent of the total) are received eight months before the actual date of arrival, whereas this proportion is not achieved in the case of the 'business' bookings until three months before arrival.

Figure 71 shows what would happen if the two booking patterns shown in Figure 70 were combined. In this (highly simplified) case, total bookings rise in a straight line until the hotel becomes fully booked during the last weeks or so before the arrival date.

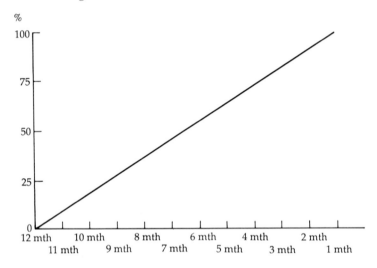

Figure 71 *Total bookings (leisure and business)*

Using bookings forecasts to maximize yield

Yield management is based on forecasts of bookings. Most hotels find that dates like 'the first Monday in September' show reasonably consistent seasonal bookings patterns for one year to the next, and allowances can always be made for changes in the economy or unusual events such as special shows.

Nevertheless, the actual bookings are likely to fluctuate unexpectedly. Figure 72 shows what might happen. The straight line represents the *anticipated* booking pattern, whereas the jagged one shows what *actually* happened. It tells us that bookings were higher than expected some ten months before the date of arrival, whereas they sagged somewhat two or three months later, before picking up again in the last quarter.

This kind of forecast can be used to 'trigger' appropriate rate adjustments. In Figure 72, the hotel could have reacted to the unexpectedly high demand in month ten by raising its average rates. It might have done this by:

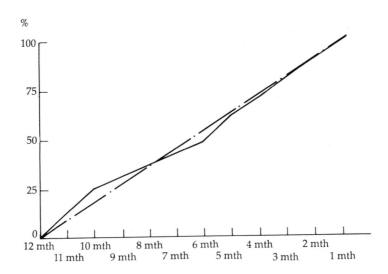

Figure 72   *Anticipated and actual bookings*

1   Reducing the discounts offered to travel agents and other intermediaries.
2   Reducing the number of lower rate 'leisure' bookings accepted, in the expectation that these would be replaced later by higher yield 'business' bookings.

Similarly, when demand began to show signs of falling off in month six, the hotel could have taken remedial action by increasing discounts and accepting more 'leisure' bookings.

This requires rapid reactions on the part of the hotel, and it is the kind of activity which responds well to computerization. The computer can be programmed to keep a cumulative bookings total for each date, and to 'signal' the receptionist every time total bookings show a significant rise or fall compared to the expected level. Human beings can do this, too, but only at the cost of maintaining additional records like the graph shown in Figure 72. The computer can do it automatically.

Experience indicates that computers are able to react more quickly to changes in bookings levels, and that this can save the hotel money. For instance, it is quite likely that the computer would react to the fall off in demand in Figure 72 at the beginning of month seven, whereas a human operator might well not react until the end. The loss of a whole month of reaction time could make a big difference.

In reality, the straight line shown in Figure 72 is much more likely to be replaced by a curve. Small variations in the number of bookings taken in any one month are to be expected and are not too important: it is only necessary to take action when the variation is substantial. If we were to graph a computer's calculations, they would look more like Figure 73. Action would only be triggered if the bookings fell outside the band between the upper and lower 'threshold' values.

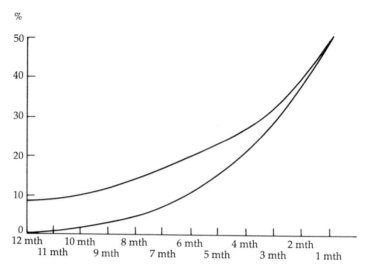

Figure 73 *Upper and lower threshold values*

Multiple rates

In practice, the division between 'leisure' and 'business' we have been using is too simple. As we have seen, many large hotels operate with up to half a dozen separate rates for different market segments.

In Table 13 we have assumed a 1,000 room hotel with standardized rooms. The ordinary Rack Rate for single occupancy is £100, but there are three other single rates depending on the type of booking:

Table 13 Differential rates and expected booking patterns

	Rates (%)	**Months:** −12	−11	−10	−9	−8	−7	−6	−5	−4	−3	−2	−1
Rack	100	12	25	37	50	62	75	87	100	112	125	187	250
Agency	85	6	12	19	25	37	50	69	87	125	162	200	250
Corporate	70					4	8	12	20	50	100	175	250
Group	55	125	150	175	200	230	250	250	250	250	250	250	250
Totals		143	187	231	275	333	383	418	457	537	637	812	1000

Table 13 shows the cumulative number of bookings expected from each market segment for each month prior to the date of arrival. These are not necessarily typical (there are considerable variation in practice), but they should help us to understand the process and some of the complications of yield management.

In this example, each market segment is expected to produce 25 per cent of the total bookings (i.e. 250 rooms at full occupancy), but each block will fill up at a different rate. For instance, the 'rack' rate will be levied on both private 'leisure' and last-minute business and professional bookings, which is why it shows a steady growth over the whole twelve-month period. Similarly, the 'agency' rate will be offered to travel agents handling both private and ordinary business travel, which explains why it follows something of the same pattern. The 'corporate' rate is for large, favoured customers who will tend to book at the last moment, while the 'group' rate will only be available to large group tour firms who, as we have seen, will book large blocks of rooms well in advance.

The operating principle is simple. The receptionist (or better still, the computer) keeps watch over the actual number of bookings taken at each rate. If in month minus 8 'rack rate' bookings are significantly higher than expected, the remaining twenty 'group rate' rooms can be switched to cope with this unexpectedly higher demand. If these can all be sold at the 'rack rate', then the hotel will have gained:

20 × £45 (the difference between the two rates) = £900.

If, on the other hand, 'rack rate' bookings are moving much more slowly than expected and only total forty in month minus 8, then twenty 'rack rate' rooms can be switched to the group market. If these can be sold, then the hotel will have earned:

20 × £55 = £1,100

which it might not have done otherwise.

Other rate adjustments are possible. In this way, by keeping a careful eye on actual demand as compared with expectations, the hotel is able to maximize its revenue or 'yield'.

Displacement

It is important to remember that the hotel will have to prepare a separate set of booking estimates for *each day*. This means that it might offer a different combination of rates for subsequent days. Demand is usually low for Sundays, for instance, so the full range of rates is likely to be on offer, whereas it tends to be much higher for Mondays and higher still for Tuesdays. Using the example above, we might assume the position nine months before arrival to be as shown in Table 14.

This indicates that demand is expected to be high for Monday and Wednesday, and even higher for Tuesday. The hotel would have allocated most of its 'group' booking block and would be unwilling to allocate any more peak-period days to this market segment, though it is still willing to sell weekend nights at the group rate.

Table 14   Rates available for specified days

	£100	£85	£70	£55
Sunday	Yes	Yes	Yes	Yes
Monday	Yes	Yes	No	No
Tuesday	Yes	No	No	No
Wednesday	Yes	Yes	No	No
Thursday	Yes	Yes	Yes	No
Friday	Yes	Yes	Yes	Yes
Saturday	Yes	Yes	Yes	Yes

However, stays of more than one night create a problem, namely, which rate should be quoted? A caller requesting a three-night stay commencing on Sunday might be quoted £100, £85, £70 or even £55 depending on how hard he pushes the question of discounts (many callers are quite prepared to bargain like this). The trouble is that he will then be occupying a room on Monday and Tuesday for which a higher price might otherwise have been obtained. Conversely, a caller requiring a three-night booking commencing on Tuesday might find only one price (£100) being quoted, leading to the risk that the hotel will lose the booking, even though it would have been willing to accept him at £85 on the two following nights.

Prospective guests who are unable to obtain rooms at a higher rate because those rooms have already been let to guests paying a lower rate are termed 'displacement'. Some of these would-be guests might well have stayed on for subsequent nights too, which produces 'secondary displacement', and they might even have found that they liked the hotel enough to become future customers too, which produces 'tertiary displacement'.

Calculating the costs and benefits of displacement can be very complicated, but we can demonstrate the nature of the problem by means of a simple example. Let us assume that we accept a four-night booking for a group of twenty guests at £55 each per night, arriving Saturday. We will also assume that although we have plenty of vacant rooms on Saturday and Sunday, demand at the full 'rack rate' would have led to our being only eight rooms short of full on Monday, and completely full on Tuesday. Finally, we will assume that half the 'displaced' guests would have stayed on for another night.

The results are shown below:

	Sat	Sun	Mon	Tue	Wed	Gain	Loss
Group @ £55 each	20	20	20	20		£4,400	
Primary displacement @ £100 each			12	14			£2,600
Secondary displacement @ £100 each				6	7		1,300
Net gain							500
						4,400	4,400

The group 'displaces' twelve 'rack rate' guests on Monday (not twenty because we would have been eight rooms short of full occupancy, remember?). Half of the twelve would have stayed on over Tuesday night (the 'secondary' displacement), which would have left fourteen rooms free for letting at the rack rate. Half of these fourteen would have then stayed on over Wednesday night (constituting further 'secondary' displacement). The total gain would have been only £500 (the difference between the revenue the group brought in and the loss incurred by not being able to accommodate the higher-priced customers), less the variable costs of servicing the extra rooms on the Saturday and Sunday nights (not included in the above calculations).

We have ignored the question of 'tertiary displacement', but even this very simplified illustration shows the difficulty of deciding whether or not to accept bookings at a reduced rate, especially when you can only guess at the likely displacement figures!

Conclusions

Yield management has proved itself to be a valuable approach to the problems of maximizing room revenue. It can be expected to increase in both importance and sophistication (the development of computerized 'expert system' applications using artificial intelligence is already well advanced). However, it is as well to keep certain limitations in mind:

1 Yield management works best when demand is high and it is possible to 'switch' blocks of rooms from one market segment to another. It will help to 'trigger' rate reductions and intensive marketing activities when demand falls significantly below the expected levels. Most experienced front office managers would probably take such action intuitively anyway, but a formal yield management approach (especially a computerized one) is likely to 'trigger' it more quickly. However, when overall demand is only around 60 per cent, *any* bookings are desirable, and the displacement effect is hardly likely to be significant.
2 Yield management is essentially a *quantitative* approach. It ignores intangibles like the need to retain the goodwill of important 'corporate' customers. These pay less and generally book later, but they can account for a significant proportion of a hotel's business. It may not be a good idea to suddenly 'close off' as far as they are concerned just because there is a temporary upsurge in transient rack rate business. What this amounts to is that a hotel has certain obligations towards its regular customers, and although the short-term cost of meeting these may be much easier to measure than the long-term costs of *not* meeting them, they are nevertheless important. We looked at this point when we were considering 'service' earlier, and found that one aspect of this was that the hotel should not be perceived to be putting its own short-term financial interests before those of its guests. This point is worth repeating. Yield management pushed to the uttermost may raise revenues in the short term, but hotels are part of the hospitality industry, and there are other important considerations as well.

Groups

We have mentioned group business at a number of places in the text, and you should have some idea of its importance. However, it is useful to bring the points together and look at the implications of group business as a whole.

Negotiating

There is a clear conflict of interests between the tour operator and the hotel. The tour operator wants to book as many rooms as possible during the peak period, at the lowest possible rates, whereas the hotel wants to use group bookings to fill up during slack periods, and to charge the highest possible rates for them.

There is nothing reprehensible about either set of objectives, and the result will usually be a bargaining process ending in a mutually acceptable arrangement. If the rooms would otherwise remain empty, the hotel's minimum position will be determined by the marginal cost of taking the group. If the rooms might otherwise be filled by customers who would have paid more, the hotel will have to calculate the effects of 'displacement' as well.

Since demand usually varies from season to season, the result may well be a 'package' agreement by which the hotel agrees to take a certain number of group bookings at the high season (thus sacrificing some revenue) in return for an undertaking by the tour operator to

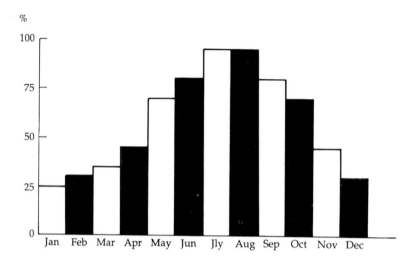

Figure 74   *'Peak' and 'shoulder' occupancy periods*

take up rooms during slack or 'shoulder' periods (Figure 74). Such agreements are sometimes expressed in terms of a formula such as 1:1 or even 1:2, depending on the relative strengths of the negotiating parties. The tour operators will have to work harder to fill whatever off-season blocks they have committed themselves to, so the bargaining is likely to be keen.

Alternatively, the hotel may raise the level of discount offered according to the number of rooms booked over a twelve-month period. There are only a limited number of rooms available over the high season, so any extra rooms must fall outside the peak season. The effect of such a quantity discount is to encourage the tour operator to sell off-peak packages.

One of the advantages of group business is that it provides the hotel with a degree of security. As long as the tour operator is reliable, the hotel knows that a significant number of bookings are 'in the bag' well in advance. Moreover, the administrative costs of handling this type of booking are lower (though this is offset to some extent by the need to spend time on negotiations). These factors help to increase the attractiveness of group bookings.

On the other hand, groups may tend to drive out higher-yielding customers. This is different from 'displacement' because it may happen even if the hotel is not turning away late bookings. Individual rack rate customers are sometimes deterred by the prospect of mixing with package tour holidaymakers or conference delegates, and switch to other hotels. This effect is difficult to measure, but it is real and needs to be taken into consideration. Because of it, hotels may restrict the overall number of rooms to be allocated to groups at any one time.

Advance booking aspects

A group represents a much larger proportion of a night's bookings than any single reservation, and a failure on the part of the tour operator to honour its contract is much more serious than an individual 'no show'. Hotels thus take even more interest in the commercial reliability of tour operators than individuals, and check them more carefully. Individual guest

Group reservation form

A/date ....   Stay (nts) ....

A/time ....   Dep/time ....

Group name ....

Tour operator ....

Address ....
....
Tel ....   Telex ....   Fax ....

Contact ....

Rooms	No	Rate	Comps	Adj/con	Z beds	Cots
SB						
TB						
DB						
Other						

Special requirements ....
T/agent ....   Ship/plane ....

Meals	D/arr.....	Day 2.....	Day 3.....	Day 4.....	Day 5.....
B/fast					
Lunch					
Dinner					
Other					

Account instructions ....

Taken by ....   Date ....

T.B.C. ☐ By ....   Confirmed ☐ Date ....

Figure 75 *Group reservation form*

histories are very much an optional feature of hotel procedures, but it is normal to maintain some such form of 'agent record card' as far as tour operators are concerned.

Hotels also protect themselves by imposing cancellation deadlines. A tour operator who allows this deadline to go by but then fails to take up the full number of rooms reserved remains liable for the full amount agreed. Cancellation deadlines are normally set at one month before the arrival date, but this may be extended to two or even three months in the case of very large groups. The point is, of course, that it is more difficult to resell large numbers of rooms at the last minute.

Group bookings are inherently more complicated than individual ones because there are a number of additional factors to consider. These include:

1   *The arrangements for payment*   The package price is simply transferred to the tour operator's ledger account in the usual way, but it may be necessary to open separate 'extras' accounts for individual group members so that they can obtain drinks, laundry and possibly room service on credit. If such credit is not extended, the situation needs to be made clear to both the guest and the other hotel departments in a manner which the former does not find offensive.

2   *Any additional administrative arrangements*   Groups are often directed to a separate area for check-in purposes, partly to foster a feeling of group cohesion and partly to avoid long queues at reception. They may also have some kind of welcoming party, or a special 'guest amenity package'. The group reservation form needs to summarize these details and spell out the division of responsibilities between the hotel and the tour operator.

3   *Arrangements in respect of couriers, etc.*   Groups are normally accompanied by a courier or tour organizer, and often by a driver as well. It is common for such functionaries to be accommodated free or at reduced rates, especially if they handle administrative tasks which would otherwise have to be undertaken by the hotel's own staff. These arrangements need to be spelled out in the group reservation form.

4   For all these reasons, group reservation forms are likely to be more complex than individual ones. A typical form is shown in Figure 75. As you can see, this form places more emphasis on the actual arrival and departure times. It is important to know these so that the hotel can be ready. It also asks for the name of any travel agent who might be handling the group locally (this is quite a common practice), and for details of any ship, flight or other form of transportation (the hotel might be well advised to ring up the local airport to confirm that the plane is actually on time). Finally, details of all meals and other refreshments agreed are included so that the food and beverage department can be advised.

As we have seen, Group bookings are often made much further in advance than individual ones. A 'time horizon' of two years or so is not uncommon. The tour operator then sells places on the group tour, which means that the actual bed spaces are booked long before they are actually taken up. This means that there may have to be last-minute adjustments to the room allocations (the group organizers may find that they have sold slightly more twins and fewer singles than they expected, for instance).

Hotels are naturally anxious to find out the exact position as far in advance of the date of arrival as possible. They need to know if the group will require more twins, for example, or whether it is going to be able to release some singles for last-minute sale to high-yield customers. The hotel will, therefore, press the group organizers for a detailed rooming list several days in advance.

The rooming list should give the names of the group members, the type of room to be allocated and other relevant information, such as details of those who want, or are willing, to share and those who want adjacent rooms. It is also helpful if it includes nationalities and passport numbers, because this allows the hotel to pre-prepare registration forms.

Unfortunately, the organizers may suffer from last-minute cancellations, or still be selling places up to the last minute, so may have difficulty in supplying a final rooming list. This is a common source of conflict between hotels and group organizers. The hotel should understand the latter's problems, but it is still its job to keep prodding and cajoling the group organizers to send the rooming list through as soon as possible. Clearly, continuing difficulties in this respect would be noted on the agent record card and taken into consideration in any further negotiations.

The hotel's other departments need to be given details of any group arrivals well in advance so that they can make their own arrangements. Even if front office does not circulate individual arrivals lists, it is almost bound to distribute a group arrivals list. This is often sent out a week in advance.

Check-in aspects

The main problem on arrival is likely to be possible overload of the reception facilities. As we have seen, groups are often directed to a separate area for registration. The hotel should consider to what extent pre-registration is possible. Ideally, it will have printed off a registration form and included this with a pre-prepared 'welcome' package for each individual guest. It is also possible to get the group tour guests to complete a registration form prior to arrival: on the coach from the airport, perhaps. Tour organizers are usually only too willing to cooperate with front office to smooth out the registration process.

Computerized systems make provision for this important type of business. It is usually possible to allocate a code reference to each group. Entering this when you are checking in the guest automatically transfers the agreed accommodation and meal charges to the master bill, while still allowing you to maintain an 'extras' account if desired.

A typical procedure for a unified group (i.e. one that all arrives at the same time) would be:

1   Enter the 'check-in with Reservation' section of the program. Skip the guest's name and address fields on the screen and enter the group code.
2   The program will then display the group's members in accordance with the rooming list previously entered. As each name is displayed, you type in the room number and hand over the appropriate room key and/or welcome package. The room number is not entered until this stage because you can't be sure that any individual group member is going to arrive until he actually does so.
3   The first name on the list should be that of the group organizer or courier, because he is responsible for the master bill.
4   The program should allow you to choose between options such as:

  (a)   Full package terms, no 'extras'.
  (b)   Full package terms, with 'extras' for some or all group members.
  (c)   Room rate only to master bill, other charges to individual bills.

This procedure still allows you to reassign rooms not taken up because of non-arrivals.

In-residence

There are no special procedural aspects, but it is sometimes necessary to guard against a tendency on the part of staff to treat group members as 'second-class guests'. The main problem is likely to centre around which 'extras' can be charged to accounts, and all departments need to be clear as to the exact terms.

Check-out aspects

These mirror the check-in procedures. The tour organizer will want to keep the group together, so a separate waiting area is a good idea. This also helps to free the rooms for servicing.

The hotel needs to ensure that all keys are returned and any 'extras' bills are paid. It is very much in the tour operators' interests to cooperate in this process, because otherwise they will be involved in chasing up any guests who have not settled with the hotel.

Conferences

Conferences are very similar to groups. They are often arranged just as far in advance, and represent just as significant a part of the night's business. Consequently, the procedures for handling conference business are very similar.

The main difference is that the hotel has to provide more in the way of facilities. Conferences require general meeting rooms and additional syndicate discussion rooms, as well as areas set aside for conference registration, press briefing (if appropriate) and any associated social events. The key points to be considered in respect of a conference booking are as follows:

1 *Accommodation requirements*   These cover not only the number of delegates expected and the types of bedroom required, but also the conference rooms themselves.
2 *Equipment*   Modern conference presentations often employ sophisticated audio-visual aids, and the hotel ought to be able to provide microphones, slide, film and overhead projectors, speaker's lecterns etc., as well as humbler items such as pencils, notepads and ashtrays. There is often a need for copying facilities or computer networks, as well as telephone and fax facilities. All this needs to be discussed and agreed with the organizer.
3 *Food and beverage requirements*   It is usual to break the conference proceedings up with a series of tea and coffee breaks, and these must be agreed with the client and arranged with the food and beverage department.
4 *VIP arrangements*   Many conferences invite distinguished guest speakers to address them. These may need to be met at the airport or station, and should be afforded every possible courtesy by the hotel as well as the conference organizers.
5 *Signs etc.*   It will be necessary to put these up so that the delegates can find their way around.
6 *Partner's programmes*   Delegates often bring their wives, husbands or children along with them, and a programme of visits, excursions and other activities may be arranged for them.

This too requires planning, and the extent of the hotel's responsibility (and the appropriate charges) needs to be settled beforehand.

A point worth bearing in mind is that unlike group tour members, conference delegates may very well have differing arrival and departure dates. Some only come for a day or two, while others may take the opportunity to stay on longer afterwards in order to get to know the area better. This represents a possible source of business for the hotel, but it also raises some problems, the main one being what kind of terms should be offered in respect of the additional days. This needs to be considered in the light of what we have said about yield management.

Timeshares

Timeshare developments are often centred around a hotel, and a number of hotels have converted some of their accommodation into timeshare apartments or are run along timeshare lines. Such developments may be found in both resort areas and in city centres.

The basic timeshare concept is that a purchaser buys limited ownership rights to a specified unit of accommodation. These entitle him to occupy that accommodation for a given period each year (the periods are usually multiples of one week) over an extended time span (twenty, forty or eighty years or more). The property is usually a self-catering apartment, but this is not always the case: the timeshare concept can also be applied to shorter periods in ordinary hotel accommodation.

The same unit of accommodation can be 'sold' to fifty separate buyers (two weeks per year are usually held back for maintenance). Each buyer is entitled to use the accommodation during his specified week, though he then has to vacate it so that the next owner can move in. Timeshare is cheaper than maintaining a separate holiday home, and has the advantage that maintenance can be taken care of by the management.

The advantage to the developer is that since the units are actually sold, the development costs can be recovered more quickly than with an ordinary hotel. However, the marketing costs are high since each unit has to be 'sold' up to fifty times, and are generally estimated to equal the actual construction costs. Timeshare selling techniques have attracted some unfavourable comment in recent years, but you should distinguish between reputable members of the industry and the 'cowboy' end of the market.

Buying a timeshare does not mean that the owner has to go back to the same destination at the same season every year for the rest of his life. There are various provisions which add greater flexibility:

1 All reputable schemes belong to one or other of the main timeshare exchange programmes. These allow owners to 'swop' their weeks with other periods elsewhere (as with foreign currency, there can be favourable or unfavourable exchange rates).
2 There are a number of hotel schemes which allow owners to take their time allocation on a day-by-day basis, to 'stockpile' entitlements (i.e. carry them forward from one year to the next), or to choose between a number of participating hotels.
3 Owners do not necessarily have to occupy their accommodation themselves. They can put it at the disposal of their relatives, for instance, or their employees (a significant proportion of timeshare visitors are in fact guests of the actual owners).
4 Owners unable to take up their allotted period can ask the management company to let it

for them instead. The company would charge a fee for this service, but the letting income can still be substantial, and some owners treat their timeshares as revenue-earning investments.

The management of a timeshare operation requires special consideration. Since there is multiple ownership of the accommodation (sometimes this is effected through shareholding, sometimes through club membership), there needs to be an owners' association. In theory this is responsible for running the complex, but in practice it often enters into a management contract with the developer or an experienced hotel company. Such contracts have to cover reciprocal duties and responsibilities, maintenance arrangements, the fees to be paid by the owners and many other matters, and are inevitably very complicated.

From the front office point of view, the main complications arising from timeshare letting are likely to be as follows:

1   In 'pure' timeshare the owner is entitled to occupy one specific unit of accommodation for a specified period. This means that it must be 'blocked' on some form of conventional chart (club style arrangements whereby an owner is entitled to a certain number of nights anywhere within a group usually require him to advise the hotel he has selected well in advance and are subject to availability restrictions). Owners might be expected to remember their own periods, but experience suggests that it is a good idea to remind them nevertheless.
2   As indicated, many timeshares are actually occupied by the owner's relatives, friends or employees, or by exchange visitors, or are let to strangers. The management's front office needs to keep track of these. The question of whether an owner needs to register when occupying his own property does not seem to have been resolved, but the safest answer would appear to be 'yes', and this is certainly true for non-owner occupants.
3   Although owners have already paid for their accommodation and are only liable for the annual maintenance charge, there will still be a need for some 'guest accounting' to cover:

    (a)   Normal lets.
    (b)   Hotel type services such as laundry etc. incurred by owners or their guests.
    (c)   Extra nights, possibly in alternative accommodation.

To sum up, timeshare management is very similar to ordinary hotel operations with some additional complications. We have discussed most of these, but the main one is that owners are likely to be even more critical of any shortcomings. This is understandable: after all, it is *their* property!

Assignments

1   Compare the Tudor and Pancontinental Hotels from the standpoint of their attitudes to yield management and group business.
2   Your hotel has 200 rooms. The forecast cumulative bookings for one particularly busy date in the future are as shown in the table below, together with the actual cumulative bookings six months prior to that date.

	Rate (%)	Months											
		−12	−11	−10	−9	−8	−7	−6	−5	−4	−3	−2	−1
Forecast bookings													
Rack	80	2	5	7	10	12	15	17	20	22	25	37	50
Agency	70	1	2	4	5	7	10	14	17	25	32	40	50
Corporate	60			1	2	3	4	6	8	10	20	35	50
Group	50	20	25	30	35	40	50	50	50	50	50	50	50
Actual bookings:													
Rack	80	3	7	10	13	18	24						
Agency	70	1	3	5	6	9	12						
Corporate	60						1						
Group	50	12	24	24	30	30	40						

What action should you take at this point?

3 You are the front office manager of a hotel with 100 beds. The average rack rate is £55, at which you expect occupancies to be as follows: Saturday 25 per cent, Sunday 25 per cent, Monday 95 per cent, Tuesday 95 per cent. You are approached by ConTours plc (a major tour operator) with a request that you take a group of sixty-five persons from Saturday night to Wednesday morning (i.e. four nights) at a room rate of £25 per person. Would you accept this booking? Ignore secondary displacement and any food and beverage aspects.

4 Prepare a flow diagram showing the major stages in dealing with a group booking, detailing the documents and procedures involved, together with the important deadlines.

5 It has been said that Gresham's Law (i.e. that the bad drives out the good) applies to hotels in the sense that group business may alienate higher yield customers. Do you consider this to be true, and, if so, what practical measures can be taken to reduce the effect?

11 Control

Introduction

The importance of the control process cannot be overemphasized. There is no point in having a well-designed, beautifully furnished establishment with highly-trained and motivated staff if it fails to reach its objectives.

The control process involves:

1 Establishing targets.
2 Monitoring performance in order to see whether these targets are being attained.
3 Taking corrective action wherever necessary.

The control of front office operations is only one aspect of general management control, which covers all the hotel's operations. These include the control of housekeeping and maintenance activities as well as food and beverage control and financial control. In this work we shall be concerned only with front office control, but it must be remembered that this has to be integrated with all the other aspects we have mentioned. Cash control, for instance, is only one part of general financial control, and similar procedures will have to be followed in the bars and restaurants.

The establishment of targets lies outside our terms of reference. Sales targets are usually set by general management or head office, though the expertise of the front office manager is clearly an important element in this process, and budgets and staffing levels are commonly decided in consultation with various other heads of department. We shall, therefore, be concentrating on the way in which front office monitors those activities for which it is directly responsible, namely, the letting of accommodation and the consequent billing and cashiering process.

The completion of various kinds of reports is an inescapable part of this process. Reports are the lifeblood of most organizations, and hotels are no exception. As we have already seen, they not only tell management what has happened, but they also form the basis for predictions regarding the future. This is particularly important with a highly-seasonal business like a hotel, where demand can often vary considerably from one day to the next.

In one respect, the nature of the hotel's 'product' makes the control process easier. The inventory is highly perishable, which is just another way of saying that an unsold room night cannot be stockpiled and offered again another day. There are thus no finished stocks or 'work in progress' to carry forward, and a twenty-four hour period can be viewed as a natural entity, complete in itself. It is relatively easy to say whether we have done well or badly, and the only factor likely to affect this is the possibility that one or two customers might not pay their bills.

On the other hand, the special nature of the hotel's business makes accounting speed and accuracy particularly important. The hotel must make sure that its bills are correct before the first guests begin to leave in the morning, which can mean six o'clock. The guests themselves often come from far away, and it is difficult to correct errors after they have left. These factors impose special strains on the control process.

There are two essential pieces of information which a front office manager needs to have in order to evaluate the success or failure of the day's operations. These are:

1   The number of rooms let.
2   The amount of revenue earned.

We shall look at each of these in turn. Before doing so, however, we must consider the very important question of verification.

Verification

Control involves records, as we have said, but these are useless unless the information they contain is accurate. Records can be incorrect for two reasons:

1   People often make silly, careless errors. They may post a meal voucher to the wrong account, for instance, or simply neglect to post it at all.
2   Occasionally, some people deliberately falsify records in order to cover up some form of wrongdoing.

Verification is based as far as possible on the comparison of records which have been produced independently. This usually catches any careless, unintentional errors because two people seldom make exactly the same mistake. It also helps to reduce the incidence of deliberate falsification, because there would have to be collusion between both parties if it were to succeed.

This comparison process has been called 'the internal audit triangle'. Strictly speaking, it is not a triangle at all because there are really only two 'sides', but it certainly has three points. These are the three departments or subdepartments which produce booking and billing records (Figure 76).

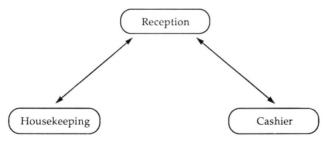

Figure 76   *Internal audit triangle*

The first side of the so-called triangle is the comparison of reception's record of rooms let with the housekeeper's report. In manual systems, the front office report is based on the room rack. A computerized system will display or print out its own summary of this information,

Housekeeper's report

Date: Time:

Summary:

	Let	Vacant	OOS	Total
SB				
TB				
DB				
TOTAL				

Analysis:

No	Tp	Let	Pers	No	Tp	Let	Pers	No	Tp	Let	Pers	No	Tp	Let	Pers
101	SB			201	SB			301	SB			401	SB		
102	TB			202	TB			302	TB			402	TB		
103	TB			203	TB			303	TB			403	TB		
104	TB			204	TB			304	TB			404	TB		
105	DB			205	DB			305	DB			405	DB		

Abbreviations: – Vacant   C/O Checked out   DND Do not disturb
                O Occupied   S/O Slept out   OOS Out of service

Figure 77   *Housekeeper's report*

which will be accessible to both departments. This printout will be internally consistent, but it is still necessary to conduct a physical check because it may not reflect the reality of the situation.

A housekeeper's report is produced independently of front office. It is compiled on a room-by-room basis and summarized by the head housekeeper. It looks something like Figure 77, though the layout and abbreviations used will vary from hotel to hotel.

'Occupied' means that the room has been used and there is still luggage in it. 'Checked out' shows that it was used but the guest has left. 'Slept out' means that the room is recorded as having been let but has not been slept in (it may mean that the guest has left the hotel for a day but has asked that his room be kept available, but it may also mean that he had paid in advance and did not bother to call in at the front office when he left). 'DND' indicates that the housekeeping staff have not been able to get into the room: if it remains this way for too long, some form of investigation may be called for. 'OOS' means that the room is being repaired or redecorated, or is otherwise unavailable.

This report has to be checked against the room rack or computerized room status display. In small hotels there are only likely to be one or two discrepancies, and these can be cleared up quickly. In large hotels it may be necessary to prepare a 'discrepancies report', which is sent back to the head housekeeper for double checking.

There will be three main types of discrepancy:

1   The rack shows 'occupied' but the housekeeper's report shows 'vacant'. The possible explanations are:

   (a)   The room rack is wrong, usually because the receptionist has forgotten to update it when the guest left. This is quite common with manual systems but much less likely with a computerized system, which will automatically update its room status records whenever a guest is checked out. Occasionally it is found that a room has continued to be shown as 'occupied' on the room rack for twenty-four hours or more after the guest has checked out. This is serious, for the room might have been let to a 'chance' customer in that time.

   (b)   There has been a 'walk out' (i.e. a guest has left without paying). This is even more serious, for it is a definite loss to the hotel, almost certainly including food, drink and services as well.

2   The rack shows 'vacant' but the housekeeper's report says 'occupied'. In this case the possible explanations are:

   (a)   The receptionist has forgotten to update the rack when it registered a guest. Again, this is almost impossible with a well-designed computerized system, especially one that issues a coded room key on registration.

   (b)   The room might have been used by staff without notifying front office.

   (c)   Someone has *deliberately* failed to check in a sleeper using the normal procedures. This is the most serious situation of all, for it suggests that the person reponsible may be indulging in one of the oldest of all the front office 'fiddles', namely, letting a late night 'chance customer' into a room on payment of a reduced sum directly to the receptionist (or night porter, since these have often been left in charge of the desk in small hotels). This is particularly difficult to detect since there will be no trace of the admission anywhere in the records, and neither the 'guest' nor the employee involved are likely to say anything. The crime (for it *is* a crime under the Theft Act) is easier to commit in a small hotel where the desk is only manned by one person, but it is not unknown even in large hotels. A computerized system is not necessarily any help since the 'transaction' bypasses it completely, and even a key issuing facility does not guarantee protection since the night staff must have access to pass keys. As we have seen, modern systems can record every use of a key, but a criminally inclined employee will probably be able to produce an explanation ('I wasn't sure if it had been cleaned, so I just nipped up to check . . .') and in any case such records are not always checked through in detail.

3   There are differences regarding the number of people who have slept in the room. This is another serious matter, especially if the rack says 'one' and the housekeeper says 'two'. One possibility here is that the guest has booked as a single and then smuggled a friend (or a prostitute) in to share his accommodation. This practice is difficult to detect since it will not appear in the records, and also difficult to prove since some single guests in twin rooms *do* change beds during the night. Nevertheless, the hotel may be losing money, and any unauthorized use must be prevented if possible.

All these possibilities underline the need for the housekeeper's report.

The second side of the 'internal audit triangle' is the checking of the financial records. This has two main aspects:

1   In manual systems it is common practice to check the room rates as shown on the room rack against the bills as shown on the tabular ledger. The object is to ensure that no accommodation charges are missed off. This is usually accomplished by adding up all the room rates as shown on the rack slips and comparing the total with that of the 'rooms' column on the tabular ledger. This process does not detect charges which have been posted to the wrong account, but it does provide a fairly simple check against simple omissions. Again, computerized systems are much simpler in this respect because the rate is automatically entered on registration and simultaneously charged to the guest's account.

2   The cash must be checked against the records. There is no point in latter being accurate if the cash itself is not there. This process is one of the main features of any front office day, because cash is uniquely liquid and will 'walk' at the slightest opportunity. Cash control is simple in theory, time consuming in reality. The main points are:

   (a)   All cash received (including foreign currency) must be properly recorded at the time of receipt.
   (b)   Manual records should be balanced regularly and reconciled with cash in hand.
   (c)   Cash must be kept under lock and key. It is usual for a safe to be provided, but this may also be used for the safekeeping of guests' valuables, so separate tills are provided for current 'floats' (i.e. cash required for the giving of change).
   (d)   Only a limited number of 'floats' should be authorized, and these must be signed for and kept under the control of the responsible individual. This implies that the cash should be checked every time the responsible individual goes off shift. This can be a chore, but is a necessary part of the routine.
   (e)   Individual cashier codes should be allocated, and these should be kept confidential. Computer systems should make it impossible for any unauthorized person to learn an individual's code.

Night audit

Although each shift is expected to 'balance up' before going off duty, hotels normally draw the line under each day's trading between midnight and 6 am the following morning. This is the most convenient time because:

1   There will be few arrivals or transactions during that period.
2   It is essential to check that the accounts are correct before the guests start to leave the following morning.

This process is known as 'night audit'. In a large hotel it is often the responsibility of a separate employee (or even a small team) known as the night auditor(s).

The role of the night auditor is as follows:

1   To ensure that any outstanding transactions have been entered. There may very well be some outstanding restaurant vouchers to be posted, for instance, or one or two late arrivals, and in a hotel offering twenty-four-hour room service it is always possible that there will be some drinks or snacks to record as well.
2   To verify that all the bills and other accounts are correct. This means checking (often on a sampling basis) to make sure that vouchers have been posted to the correct accounts, that cash balances as shown are actually represented by cash in the safe, and that miscellaneous items such as guests' property deposited for safekeeping are actually there.
3   To verify that front office's guests in residence records are up to date and accurate. As we have seen, this involves using the 'internal audit triangle'.
4   To prepare a management report summarizing the day's trading activities.

Computerized control systems

One of the great advantages of a computerized system is that it reduces the need to duplicate entries, thus eliminating many common types of error. The computer's accounts will always be 'in balance', and the tally of rooms let should always agree with the total number of room charges.

This apparent infallibility creates a risk that the control procedures will be reduced or even eliminated. Front office staff using a manual system are always aware of the possibility that a minor error may lead to a discrepancy when they come to 'balance up' at the end of their shift. The fact that the computer will always be 'in balance' tends to lead to a complacent assumption that those balances are necessarily correct, which is not so. As the well-known computer saying 'garbage in, garbage out' reminds us, a computer is only as accurate as its information input allows it to be. If room rates have been entered incorrectly, or charges posted to the wrong accounts, then the final bills will be just as wrong as if they had been done by hand.

It is, therefore, necessary to check computerized records in the same way as manual ones. There are four steps in this process:

1   The records must still undergo the verification processes we have already described. In particular:

   (a)   Room rack printouts should be compared with some form of housekeeper's report. The fact that the computer shows a room as occupied does not necessarily mean that it is.
   (b)   All cash balances and items on deposit must be physically checked. Once again, the fact that the computer says they should be there does not necessarily mean that they are.

2   The records also need to go through the night audit process. Systems will vary somewhat in this respect, but are likely to include the following:

   (a)   It should be possible to print out a comparison between the rack rates and the actual rates charged for all occupied rooms, with the reasons for any differences. This allows the auditor to check that all discounts and other allowances are properly accounted for.
   (b)   It should also be possible to print out a complete record of all transactions posted during the day. This provides the necessary 'audit trail'.

3 After completion of the night audit process, the computer will probably have to be 'reset'. This is because its memory is not unlimited, and it is necessary to 'clear' it of unnecessary detail before starting to enter the following day's transactions. This process will involve, among other things:

- Setting all daily totals back to zero.
- Updating any cumulative figures.
- Automatically reducing all current stays by one night.
- Deleting all cancellations and departures, and transferring the latter to guest history files.

In the interests of safety, it is essential to make a back-up copy of all the files being deleted, in case there turns out to have been a mistake and it is necessary to go back and rerun. The system in use ought to make all this as easy as possible. As we have said before, many hotels find it advisable to back-up more than once per day. It may also be desirable to obtain a printed record of the items being deleted for future reference.

4 Preparing reports summarizing the day's activities. These are usually much more varied and detailed than is possible with a manual system because of the computer's ability to scan all the data already in the system. With a well-designed program, pressing the appropriate key or keys can produce any or all of the following reports:

- Arrivals List
- Departure List
- VIP Guest List
- Group Tour List
- Chance Guest List
- Regular Guest List
- Cancellations Report
- No Shows Report
- Room Availability
- Vacant Room List
- Rooms Out of Service
- Extra Bed/Cot List
- Room Vacate Times
- Room Changes List
- Maintenance Report
- Messages Report
- Revenue Report
- Deposits Report
- Credit Limit Report
- Commissions Due List
- Corrections Report
- Rate Analysis Report
- Folios (Bills) List
- Currency Report

All of these (and others, too) contain information which can be useful to the front office manager. In addition to these simple lists and summaries, the computer can also produce a variety of management statistics. This task needs to be done within manual systems, too, and is such an important part of front office duties that we ought to consider it separately. Before that, however, we should discuss the various measures of performance which might be used.

Occupancy and revenue reports

The main figures required are simple enough to understand. There are two traditional calculations (occupancy and average rate), each usually subdivided into two (room and guest). In recent years there has been increasing interest in a third (income occupancy). They are calculated as follows:

Occupancy percentages

These are subdivided into:

1   Room Occupancy, i.e.

$$\frac{\text{Rooms occupied}}{\text{Total rooms available}} \times 100$$

2   Beds occupancy, i.e.

$$\frac{\text{Beds occupied}}{\text{Total beds available}} \times 100$$

Both of these are needed in order to check on the incidence of double occupancy. If room occupancy was 95 per cent, for instance, and bed occupancy was only 78 per cent then you could tell at a glance that a significant number of your twins or doubles had been occupied by single persons. This might not appear to matter very much if the hotel has a 'per room' tariff, but don't forget that a single guest can only consume one meal at a time, and that restaurant and bar takings may suffer.

Sometimes management will ask for an additional statistic, namely:

Double Occupancy, i.e.
$$\frac{\text{Double/twins let to two persons}}{\text{Total doubles/twins}} \times 100$$

This is self explanatory.

The main problem likely to arise when calculating occupancy percentages is that of the base figure. The number of rooms available tends to fluctuate for a variety of reasons. Sometimes whole floors or wings are taken out of service during the 'off' season, or individual rooms are closed off for redecoration or staff use.

There is a certain amount of disagreement as to how this should be handled. Some hoteliers prefer to base their occupancy percentages on the number of rooms actually available, arguing that you can't let a room which has been taken out of service. However, we believe that it is best to use a standard base figure throughout. This allows you to see:

1   The real level of occupancy during the 'off' season (after all, you are still incurring overheads like insurance and depreciation on the empty rooms).
2   The proportion of rooms set aside for non-revenue earning purposes such as complimentaries or staff use (especially if they *could* have been let).
3   The proportion of rooms out of service at any time (again, especially if they could have been let. Planned maintenance should ensure that rooms are only redecorated during slow periods: it is important to know if this is not being done).

A second problem may occur should you manage to squeeze more guests in than you appear to have rooms or beds for. This can happen because of 'day lets', or because you have put in some 'Z' beds, or managed to convert a spare room of some kind, as occasionally happens during periods of very high demand.

A few hoteliers argue that you ought to increase the base figure in these circumstances, because you can't really have an occupancy of more than 100 per cent. However, this is an accepted convention within the industry, and almost everyone knows what it means.

Average rate figures

These are subdivided into:

1   Average room rate, i.e.

$$\frac{\text{Total room revenue}}{\text{Total rooms let}} = \text{Average room rate}$$

2   Average guest rate, i.e.

$$\frac{\text{Total room revenue}}{\text{Total sleepers}} = \text{Average guest rate}$$

Again, it is useful to have both figures in order to provide another check on the incidence of single letting of twin or double rooms. If a hotel had 100 standard twin rooms, each occupied by only one sleeper at a per person rate of £40, the figures would be as follows:

1   Average room rate: $\dfrac{50 \times £40}{100} = £20$

2   Average guest rate: $\dfrac{50 \times £40}{50} = £40$

The difference between the two rates would make it clear that there had been a significant amount of single letting.

The main value of these figures is that they give us a quick indication of the extent to which discounting is taking place. It would be easy to achieve 100 per cent occupancies night after night by reducing the room rate to £1 per night, but this wouldn't be very profitable.

It is possible to compare these average rates with a break-even figure and thus tell whether the accommodation department has made a profit or a loss on any particular night.

Income occupancy percentage

A major disadvantage of the average rate figures is the difficulty of comparing one year's figures with another, especially during a period of high inflation. Imagine, for example, that you are told that your hotel's current average guest rate is £74.50 whereas in 1970 it was £9.75 and then asked to say whether it was doing better or worse. What you need is a handy yardstick for this kind of comparison.

This has led to increasing interest in the 'income occupancy percentage'. It is calculated as follows:

$$\frac{\text{Total room revenue}}{\text{Optimum room revenue}} \times 100 = \text{Income occupancy } \%$$

The optimum room revenue is of course the maximum obtainable given 100 per cent occupancy at full rack rates.

The income occupancy percentage allows us to compare performance over a period of years. Returning to our hypothetical example, let us assume that our 100 room hotel had an optimum room rate of £10 in 1970 and £80 today (which is not too unrealistic). Its average occupancies were 90 per cent in each case. The income occupancy percentage calculations are as follows:

$$1970 \quad \frac{90 \times £9.75}{100 \times £10.00} \times 100 = 87.75\%$$

$$\text{Today} \quad \frac{90 \times £74.50}{100 \times £80.00} \times 100 = 83.81\%$$

Now it is easy to see that our hotel was doing better in 1970.

Income occupancy percentages assess both our ability to fill the hotel *and* our ability to obtain something close to the full rates for the rooms. A high but heavily discounted occupancy pattern would produce a relatively low percentage, as would a low occupancy pattern at the full rack rate.

This calculation is thus the single most important one available to management, though it needs to be supplemented by occupancy and average revenue figures to explain just why it may have gone up or down. In turn, these can be further split down according to room types to

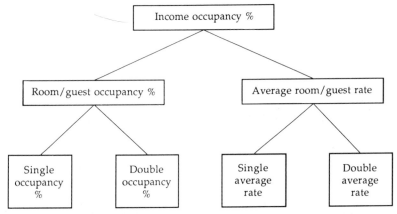

Figure 78   *Control pyramid diagram*

give even greater control. The process might be illustrated diagrammatically as shown in Figure 78.

Daily occupancy reports

The various figures we have been discussing need to be combined in a regular daily report. Five desirable features of such reports should be noted:

1 *The figures should be comparative*   In other words, they ought to compare what did happen with what you thought should have happened, thus allowing you to assess the accuracy of your predictions. You should be familiar with the concepts and practices of budgetary control, and be able to see how these apply here.
2 *Space should be allocated to an 'analysis of business'*   We have already pointed out when discussing yield management that different types of customer may very well be paying different rates. The overall results of the actual sales mix achieved will be revealed by the average room and guest rates, but it is useful to be able to explore this further. The categories will not be the same for all hotels, of course, but most are now taking much more interest in the kind of business they are attracting.
3 *Space should also be set aside for a detailed analysis of house use and complimentaries*   This is necessary because otherwise a devious employee might put a friend in a room under one of these headings, trusting that no one would notice. Comparison of the room rack with the housekeeper's report would reveal no discrepancy, and the Housekeeper's department would not usually query the allocation. It is thus necessary to scrutinize any such use carefully.
4 *It is useful to note any groups or conferences being hosted*   These can have a significant effect on total occupancies, and should be recorded for future reference.
5 *Finally, space should be set aside for 'comments'*   This is not (as you might suppose) to allow you to note any unusual incidents, but rather to record anything else which is likely to have affected the occupancy level, such as 'heavy fog', 'rail strike' or 'major exhibition'. These are all events which will make the occupancy percentages non-typical, and it is important to record them for future reference.

A possible layout for such a report is shown in Figure 79. There will be many variations in practice.

Forecasts

Control is not just a historical process. In fact, there is no point in calculating *any* of the figures we have been discussing *unless* they are used to improve future performance.

An important part of this process is forecasting. We have already looked at this in connection with yield management. However, there is also a need for relatively detailed short-term forecasts in order to help receptionists to make last-minute booking decisions, and also to assist other departments in their planning.

The forecast period is usually five to ten days. The forecast is prepared daily, so that each

Day:.................... **Daily occupancy report** Date:....................	Actual		Budget	
	Today	To date	Today	To date

Rooms sold:
  Singles
  Twins (single rate)
  Twins (double rate)
    Total rooms sold
  Complimentary
  Company use
  Out of service
  Vacant
    Total rooms				

Sources of business:
  Individual
  Travel agent
  Airline
  Group tour
  Conference
    Total guests				

Room revenue				
Room occupancy % Guest occupancy % Average room rate Average guest rate Income occupancy %				
Company and complimentary use: Room Name Company Explanation				
Groups:				
Comments:				

Figure 79 *Daily occupancy report*

day is recalculated up to ten times with ever-increasing accuracy. A possible layout for a five-day forecast is shown in Figure 80.

This assumes standard rooms and ignores possible single occupancies of twins. It could be made more detailed if required. However, it does indicate the kind of factors which need to be allowed for when preparing such forecasts, namely:

Day/date	Five-day forecast				
	☐ ☐	☐ ☐	☐ ☐	☐ ☐	☐ ☐
Stayovers					
Departures:					
Check-outs due					
Extra departures					
Total departures					
Arrivals:					
Reservations					
Less no shows					
Add 'chance'					
Total arrivals					
Stayovers (next night)					
Vacant					
Total rooms					

Day:....................   **Five-day forecast**   Date:....................

Figure 80 *Five-day occupancy forecast*

1 The number of extra or unplanned departures likely.
2 The likely 'no-show' rate.
3 The likely number of 'chance' guests.

All these can be forecast with considerable accuracy on the basis of experience. Obviously, your predictions will not be exactly correct, but the stayovers figure can be updated daily on the basis of the actual arrivals.

Other statistics

There are a number of other control statistics which management will find useful. They include the following:

1   Average daily spend per guest

This is particularly helpful if it is broken down by guest category, because then it reveals which market segments are worth attracting on the basis of their spending within the hotel and its various facilities. Casino hotels, for instance, are well aware of differences in the amounts wagered by the single booking 'high roller' on the one hand and the 'package tourist' on the other.

The figure is easily calculated:

$$\frac{\text{Total guest bills}}{\text{Total guests}} = \text{Average daily guest spend}$$

2   Average stay per guest

This is also useful in terms of deciding which type of guest to attract, but more so in determining the kind of facilities which need to be offered. In general, the longer the stay, the more varied the meal and other 'experiences' required. A careful watch on the length of stay figures will enable mangement to make sure that they continue to make proper provision for these needs.

The figure can be obtained relatively easily by taking an appropriate period such as a week or a month and then calculating it as follows:

$$\frac{\text{Total room nights}}{\text{Total guests}} = \text{Average stay per guest}$$

An alternative approach is to take the 'nights stay' figure from the registration forms, add them up, and then divide by the total number of forms. This figure will not be precisely accurate because of overstays and early departures, but experience suggests that these tend to cancel each other out and that the final figure is accurate enough for most purposes.

3   Analysis of guests by nationality

It is useful to be able to see where guests come from in order to be able to discern trends and assess the effectiveness of particular marketing campaigns.

This figure is easily obtained by analysing the registration forms and then turning the figure for each country into a percentage. For instance, if a hotel had 1340 visitors during the period under consideration, of whom 265 were from the USA, the percentage of American visitors would have been 19.78 per cent.

4   Analysis of business by region of origin

This is very similar to a nationality analysis, and may in fact form a continuation of that process. It is often helpful to know from which regions one's guests are coming.

This information is obtained by analysing the addresses given on the registration forms. A highly-detailed breakdown is not usually necessary: it is usually sufficient to use standard regions such as 'South East' or 'North West'.

5 Analysis of bookings by source of business

This is another useful statistic. It allows us to measure the effectiveness of different bookings channels, and also offers some guidance as to yield.

   This figure can also be obtained by analysing the registration forms, providing these note the source of the booking. It is simple to add the bookings from different sources together and then turn these into percentages as you did with the guests' nationalities.

6 Lost room revenue

This is the number of rooms unsold multiplied by the average rate achieved (in practice, since most hotels fill up 'from the bottom', this will understate the amount of the loss slightly). It represents what we *might* have done given better marketing and sales techniques. There is a school of thought which argues that this is the most important statistic of all, because it creates a greater sense of urgency. A 90 per cent occupancy rate can lead to a certain degree of complacency, whereas 'There were ten rooms we *didn't* sell last night' creates a much greater feeling of urgency.

7 Denials (business turned away)

It is very useful to know how many requests for accommodation are being turned away. In practice, late cancellations and no shows mean that a high level of requests can still result in an occupancy percentage of less than 100 per cent.

   Table 15 shows how this can happen. It shows the booking position in respect of 100 standard rooms over a six-month period up to the date of arrival.

Table 15

	Month						
	−6	−5	−4	−3	−2	−1	Totals
Requests per month	25	25	25	25	25	25	150
Cancellations per month		2	3	5	10	15	35
Bookings per month	25	25	25	25	10	10	120
Cumulative bookings	25	48	70	90	90	85	
No shows						10	10
Arrivals						75	75

In this example, requests remain steady at twenty-five per month, while the number of cancellations increases steadily (we have assumed that these come in *after* the requests, which is not entirely true but helps to simplify the calculations). The other figures are obtained as follows:

1 The first requests are received during month minus-six (i.e. six months before arrival), and all can be accommodated. The cumulative bookings figure (i.e. total bookings taken) is thus twenty-five.
2 During month minus-five the hotel accepts another twenty-five requests, making fifty bookings in all, but it also has two cancellations, so the cumulative bookings total is reduced to forty eight ($25 + 25 - 2 = 48$).
3 During month minus-four the hotel accepts another twenty-five requests, but since it also receives three more cancellations the cumulative bookings total is only seventy ($48 + 25 - 3 = 70$).
4 During month minus-three it accepts twenty-five more bookings and has five more cancellations, yielding a cumulative bookings total of ninety ($70 + 25 - 5 = 90$).
5 During month minus-two it receives another twenty-five requests. However, it can only accept ten of these since it already has ninety bookings and there are only 100 rooms. It also receives ten cancellations, so the cumulative bookings total remains at ninety ($90 + 10 - 10 = 90$).
6 During month one (the last month), it receives a further twenty-five requests, of which it is able to accept ten. However, it also receives fifteen cancellations, so that the final figure for expected arrivals is only eighty-five ($90 + 10 - 15 = 85$). Of these, ten turn out to be no shows, so that the eventual arrivals total is only seventy-five.

In this case the hotel received 150 requests in all. Admittedly thirty-five of these cancelled later, and ten more turned out to be no shows, but there were still thirty unsatisfied requests for accommodation (150 requests less 120 actually booked). True demand, in other words, was closer to 110 per cent rather than the 75 per cent occupancy actually realized (seventy-five completed bookings plus the thirty refused, though this does not allow for those of the latter who might have cancelled later or turned out to be no shows).

In practice, few hotels record 'denials' because they involve making a separate entry, often when the front office staff are very busy. However, we have already suggested that a wait list is a good idea. If brief details of any unmet requests can be entered on this (name, contact number, room type and dates required), then the production of denial statistics becomes much easier. Any name not crossed off the wait list (i.e. not eventually roomed) will be a 'denial', and these can be added up. Usually this will only involve a limited number of nights, so the administrative burden is not as excessive as it might at first appear.

We have already indicated that overbooking can help to reduce the impact of late cancellations and no shows. However, it is still useful to know just how much demand there really is. It may justify management in adding some extra rooms!

It should be obvious that you will obtain the greatest benefit from putting all these different statistics together. You may for instance find that certain nationalities stay longer and occupy higher priced rooms than others, or that group tour business produces a lower average spend overall. Many of these results are likely to be self evident, but you may well get one or two surprises.

Assessing guest satisfaction

Since the guest is the focus of all the hotel's services, it is important to try to find out how successfully his needs are being satisfied. Upward or downward trends in the occupancy percentages will indicate this in an indirect way, but these might be influenced by all kinds of other factors, from changes in the economic environment to the arrival of new competition in the vicinity.

Guest questionnaire

Please help us to maintain the standard of the service we offer by answering the following questions:

How did you hear of the hotel?

From friends ☐	From travel agent ☐
From advertising ☐	From tour operator ☐

Other (Please specify):...

How did you make your reservation?

At reception ☐	Tour operator ☐
Phone ☐	Central reservations ☐
Letter ☐	Other hotel ☐
Travel agent ☐	

Other (Please specify):...

How do you rate the following (please tick appropriate column):

	Excellent	Good	Fair	Poor
Reception?				
Telephone service?				
Room cleanliness?				
Room facilities?				
Room prices?				
Restaurant food quality?				
Restaurant menu choice?				
Restaurant service?				

Your name (optional):...........................   Date of stay...........................

Profession:...........................   Room:...........................

We are very grateful to you for your comments. They will be given careful attention. Thank you for staying with us, and we hope to see you again!

Figure 81 *Guest questionnaire*

One way in which managers have tried to do this has been to get people to stay at the hotel as guests and then report back on their experiences. However, there is really no substitute for the real guest's own comments. Unsolicited letters are perhaps the most genuine type of feedback you can have: only a small minority of visitors take the trouble to sit down and write a letter afterwards, and it is a good rule of thumb to assume that one letter represents around ten or so satisfied (or dissatisfied) customers. In other words, they should be taken seriously.

'Prompted' comments can also be useful. If you are serious about wanting to find out whether your package is really satisfying the guest, the quickest and simplest method of finding out is to ask him directly. However, such replies need to be kept confidential. Old-fashioned hotels often used to maintain a visitor's book in which guests were invited to write their comments. In theory these could be critical: in practice they hardly ever were, mainly because the writers knew that their comments could be read by everyone else who stayed at the hotel.

Guests' views are best obtained by means of a 'guest questionnaire'. This is usually left in the guest's room. Not all guests actually complete it, but those who do can provide useful data. Such questionnaires should:

1 Be as short and easy to complete as possible (this means using boxes for ticks rather than asking for extended comments).
2 Commit the guest to expressing a positive opinion rather than just 'ticking the centre column'.
3 Allow the guest to remain anonymous if he so desires.
4 Contain an explicit promise that the guest's opinions will be studied and if necessary acted upon.
5 Thank the guest (in advance) for any information provided. This is only normal courtesy but it is particularly important within the context of an establishment dedicated to 'service'.

Normally such a questionnaire will cover the whole of the hotel 'package' rather than just its accommodation aspects. It may look something like Figure 81.

Assignments

1 Compare the control systems likely to be found in the Tudor and Pancontinental Hotels.
2 Obtain specimens of the type of control vouchers and other documents used at a selection of local hotels, and compare these with one another, relating the characteristics to the types of hotel involved.
3 You are acting as front office manager in a large hotel. At 11.00 am you discover that there is a discrepancy between the room rack and the housekeeper's report regarding occupancies for the preceding night. According to the latter, rooms 802 (single) and 1125 (twin) have been occupied, whereas the room rack does not show this, and no bills have been made out. What steps would you take?
4 Describe how the front office control system relates to the management control system of a hotel as a whole.
5 The following shows a room rack at the start of the evening:

101 S Mr Blake (1) £24	201 S	301 S Mr Singh (1) £24
102 T Mr/s Snow (2) £38	202 T Mr/s Rowe (2) £38	302 T
103 S	203 S Mr Harris (1) Comp	303 S
104 T Dr/Mrs Jenks(2) £40	204 T	304 T Mr/s Ryan (2) £40
105 T Mrs Carter (1) £30	205 T	305 T
106 T	206 T Mr/s Keys (2) £40	306 T Mr/s Scott (2) £40
107 S	207 S	307 S
108 T Mr Toms/fam(3) £50	208 T Ms Morris (2) £40	308 T
109 T U/s (Repairs)	209 T Mr/s Thomas(2) £38	309 T U/s (Repairs)
110 S Mr Lucas (1) £24	210 S	310 S Mr Croft (1) £24

The following amendments were recorded during the remainder of the evening:

- Mrs Carter negotiated a change to Room 107 @ £24.
- Mr/s Nolan arrived and were allocated Room 204 @ £40.
- Mr Clark arrived and was allocated Room 201 @ £24.
- Miss Drury arrived and was allocated Room 207 @ £24.
- Mr/s Creery and their two daughters arrived and were allocated Rooms 105 and 106 @ £40 and £30 respectively.

Design a simple room occupancy and revenue report to record letting performance, and complete it for the night in question.

12 Staffing and equipment

Introduction

We need to look at this aspect before concluding our survey of front office operations. It is of course the business of the front office or accommodation manager, but that is no reason why you should not consider it too. You may reach that rank yourself some day, and in any case it is useful to know the kinds of criteria such managers ought to be applying.

The provision of an effective front office service is a matter of selecting the right staff, giving them the right equipment, training them properly, and then letting them get on with it, using the control process we have already described to monitor their performance.

Unfortunately, these activities overlap into other management subjects. Staffing, for instance, covers the establishment of appropriate staffing levels, recruitment, selection, induction, training, motivation, staff welfare and appraisal. Most of these are the province of the personnel expert, and we do not intend to try to cover them here. You are advised to consult a good personnel textbook. What we *do* propose to look at are the questions most likely to be asked of the front office manager, namely:

- What staff are required?
- What kind of recruits are needed?

This should allow us to prepare a specimen job description and a specimen personnel specification (the latter as a basis for interviews), which is what the personnel department would ask the front office manager to do in a large hotel. We would have liked to go further and explore the question of training, but this is a specialized field. Our chapters on procedures, social skills, selling and marketing should give you some idea of *what* skills you would want your staff to acquire; *how* to get these across effectively is perhaps best left to the experts.

As far as equipment is concerned, this mainly concerns computers. Once again, there is a lot of overlap with other specialisms. Hotel computers often handle a great deal more than just front office routines (they are used for general accounting purposes and food and beverage control, for instance), and you should consult one of the growing number of excellent textbooks on this subject for a full study of such integrated systems and their more technical aspects. All we are concerned to do here is to provide a general and non-technical account of:

- What computers can do for front office now, and
- Their implications for future front office operations.

It should be obvious that one possible consequence is the substitution of technology for staff. Nevertheless, our conclusion is that machines are no substitute for human beings as far as the provision of 'hospitality' is concerned, and that there will continue to be a major role for the warm, cheerful, genuinely hospitable front office employee.

Staffing

Introduction

No matter how well designed a system may be, it can only be as good as the people who run it. Well-qualified, well-trained and well-motivated staff are an essential element of any successful front office operation.

We have already looked at the general organization of front office and its place within the hotel as a whole. All we need to remind you of here is that front office has five main responsibilities, namely:

- Advance bookings
- Switchboard
- Reception
- Billing
- Cashier

In a large hotel, these are all separate sections, each with its own supervisor. In small establishments, all the duties may have to be undertaken by a single receptionist, who may find herself taking bookings, registering arrivals, putting calls through, posting charges and taking payments at different times (occasionally all at once, or so it can seem!).

In addition, there must be management staff on duty in order to deal with major problems or the kind of guest who says 'I demand to see the manager.' In a small hotel these responsibilities will be undertaken by the manager or assistant manager. In a large hotel there may well be a number of 'duty managers', who cover a twenty-four hour period between them and whose job it is to make sure that the various section supervisors cooperate in solving any problems which arise.

Even in large hotels, it is a good policy to move front office staff around so that they can experience different aspects of the job. This helps to maintain their interest and enthusiasm, and increases staff flexibility. Some such hotels start new staff in the back office so that they can learn about the rooms and the systems in operation before going onto reception to meet real live customers on a face-to-face basis. All-round experience is also valuable because the work often comes in peaks and troughs, and it is useful to be able to pull somebody out of the back office, say, and put them on the desk to help deal with a sudden rush of arrivals.

All this means that it is desirable that front office staff should have some experience of the work of the department as a whole, and should not be confined to their own narrow specialism, no matter how large the establishment may be. This is particularly important with regard to potential supervisors or managers.

'Job enlargement' has been advocated by many industrial psychologists, and some attempts have been made to apply this on a more extended scale. One major company experimented with appointments inspired by the airline's 'air hostesses'. These employees were expected to handle not only reception duties but also housekeeping and food and beverage service, with the emphasis placed very much on customer relations. However, the range of duties involved was too wide, and the experiment was not a success.

Other attempts have been made to apply the concept within front office. The idea is to encourage a single receptionist to deal with a particular guest or group of guests throughout their stay as far as possible. Shift patterns make this difficult to achieve, but it certainly develops a feeling of involvement on both sides, and helps to counteract the feeling of anonymity that guests sometimes get in very large and busy establishments.

The 'host' or 'hostess' concept has also been tried occasionally. Guests are greeted by a pleasant, attractive, well-groomed person who directs them to the appropriate clerk and makes sure that the clerical functions are handled smoothly. However, there is an element of artificiality about trying to separate the 'hospitality' side of the job from the 'clerical', and our view is that all front office staff should employ social skills as an integral part of their job.

Numbers and hours

How many receptionists are needed? This is a very difficult question to answer. An old rule of thumb sometimes quoted was that a receptionist ought to be able to handle 50–60 occupied rooms. However, this excluded switchboard operators and back office staff. If the receptionist was also required to handle guest billing and cashiering duties, this figure would have to be substantially reduced. All we can usefully say is that it depends on:

1 *The number of* occupied *rooms*   Empty ones do not give rise to any clerical activities or customer contact, though the loss of revenue ought to be a cause for concern.
2 *The average length of stay*   Guests who stay for seven nights on inclusive terms put less of a burden on front office than one night stays (they only need to be registered once, and their bills are simpler).
3 *The pattern of activity*   Most hotels experience departure and arrival 'peaks' in the early morning and the late afternoon, and these may call for extra staff to be on duty. Resort hotels may have similar, weekend 'peaks'. On the other hand, a busy airport hotel may have a much more even distribution of arrivals and departures.
4 *The amount of personal contact required*   This can be reduced by various means. Groups can be pre-registered, or some of the formalities can be looked after by the group organizers. Automated check-in and check-out can reduce the amount of time the guests needs to spend at reception. Experienced 'FITs' (frequent independent travellers) may welcome such innovations, but other guests still prefer the personal touch, and contact times should allow for the pleasantries which help to create that impression of 'hospitality'.
5 *The character of the hotel*   A few minutes' wait might be acceptable in a small country hotel catering for a leisure market, whereas it is quite inappropriate in a busy city centre environment. Luxury hotels in particular must try to avoid exposing their guests to the indignity of having to queue, even for a few minutes.
6 *The technology employed*   Manual methods are more expensive in terms of clerical time than mechanized or computerized ones. Automated telephone exchanges reduce the number of telephonists required, for instance, and POS (point of sale) terminals can considerably reduce the amount of voucher posting that has to be done.

The best way to approach the question of staffing requirements is to consider *what* has to be done, and *when* it must be done by. This must be determined by the guest's requirements, not the hotel's. The guest wants to be checked in smoothly on arrival, shown to a clean, vacant room, allowed to eat, drink and enjoy an undisturbed night's sleep, and then checked out again swiftly and efficiently when he leaves, and it is up to the hotel to arrange its staff schedules to make sure that this happens. Let us consider the activity patterns of the main front office areas:

1   Advance bookings for a large international hotel may come in at any time of the day or night, but in most establishments they will tend to be concentrated during normal business hours, with something of a 'peak' when the morning mail arrives.
2   The switchboard will also be busiest during normal business hours.
3   The reception desk will have to be staffed from the early morning to the late evening, and large, busy hotels will need somebody on duty overnight as well. The main 'peaks' will come when guests depart (usually 7.30 to 10.30 am) and arrive (about 3.00 to 7.00 pm).
4   The billing and cashiering 'peaks' will be concentrated in the morning (when early morning teas, breakfasts etc. have to be posted), middle of the day (lunchtime postings and dealing with bar and restaurant takings), and the evening (opening bills for new arrivals, posting accommodation charges and bar and restaurant vouchers).
5   The control process should go on all the time, but the natural time for a general review of the day's activities is overnight, when most guests are asleep and there is time to check the figures before they wake up and start demanding their bills. This is so common that the process is almost universally known as 'night audit'.

What this activity pattern calls for is a series of shifts. With a normal working day of eight hours, the whole twenty-four-hour period can be covered by three consecutive shifts, an 'early' one starting some time between 06.30–07.30, a 'late' one from 14.30–15.30, and a 'night' (or 'graveyard') shift from 22.30–23.30 to 06.30–07.30 again. The night shift does not usually require so many staff as the other two, and often attracts specialists who for some reason or other don't mind working at night.

This shift pattern undoubtedly creates problems. Staff have to start or finish earlier or later than in most jobs. There are sometimes transportation difficulties, and the personal security of staff (especially females) going home late at night is a legitimate cause for concern. Weekend work is also necessary because hotels have to remain open seven days a week, but it is not always popular.

Some of the stress can be reduced by introducing a supplementary 'middle' shift, which might last from mid-morning to early evening (08.30–10.30 to 16.30–18.30). This covers the normal business hours and many of the back office activities like taking advance bookings. It might suit an older, experienced person with a family, or could be introduced as part of a rota scheme to allow ordinary staff a 'normal' day at regular intervals.

Arranging staff rotas is one of the most challenging of the front office manager's duties. The front desk must be covered at all times (except in small hotels), on weekends as well as weekdays. Holiday entitlements need to be built in, and rotas arranged in advance so that staff know when they are going to be off duty, even though the hotel may have to cope with considerable variations in terms of occupancy. The rotas must be seen to be fair to all concerned, but there must be a judicious mixture of youth and experience on duty at any time. The need to draw up staff rotas (in the housekeeping and food and beverage departments as well as front office) is one of the main reasons for producing medium-range occupancy forecasts.

Assuming a medium-sized hotel operating a standard three-shift pattern, the day's work might be programmed as follows (this is a simplified example: most hotels will have their own terms relating to the specific equipment and procedures being used):

07.00–09.00   Early shift take over from night shift; check float; early morning calls, post early morning teas, papers etc.; check-out departures; present bills; deal with payments; file registration cards.

09.00–12.00   Mail (advance bookings and confirmations etc.); check stopovers on chart and liaise with housekeeper; check stopovers for credit limits; check room availability and ring round other hotels if necessary; check housekeeper's report and account for discrepancies (if any); run key check if appropriate.

12.00 on   Post lunches to bills; cash up lunch and bar receipts.
15.00   Check float and safe; reconcile cash etc.

15.00–17.00   Late shift takes over; check float etc.; check room availability and current arrivals list; check any VIP arrivals and confirm arrangements; prepare arrivals and departures lists for next day; prepare registration cards for next day; file correspondence; check-in early arrivals.

17.00–20.00   Check-in normal arrivals; check 6 pm releases and ensure these rooms are available for chance requests; check any no shows; deal with book-outs (if necessary).

20.00–23.00   Post room charges, dinner and bar vouchers; check float and safe; reconcile cash etc.

23.00–07.00   Night shift takes over; check float etc.; check-in late arrivals and chance guests; check room status report; carry out night audit; run back-up procedures.

Staff selection

One of the accommodation manager's tasks is to recruit new front office staff. In a new hotel she must start from scratch and select a complete team. This will generally be built around one or two experienced staff, but many of the employees will be new to the job, and they will certainly be new to each other. In an established hotel, it will generally be a question of filling individual vacancies. Labour turnover among receptionists varies from hotel to hotel, but some changes are inevitable.

The aim of the recruitment process is to select the best person for the job. This means that the person doing the recruiting must have a clear idea of what the job entails. The best method of ensuring this is to prepare a detailed job description. These will vary in detail from hotel to hotel, according to the systems, procedures and equipment used, but will bear a general resemblance to Figure 82.

It is also desirable to have an idea of what kind of person you are looking for to fill the vacancy in question. The recommended method of achieving this is to prepare a personnel specification. This ought to cover the main points against which you will be assessing applicants. There is no need to work these out for yourself: personnel experts have already produced well-tried Interview Plans, and it makes sense to follow one of these in preparing

---

Job title:	Senior Receptionist
Place of work:	Queen's Hotel, Melcaster
General scope of job:	To carry out reception duties as laid down in the hotel's operating manual, and to assist the front office manager in maintaining an efficient, helpful and sales orientated department.
Responsible to:	Front Office Manager
Responsible for:	Receptionists, telephonists, reservations staff

Main duties:

1 To have full knowledge of, and be able to act in accordance with, the hotel's fire plan and the Fire Act 1971.
2 To be fully conversant with, and be able to implement, the Hygiene and Safety Act of 1974 to the highest possible levels.
3 To ensure that all guests and their requests are dealt with efficiently, courteously and promptly.
4 To maintain a high standard of personal hygiene and appearance.
5 To ensure that strict security is maintained in respect of all monies, keys, guest property and hotel equipment.
6 To ensure that all reservation, registration and check-out duties are carried out as laid down in the hotel's operating manual.
7 To carry out the duties of reservations clerk, receptionist or telephonist as necessary.
8 To be responsible for the reconciliation and banking of all receipts and floats as laid down in the hotel's operating manual.
9 To prepare all relevant statistics as laid down in the hotel's operating manual.
10 To carry out any reasonable duty required by management for the efficient operation of the hotel.

Occasional duties:

- To carry out general clerical or administrative duties as required by management.
- To assist management with the induction and training of new front office staff.

Figure 82   *Job description*

your personnel specification, since this allows you to conduct an effective and comprehensive interview.

The National Institute of Industrial Psychology's well-known 'seven point interview plan' allows us to consider the following points:

1   *Physical requirements*

The job has few taxing physical requirements, except that receptionists do rather more standing than is usual in clerical jobs (even if this is not true of back office personnel or telephonists). However, the hours *do* impose a certain amount of stress, which is why many accommodation managers have a preference for younger applicants, who can be expected to be more resilient.

Physical appearance is an important factor, since the receptionist is one of the chief representatives of the hotel as far as the guest is concerned. However, you do not have to look like a film star to get a job in front office. Attention paid to grooming is far more important: neat hair, a clean face and hands and tidy clothes will normally be sufficient for most situations, especially if they are accompanied by a pleasant smile.

2   Attainments

An applicant's previous experience can be a valuable guide to her likely effectiveness. Obviously, previous front office experience is the best recommendation, though this needs to be tempered with common sense: what is right for one hotel is not necessarily right for another, and you don't want to recruit the kind of person who is always saying: 'That's not the way we used to do it at the Superbe.'

If this is not available, then clerical experience of some other kind is useful, especially if it involved dealing with the public in a customer service context. Such applicants will be prepared to meet the occasional rude or even hostile guest, and should have evolved their own strategies for dealing with them. This aspect of the job needs to be made clear to them, so that if they *aren't* willing to be civil they can withdraw their application before it is too late.

Records of previous employment can be read with an eye to spotting significant unexplained 'gaps' or unusually rapid job turnover patterns. Front office staff are often in a position of trust as far as guests' valuables are concerned, so honesty is an essential quality. They will have to relieve their colleagues at awkward times, so reliability is another important quality. Someone who has never worked early or late hours, or in a situation calling for the display of individual initiative is an unknown quantity as far as front office is concerned.

3   General intelligence

The clerical aspects of the job call for staff who are reasonably literate and numerate. Clerical entry requirements are usually expressed in terms of school-leaving qualifications: there is no such thing as a rigid requirement, but a commonly accepted standard is three or four GCSE 'O' level passes or their equivalent, preferably including English and Mathematics.

4   Special skills and aptitudes

Obviously, a qualification in reception work is a very considerable recommendation, since the applicant has already demonstrated both interest and aptitude, and will require less training.

Other than this, the skills called for fall into two main groups:

(a) *Keyboard (i.e. typing, machine operating or computer) skills*   These are highly desirable in most front office situations. There are still many small establishments which use manual tabular ledgers and produce handwritten bills, but few of these would dream of sending out a handwritten letter. Keyboard skills of some kind are thus essential, and familiarity with the layout of a typewriter keyboard can easily be transferred to a computer. A knowlege of computer programming or how a computer actually works is not necessary: far more important is the ability to follow manuals which are still, alas, not particularly 'user friendly'.

(b) *Linguistic skills*   A knowledge of any of the main foreign languages likely to be used by guests is a valuable asset, especially if it covers what the language specialists call 'oral/aural' skills (i.e. the ability to understand what people are *saying* to you, and to respond effectively). Associated with this is an awareness of the existence of intercultural differences. This tends to come with a knowledge of languages, but it can also be the product of foreign travel.

5   Interests

This heading is mainly of use because it provides some clues as to the applicant's personality traits, which are assessed next.

6   Disposition

This is perhaps the most difficult area to assess, and also the hardest to sum up in words. Nevertheless, it is very important. We all know that our friends tend to behave in fairly predictable ways: 'X' is always cheerful and enthusiastic, for instance, whereas 'Y' can be grumpy and irritable, and 'Z' is often timid and lacking in initiative. There is a good deal of argument regarding the extent to which these characteristics are innate or acquired: for our purposes this is less important than the fact that people do exhibit differences of personality.

Let us consider what personality traits are required by front office staff. As we have seen, the job has three main elements:

(a) *Clerical*   This requires staff to be conscientious, methodical, and accurate. Because they may have to be on duty alone, they also need to be self-reliant, and since the problems are often 'immediate' ones, they must be prepared to accept responsibility.
(b) *Hospitality*   This requires staff to be friendly, sympathetic and understanding, and to possess the behavioural skills necessary to project these qualities. We have discussed these skills in some detail earlier: to some extent they can be acquired, but it is still true that some people possess them naturally to a greater extent than others.
(c) *Selling*   This requires staff to be knowledgeable, enthusiastic and persuasive. In these days of yield management, it also requires them to be reasonably numerate, and tough enough to be able to negotiate successfully with people who make a living out of driving hard bargains.

To some extent these qualities are mutually exclusive. It is not easy to be tough when you are naturally sympathetic, or to sound understanding when your feet hurt and there are several reports and reconciliations to be completed before you can hand over.

The real clash is between the 'introvert' and the 'extrovert'. Introverts are naturally self-absorbed, shy and withdrawn. They are not easily distracted, and are generally careful and methodical: useful qualities, in fact, for the 'clerical' side of the task. Extroverts, by contrast, are naturally gregarious and spontaneous, but they are more easily distracted and not always as careful as they should be.

The question is, which set of qualities should you put first? Ideally you want a combination of both, but this is not always possible. The choice is influenced by three considerations:

(a) The procedures are not hard to master, whereas it is much more difficult to teach social skills.
(b) An effective control process should 'catch' any serious procedural errors.

(c) The effect of any such errors can usually be cancelled out by the effective exercise of social skills.

Personal specification:
Post: Junior receptionist

		Essential	Preferred
1	**Physical**		
	Age		18–25
	Health	Good	
	Appearance	Neat, well groomed	Attractive
	Voice	Pleasant, clear	Acceptable accent
2	**Attainments/Experience**		
			Full time work in equivalent hotel
			Good reference
3	**General Intelligence**		
	Secondary	GCSE or equivalent with English and Maths	
4	**Special Skills/Aptitudes**		
	Secondary		Typing
			Language(s)
			Computer Studies
	Advanced		
	Further		C&G reception
			BTEC Diploma
			First aid certificate
	Higher		
5	**Interests**	Sociable, gregarious, fluent, self-reliant,	Persuasive, numerate,
6	**Disposition**	Honest	Initiative, mature
7	**Circumstances**	Local	Live-in

Figure 83 *Personnel specification*

These suggest that if it is necessary to choose, it would be better to go for the applicant who is naturally hospitable.

The extent to which applicants possess these traits can be assessed both before and during interview. The completed application form often offers indications as to the presence or otherwise of desirable qualities. Examination successes not only indicate the possession of specific skills and a certain level of general intelligence, but also (by implication) a methodical approach and a degree of self-motivation. Many forms contain an 'interests' section, and this can tell you much about an applicant. Indications of sociability are valuable (club membership, for instance), as is any evidence of organizing ability or a constructive concern for other people (someone who shows such concern in their private life is likely to project it in their professional guise too).

The interview has many limitations as a selection method, but as far as front office staff are concerned it does have the advantage that it enables you to assess the applicant's social skills directly. An applicant who turns up untidily dressed, who mumbles her answers and who fails to respond to your welcoming smile is hardly likely to behave very differently when she is behind the desk, and should not be employed. Interviewees who recognize the importance of being well turned out and who can be fluent and outgoing in what is admittedly a stressful situation are likely to exhibit the same qualities in employment. However, allowances have to be made for differences in background: a school leaver attending her first interview is unlikely to be as confident as someone with several years' experience.

7   Circumstances

This is of some importance because of the special requirements of the job. Applicants who are restricted to regular business hours for some reason or other (husbands, wives, children etc.), or who would have to travel long distances at inconvenient times, are clearly at a disadvantage, and the likelihood of their being able to perform their duties regularly and successfully needs to be examined carefully.

Flexibility often requires that preference be given to single applicants who are prepared to live in. However, this group tends to be more job mobile than most, so the policy more or less guarantees a high labour turnover rate. It is up to the front office manager to decide to what extent this outweighs the advantages of having staff to hand to cover emergencies.

A personnel specification ought to describe the kind of person who could fill the job reasonably satisfactorily, not an ideal candidate who might well turn out to be overqualified for the job. This means that it is sensible to divide the qualities you are looking for into 'essential' and 'desirable', since you are unlikely to find many applicants who have everything you could possibly want. A possible personnel specification is shown in Figure 83.

Computers

The computer is a relatively recent innovation which is revolutionizing many aspects of front office work. We have discussed the differences between manual and computerized procedures in a number of places, but it would still be useful to bring these points together and to try to come to some general conclusions.

In doing so, we must recognize that this is very much an unfinished revolution. The first hotel computers were installed during the 1960s, but they were cumbersome and expensive. Even in the later 1970s it was estimated that a hotel needed to have 200 rooms or more to justify a computer. The introduction of powerful but inexpensive business personal computers has changed all this, and now all but the very smallest hotels can afford their own. The technology is continuing to change, and we can expect more and more functions to be computerized during the next decade.

That being so, you should try to acquire some knowledge of computers. It is not really necessary to know how they work, or be able to write programs, but some awareness of what is meant by 'processing speed' or 'memory capacity' would be useful when (as is likely) you have to evaluate new models. It is also important to know enough to avoid careless mistakes. Trying to move a machine when its hard disk is running is a recipe for a very expensive disaster, and leaving floppy disks around exposed to sunlight, radiator heat, cigarette smoke or the odd coffee stain is also bad practice. Almost everybody loses some data sooner or later, but you should try to be one of the exceptions. In particular, observe the 'back-up' routines absolutely scrupulously. There are few things worse than losing twenty-four hours' worth of bookings and transactions, and then having to recreate them all by hand!

You should also familiarize yourself with the standard business software, namely:

1 *Word processing* Front office will often be called upon to send out non-standard letters, and you need to be conversant with the word processing software in use in your establishment.
2 *Desktop publishing* Linked with a good printer this allows you to produce good quality brochures, posters, display cards and many other items for which you would normally have to go to a printer. This could save your establishment both time and money.
3 *Spreadsheets* We mentioned this in our introduction, and we have offered one or two suggestions as to where spreadsheets could be useful, but there are likely to be other areas as well.
4 *Graphs packages* Many of the statistics we have discussed can be presented more clearly and more excitingly in the form of a graph or pie chart. Computers can handle this task, too.

The advantages of computers

As far as the purely front office applications are concerned, computers offer a number of significant advantages over manual systems. We have already mentioned some of these in connection with various aspects of front office operations, but it is useful to bring the points together in a more general summary:

1 Reduction in entries

This arises because of the computer's ability to analyse information once it has been entered (this is a 'data base' function: as you should know, the main task of this type of program is to allow you to sort and classify data entered in a variety of 'fields').

This point can be demonstrated by means of a simple example. A manual system normally requires *two* separate records in order to keep track of a guest in residence. One appears on the room rack (to show who is occupying that particular room), while the other appears in the switchboard's guest index (to enable them to find out which room the guest is occupying). Patent systems allow you to produce duplicate copies, so reducing the amount of writing involved, but they still require two separate cards or slips. A computer, on the other hand, can produce *either* a rooming list *or* an alphabetical guest list from the same set of registration entries, and it can go further and do a guest search for you providing you type in the guest's name (modern systems will even accept 'fuzzy' inputs and produce near equivalents even if you don't get the name right).

2   Automation

The computer can be programmed to make a whole range of necessary entries quite automatically. This means that nightly room charges need never be omitted, and that complicated breakdowns of inclusive rates (so much for the room, so much for breakfast, lunch, dinner etc.) can be handled quickly and accurately.

It also means that the necessary updating of records can be handled automatically. When a guest arrives and is allocated a room, the room display (room rack) is automatically amended to indicate the fact. When he checks out, the room is automatically shown as having been vacated and all the room total figures are altered. Some systems also allow a guest history file to be created when the guest leaves: if there is already such a file, this is updated automatically.

3   Processing speed

Once data has been entered, the computer can process it very quickly. This applies to all the normal mathematical functions (e.g. addition and subtraction), which means that the long drawn out process of balancing the tabular ledger becomes a thing of the past, and that running totals of all guest bills can be maintained without difficulty. It also applies to most 'search and sort' activities, which means that it is usually quicker to run a guest search on the screen rather than to scan a manual room rack visually.

In addition, it means that reports and statistics can be produced very quickly. Since the computer can handle complex calculations without difficulty, a much wider range of statistics can be produced. This facility also allows you to exercise much tighter control with respect to overbooking, pricing and yield management decisions, all of which can be made much more responsive to changes in demand.

4   Accuracy

This quality is implied in all we have said so far. The computer's figures will always be correct (just so long as the input is not 'garbage', of course), which helps to inspire confidence. It also reduces much of the burden of night audit.

5   Networking

What we mean by this is the computer's ability to handle entries from a number of different sources simultaneously (technically, this is not strictly accurate, but from the operator's point of view the necessary 'switching' appears to be instantaneous).

This allows items to be fed into guest bills from a variety of POS (point of sale) terminals scattered throughout the hotel building. It also allows front office and housekeeping to exchange information about the current state of rooms virtually instantaneously (in the precomputer era this could only be done by installing elaborate wiring systems terminating in room racks with coloured light displays).

Even more important, it permits entries to be made from considerable distances away.

As we have seen, this opens the door to automated guest check-in (where a guest inserts his credit card into a cash dispenser type machine and is issue a coded room key in return). It also means that receptionists at other hotels (or even independent travel agents) can make bookings at your hotel without the intervention of any of your front office staff.

These advantages are real, and they are the reason why computers have been adopted so widely and so quickly. To summarize, they allow:

1 Most traditional front office activities to be carried out more quickly, more accurately and more economically.
2 Many *additional* activities to be undertaken by front office. These either offer higher levels of service (the facility to preview bills, for instance) or increase the hotel's commercial efficiency (yield management).

Some limitations

Nevertheless, computer systems still have certain drawbacks. Not all hotels which have bought computerized systems have been happy with their choices. These problems will no doubt be reduced or eliminated in time, but at the moment they consist of the following:

1 Breakdowns

The systems are still not 100 per cent reliable, and occasionally 'crash' at awkward moments. This means that it is necessary to make hard copy back-up records at frequent intervals (how frequent depends upon the number of transactions being handled: some very large and busy hotels 'save' their data every half an hour, though twice daily is more usual).

2 Audit trail requirement

Coupled with the reliability problem is the need to provide a written or printed 'audit trail' just in case anything goes wrong. This again means that all transactions need to be printed out, which in turn means that the 'paperless hotel' forecast by the enthusiasts is further off than ever (in fact, computer systems often generate *more* paper than manual ones).

3 Memory restrictions

Although there have been tremendous advances in terms of data storage, the computer's memory is still finite. As we saw when we considered control, it is necessary to 'clear' it of a lot of out-of-date or unwanted records in order to free space for the following day's transactions. Thus, although night auditors have been freed from a lot of tedious balancing and reconciliation work, there is still a certain amount of essential computer 'housekeeping' to do every twenty-four hours.

4 Training time

The immense range of things that front office computers can do makes the programs complicated and thus difficult to master. This necessarily increases the length of time it takes to train front office staff, and this problem has been made worse by the fact that not all the software available to date has been particularly 'user friendly'.

5   *Speed restrictions*

Although computers process information incredibly quickly, the actual data entry process can take a surprising amount of time. One obvious reason for this is that it all has to be keyed in (so that the computer can only be as fast as the operator's typing speed), but another reason is that the computer has to be told what to do every step of the way. This means that you have to go through a particular series of steps in strict sequence.

Typically, you would have to start with the 'main menu' screen and then select the subsection you want. If this happens to be 'reservations', you then have to tell the computer which particular date the booking is for, and there will be a short delay while the computer loads the bookings for that date. Making the booking itself will involve moving through a series of 'fields' on the screen, some of which may be irrelevant as far as that particular booking is concerned. The programmers will probably have built in a series of short cuts, but the process still takes time.

So do the safety routines. Computers have to be made 'idiot proof' because once you lose electronic records they are gone for ever. Consequently the program will frequently stop, give an annoying little 'bleep' and ask you 'Do you really want to do this?' Only when you type 'Y' will it go ahead. This is all very necessary, but it is also time consuming.

6   *Compatibility and expandability*

Not all computer systems can 'talk' to one another easily, and it is frustrating not to be able to link up with a larger group or national network simply because of technical limitations. This can be a problem when groups merge. On a smaller scale, businesses often find that their initial choice of hardware (often made with cost considerations in mind) turns out to be too limited once they begin to appreciate the possibilities of the new technology.

7   *Dependence upon suppliers*

A small hotel buying a computerized system becomes heavily dependent upon its suppliers for:

(a)   Servicing
(b)   System documentation, training and support

This is fine as long as the supplier is reliable, but computing in a dynamic field and there have been casualties.

The result of all these limitations is that a small hotel with a limited number of rooms may still find it quicker and simpler to use a simple conventional chart and tabular ledger. Instead of having to jump backwards and forwards from the reservations program to the billing program and back again, the receptionist can simply glance up at the chart, make a quick entry in pencil, and then turn back to the 'tab'. Moreover, as at least one disillusioned front office manager was heard to say, neither chart nor tab are dependent on the **** electricity supply!

Front office applications

A typical front office computer program starts with a main menu which may look something like Figure 84 (note that this is a generalized example, not a specific program).

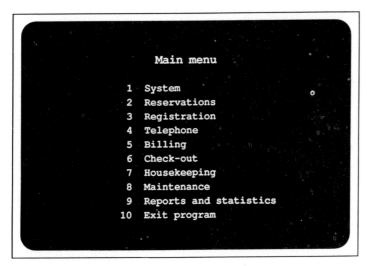

```
                    Main menu

            1   System
            2   Reservations
            3   Registration
            4   Telephone
            5   Billing
            6   Check-out
            7   Housekeeping
            8   Maintenance
            9   Reports and statistics
           10   Exit program
```

Figure 84   *A computerized system's main menu screen display*

Most of these headings are self-explanatory, but one or two may need explanation. The 'system' option is reserved for management. It will be used to set up the various parameters for the hotel, such as the number and type of rooms, the rack rates and the various special rate 'packages', the types of report required and so on. Somewhere within it will be a subroutine allowing the front office manager to allocate individual codes to receptionists. Obviously, some of these items may need to be changed from time to time. Equally obviously, some will need to be kept confidential. Consequently, this section of the menu will be 'restricted' to persons holding an appropriate management level code.

An 'exit from program' option is necessary because you may want to use the computer for other purposes, such as normal word processing or standard hotel accounting.

This example indicates something of the range of tasks which the computer can handle, but it does not show the menu options in detail (some have been displayed earlier in this book), nor does it show some of the wider range of activities which hotel computers can undertake. This is expanding all the time. It includes the following (though the list is not intended to be exhaustive):

Reservations

- Room availability displays (by floor or room type).
- Group or single reservation handling.
- Automatic confirmation letters.
- Arrival lists for any date.
- Cancellation retrieval and reinstatement.

Interfacing

- With head office.
- With other group hotels.
- With airlines.
- With travel agents.
- With Tourist Information Centres.

Check-in

- Automated check-in.
- Pre-registration.
- Room allocation (automatic or manual).
- Room status displays (room rack).
- Guest search by name, group or room.

Billing

- Guest accounts.
- Point of sale terminal charging (including drink dispensers).
- Automatic additions, subtractions etc.
- Automatic item totals.
- Phone logging and charging

Check-out

- Automatic bill presentation.
- Self check-out.
- Direct debiting facilities.
- Automatic room status updating.
- Automatic guest history upgrading.

Control

- Room occupancy reports.
- Itemized room and guest revenue reports.
- Guest analysis reports.
- Forecasts.
- Yield management cumulative totals with action indicators.

Security

- Black list checks.
- Automatic credit control checks.
- Room access control via coded keys.
- Fire/intruder/theft sensing.
- Child monitoring.

Guest services

- Automated wake-up services.
- Bill preview facilities.
- Guest message displays.
- Data network access.
- Video/computer entertainments.

Room management

- Controlled room allocation.
- Automatic room record upgrading.
- Energy monitoring.
- Housekeeping scheduling.
- Maintenance scheduling.

A projection of the hotel of the near future indicates that it will be possible for a guest to make an advance booking from the comfort of his own home or office by contacting the hotel's computer directly. The computer will check room availability and the would-be guest's credit status and, if satisfied, will issue out a reservation confirmation code.

On arrival, the guest will insert his credit or 'smart' card and type in his reservation code. Registration data will then be displayed on the screen for checking and confirmation, after which the computer will allocate a suitable room and issue an electronic room key.

During the guest's stay, the computer will automatically post all charges to his account as they arise, and he will be able to review his bill at any time via the TV screen in his room, which can also be used to display personal messages and hotel advertising, or screen programmes, films or games. Fax facilities will be able to deliver hard copies of messages and news sheets as and when required.

On departure, with the bill previously checked and agreed, the computer will simply

Table 16

	1940s–1960s	*1960s–1970s*	*1980s–1990s*
Reservations	Bookings diary and conventional chart	Whitney rack and density chart	Electronic bookings records
Registration	Registration book	Registration cards	Automatic check-in via VDU screen
Room allocation	Based on chart (reserved) or housekeeper's lists (chance)	On arrival via room rack with room status display	By computer on basis of cumulative room usage
Accounts	Voucher posting to tabular ledger	Voucher posting to billing machine	Direct entries from POS terminals to electronic accounts
Payments	Cash or pre-cleared cheques	By credit card or travel agency voucher	Direct debiting

revalidate the guest's credit card and debit his account instantaneously. Security routines will guard against 'walk-outs' and the unauthorized removal of hotel property.

Many of these features are already in operation now, and the others are technically feasible. They should be seen in the context of the changes which have occurred over the past half century (Table 16).

Some implications of computerization

This is a difficult area because computerization is relatively new and the technology is still developing. However, any technological change is bound to have wider implications, and we ought to end by trying to consider what these might be. There are three in particular which need to be discussed.

1   The effects on staffing

It is clear that computers do reduce the need for staff to some extent. Automatic or self check-in is one fairly extreme example, but there are others. The reduction in time-consuming account balancing and reconciliation duties reduces the need for night audit staff. Less obviously, networking arrangements whereby bookings can be taken at distant locations has reduced the need for expensive central reservations offices, and the ability to print out standard confirmation letters eliminates much back office typing.

These examples (and there are many others) indicate that computers reduce the overall clerical burden on front office staff. However, there are three alternative ways of responding to this development:

(a)   To reduce staff, either through natural wastage or straightforward redundancies. This is particularly likely to apply to the relatively expensive and unpopular night clerk/night audit tasks, to switchboard operators (increasingly being displaced by automatic telephone logging equipment), and to back office typists.
(b)   To seek to handle more business without taking on any extra staff. In effect this is also a form of staff reduction since it reduces the guest:staff ratio. Of course, the process of gaining the extra business may involve taking on more staff in the marketing department.
(c)   To maintain existing staff numbers, using the extra time to provide greater guest/staff contact time, and thus more 'hospitality'. This approach is most likely to be adopted with reception desk staff, since they are most likely to come into face-to-face contact with the guest.

2   The effects on organization

It is probable that computers will break down traditional departmental barriers in terms of both information handling and responsibilities.

In hotels using manual systems the work of the housekeeper has been clearly separable from that of the front office manager, and liaison between the two has not always been satisfactory. There is now a clear trend towards what are called 'integrated room management systems'. Since the computer holds all the normal room rack data, it can produce sophisticated housekeeping schedules on demand, and systems which control and record actual room access can produce housekeeping productivity reports as well (these are based on the monitoring of the actual time spent by housekeeping staff within rooms). Maintenance operations can be controlled in the same way.

The effect may well be to encourage a greater degree of centralized control by the accommodation manager, rather than the older system of delegated responsibility to section heads.

3 *The effects on the guests*

These are the most difficult to predict. We have already suggested that the 'computer-literate' guest of the future will experience little difficulty in adjusting to automated check-in or checkout facilities, and will come to accept them as a convenience in the same way that we now regard cash dispensers. This type of guest may well not regret the disappearance of old-fashioned personal service, especially if he has never experienced it anyway.

Taking the broader view, it is also possible that developments such as 'electronic conference' may even affect the market for business travel. After all, if one can talk face-to-face to people in other countries over two-way TV-telephone links, and pass them documents by means of fax connections, is there any real point in wasting valuable time (not to mention incurring jet-lag) in travelling to their offices?

However, we think that both these worries are misplaced. For us, 'hospitality' is an essential element of any hotel experience, just as it is in any significant business relationship. A hotel is a surrogate home, with all that implies in the way of intangible but essential features. Most of us would agree that an apartment filled with the most modern and sophisticated electronic equipment is still not much of a 'home' unless there is someone to provide a welcoming smile when we return, and the same is true of hotels.

In the same way, face-to-face contacts and entertaining will remain an essential feature of business for a great many years to come. People do not like making important deals with someone they have never shared a smile, a handshake and a relaxing and companionable drink or meal, and these basic psychological needs will continue to make business travel necessary. In any case, tourism and leisure travel will undoubtedly continue to expand because no electronic image can ever take the place of the real thing.

What all this means is that we firmly believe that there will continue to be an important role for front office staff, particularly those possessing the all-important social skills.

Assignments

1 Prepare outline organization charts for the Tudor and Pancontinental Hotels.
2 Assign staff names to the front office posts you have designed for the Pancontinental, and prepare a specimen four-week duty rota.
3 Detail the front office equipment you would expect to find in the Tudor Hotel, and obtain approximate costs.
4 List and explain the range of functions you would expect to be carried out by a front office computer.
5 Draw up a checklist of factors to be taken into consideration by a small hotel contemplating the purchase of a computerized front office system.

Index